Webbing with Literature

Webbing with Literature

Creating Story Maps with Children's Books

Second Edition

Karen D'Angelo Bromley

*Binghamton University,
State University of New York*

Allyn and Bacon
Boston   London   Toronto   Sydney   Tokyo   Singapore

Senior Editor: Virginia Lanigan
Editorial Assistant: Nihad Farooq
Marketing Manager: Kathy Hunter
Editorial-Production Administrator: Annette Joseph
Editorial-Production Coordinator: Helen Shaw
Editorial-Production Service: Colophon
Composition Buyer: Linda Cox
Manufacturing Buyer: Megan Cochran
Cover Administrator: Suzanne Harbison

Copyright © 1996, 1991 by Allyn & Bacon
A Simon & Schuster Company
Needham Heights, MA 02194

Library of Congress Cataloging-in-Publication Data
Bromley, Karen D'Angelo
    Webbing with literature : creating story maps with children's
books / Karen D'Angelo Bromley. — 2nd ed.
        p.   cm.
    Includes bibliographical references and index.
    ISBN 0-205-16975-9
    1. Literature—Study and teaching (Elementary)   2. Language arts
(Elementary) 3. Children's literature.   4. Children—Books and
reading.   I. Title.
LB1575.B73   1996
372.64044—dc20   95-31348
                                                       CIP

Printed in the United States of America

10 9 8 7 6 5 4 3 2 1 00 99 98 97 96 95

Photo Credits: pp. 1, 41, 67, and 109: Will Faller; p. 23: Jim Pickerell; p. 83:
Stephen Marks.

contents

preface

Webbing with Literature: Creating Story Maps with Children's Books, Second Edition, is a book about literature and about sharing it in the classroom with K–8 students. My intention in writing this book is to support you in using webbing and literature in literacy programs and language arts, and with thematic instruction or an integrated approach to curriculum as you connect literature with science, social studies, mathematics, or other areas.

For me, webs are a useful way to organize and represent ideas and information. The process of webbing often allows me to see new relationships and have fresh insights. I use webs to structure my thinking, prepare for and teach classes, and plan writing. In the classroom, webbing invites students to participate together and construct knowledge collaboratively. Over the years, I have worked with many teachers and students who also realize the power of webbing, and in this second edition, I describe many of their classrooms. In so doing, I have tried:

■ To make this book practical and authentic by telling the stories of many teachers and students as they use webbing in many ways and by including the webs they created.

■ To provide a resource by including 125 webs and annotations for over 200 children's books organized by genre (folktale, fantasy, realistic fiction, historical fiction, biography, poetry, and information books) and by noting multicultural titles with an asterisk (*).

The ideas suggested here are meant to introduce you to webbing. As you and your students use this book, you will discover many ways to adapt, innovate, and use webbing creatively in teaching and learning.

=== *Acknowledgments*

The names of many teachers and students who shared their work with me appear here. They described to me what did and did not work as they used webbing, and both teachers and student allowed their webs to be reproduced. I am grateful to them for their application of the theory and research that underlie webbing.

The teachers I want to thank include: Mary Bonner, Carolyn Curren, Christine Czarnecki, Charlotte De Almeida, Diane Doherty, Jill H. Baker, Merri J. Earl, Suzanne S. French, Kim Gagnier, Kelly Haight, David K. Hall, Kelly Hawley, Donna Hein, Linda Hopkins, Renée A. Jahelka, Meredith Jewett, Mary S. Johnson, Terri A. Judge, Charlene Kempa, Nancy Mangialetti, Diane Mannix, Regina Mardex, Michele McDonald, Jennifer McManus, Lisa Milano, Maria Moy, Jennifer A. Nowacki, Maryann Parker, Barbara Patten-Skellett, Deborah A. Pease, Pam Pignatelli, Lisa Rieger, Lisa K. Shrot, Shannon Smith, Karen M. Wandell, Jill Zavelick, and Ann Maria Zevotek. I am very grateful to the students who illustrated selected children's books for Chapter 3: Derrick Ryan Brundege, David Caramore, Kimberly Clark, Rachel Daddezio, Katie Karcher, David Law, Daniel Ray, and Michele Reynolds. My special thanks to Karen M. Wandell who helped in many, many ways in the preparation of this book and to the reviewers Nancy B. Cothern, Indiana University; David D. Hall, Central Connecticut State University; Armin R. Schulz, California State University, Stanislaus; and Janet H. Towell, California State University, Stanislaus, whose thoughtful comments helped shape this revision.

=== *Dedication*

For Christopher, Westra, Karen, and Hanlon

Dr. Karen Bromley is the coordinator of the reading–language arts program at Binghamton University, State University of New York, where she has been a professor since 1979, teaching courses in reading, writing, children's literature, and language arts. In 1992 she received the Reading Educator award from the New York State Reading Association. *Webbing with Literature: Creating Story Maps with Children's Books,* Second Edition, is her fourth book.

She lives in Vestal, New York, with her husband and two Maine coon cats.

chapter 1

Webbing

This chapter discusses *webbing,* a visual strategy for representing and organizing ideas and information. It explores different types of webs and the versatility of webbing as a tool for encouraging response to literature, comprehension, literacy, and learning. It includes examples of K–8 teachers using webs with children's literature across the curriculum.

What Is Webbing?

In nature, a web is a network of fine threads that a spider weaves. This network forms a complicated structure that is the means by which the spider snares its prey. A web can also be a complex work of the mind that represents objects or concepts and the relationships a person perceives among them. In a classroom, the term *web* borrows something from both definitions.

In the classroom, a web is a visual display of categories of information and of their relationships that teachers and students create to structure ideas and aid learning. Webbing is the process of constructing a web, or graphic representation, of organized relationships among those ideas or categories of information.

Webs are sometimes called *semantic maps, concept maps, semantic networks, diagrams,* or *graphic organizers,* and webbing is called *semantic webbing, mapping, semantic mapping, networking,* or *concept mapping.* The variety of names for both the product and the process indicate the versatility of the strategy.

A web usually contains a *core concept,* or idea, at its center (Freedman & Reynolds, 1980). Different categories of related information occur at various points beyond the core concept. Specific facts, information, ideas, or examples support each of these categories (see Figure 1.1).

Webbing is one way of representing knowledge (Bromley, Irwin-DeVitis, & Modlo, 1995). Webs illustrate knowledge using a *conceptual pattern.* Knowledge can also be represented in a *hierarchical pattern* with a main concept and ranks or levels of subconcepts under it, in a *sequential pattern* including events in chronological order with a specified beginning and end, or in a *cyclical pattern* using a continuous series of events in a circle.

Webbing is a flexible instructional strategy at all grade levels. In a college or university chemistry class, a concept web helps students organize and represent information about the element *tritium,* for example, so they can more easily understand its properties. In an education course, a student creates a literature web to represent and organize a variety of activities for studying the interdependence of plants and animals, using books like *The Lorax* by Dr. Seuss (T. Geisel). In a sixth-grade classroom, a teacher uses a web to represent the causes of the Civil War and to show students how the North and South participated. In a third grade classroom where students are learning about a community in Brazil, children brainstorm for written reports while their teacher constructs a web of the topics. In a first-grade classroom, a teacher uses a web to show children the stages in the life of a butterfly.

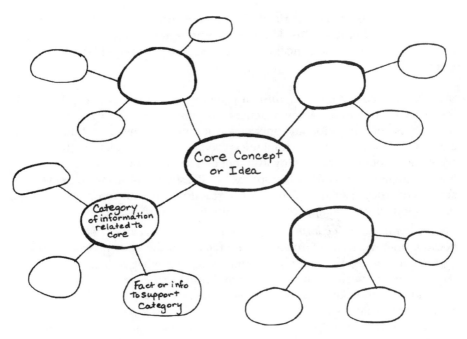

Figure 1.1 The basic structure of a web.

== *Why Use Webbing?*

The connection between webbing and learning is clear. We know that learning occurs in an organized way (Ausubel, 1968; Novak & Gowin, 1984), so it is not surprising that graphic material, such as webs used to illustrate the organization of ideas and information, aids the development of vocabulary, comprehension, and learning (Flood & Lapp, 1988; Heimlich & Pittelman, 1986; Pearson & Johnson, 1978). Reviews of research dealing with the generation of visual material like webs conclude that students' comprehension and learning improve when they use such visual graphics (Dunston, 1992; 1986; Moore & Readance, 1984). These studies show that the effects of visual graphics are greatest when students have in-depth instruction in their use and are actively engaged in the construction of the graphics themselves.

Creating graphic displays encourages students to talk, share information, discuss and analyze ideas and relationships, and construct knowledge together, all of which are central to literacy and learning (Alvermann, Dillon, & O'Brien, 1987; Bromley, Irwin-DeVitis, & Modlo, 1995), so you can see that the collaboration that occurs during the process of constructing webs is a key to their success.

Several benefits of webbing appear in Figure 1.2 where the core concept is *webbing with literature* and four web strands or categories of information related to the core, for example, *encourages response,* appear beyond the core.

Each strand is supported by related information such as *promotes sharing* and *promotes personal reactions.* The strands represent different functions of webbing and *function* is the concept that ties the strands together. The benefits of webbing are:

- *Webbing encourages response.* It promotes, supports, and helps structure response to literature. Many teachers attempt to evoke literary response through use of a question and answer format, unwittingly contributing to creation of a classroom in which thinking is too often defined solely by the teacher. Webbing encourages student involvement and sharing as you encourage a genuine exchange that reveals rich responses to literature. Allowing students to react to what they read and to share those reactions gives them opportunities to understand, enjoy, and appreciate literature from a variety of perspectives.

- *Webbing extends comprehension.* It promotes and extends comprehension because it allows new information to be related to the known. *Schema theory* suggests that what we comprehend and learn from what we read or hear is directly related to what we already know and bring to a given situation. So assessing students' prior knowledge, *schema* (singular) or *schemata* (plural) before reading or learning is very important. Create webs to assess and organize your students' prior knowledge about a topic and establish purposes for learning. After a lesson or unit, add new information to the existing web. Meshing the *new* with the *known* makes sense and makes all information easier to remember.

- *Webbing builds literacy.* It supports the growth of literate thinking, talking, reading, and writing. When students create webs together, they use language in authentic ways to share and learn from one another, and in so doing they build their literacy. Webbing helps students connect reading and writing naturally as they create webs before, during, or after reading. When they see spoken language being written down on a web or write it themselves, they learn about the form of language and how to spell words. When they read what is on a web and talk about it together to decide whether it is accurate or to add information, they practice using literacy authentically. You can use webs as springboards for discussion, retellings, or analysis of stories; and they can also support the writing process by helping your students plan and organize what they will write.

- *Webbing enhances learning.* Since webs display concepts and relationships among concepts in a visibly structured format, they enhance the probability that your students will learn and retain what they have read and talked about. Webbing promotes student involvement and interactions that are catalysts for rich response and insights. It provides opportunities to interpret critically and to analyze what is read. As your students hear and see what others feel, believe, and know about a topic, each can add beliefs and knowledge, and through negotiation, the group's collective knowledge can be represented in a web. Your students will learn to appreciate the perspectives of others and realize that stories can have various meanings and evoke various emotions.

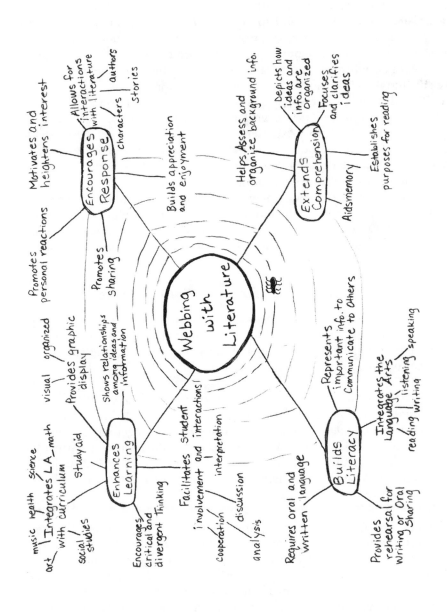

Figure 1.2 Using webs with literature serves many functions.

Webbing with Literature

Encourages Response
- Motivates and heightens interest
- Allows for interactions with literature — authors — stories — characters
- Promotes personal reactions
- Promotes sharing
- Builds appreciation and enjoyment

Extends Comprehension
- Helps Assess and organize background info.
- Depicts how ideas and info. are organized
- Focuses and clarifies ideas
- Aids memory
- Establishes purposes for reading

Enhances Learning
- Provides graphic display
- visual — organized
- Integrates LA—math with curriculum
- music — health — science — art — social studies
- Study aid
- Shows relationships among ideas and information
- Encourages critical and divergent Thinking
- Facilitates Student involvement and interactions
- interpretation
- cooperation — discussion — analysis

Builds Literacy
- Represents important info. to Communicate to Others
- Integrates the Language Arts
- reading — writing — listening — speaking
- Requires oral and written language
- Provides rehearsal for writing or Oral Sharing

5

Getting Started with Webbing

Two cautions are important to remember before you begin using webbing. First, when you use children's literature to teach, it is important to remember that your students' enjoyment and appreciation of stories is paramount. Everything you do should foster personal response from which students can learn about literature. Second, teaching students literary elements does not ensure their comprehension of, or personal response to, children's literature. Even young children who have no explicit knowledge of story elements or structure can recall, understand, and respond to stories, but better understanding of literary elements can promote comprehension and deepen response. Webbing can lend structure to readers' story experiences and responses and help them think about literary elements as they untangle the plot, connect related ideas, track character traits, consider the influence of setting, recall the creation of mood, identify themes, or visualize aspects of the story in myriad ways.

Of course, you should also remember that webbing is only one of many ways to connect children with literature and that overuse will certainly dilute its effectiveness. When you use it appropriately, it is a rich avenue for sharing and responding to literature as well as a useful tool for planning and assessment.

Planning with Webs

Typically, webbing is used in the classroom as a planning tool to organize thematic instruction, integrated curriculum, or interdisciplinary units. Three teachers' comments about, and descriptions of, how they use webbing suggest its potential for planning:

Charlene: "Webbing is a way of illustrating what's in my mind. Webs help me organize my thoughts and branch out from them." Charlene and her primary-level special education students planned a unit together on weather and put the web in Figure 1.3 on a bulletin board to initiate and guide their inquiry. A bulletin board web like this one provides a place to record progress, too. Charlene could use the bulletin board web to chart the activities and projects as her class completes them.

Joanne: "I see webbing as having a lot of potential for planning. You can add ideas as they come to you and see how they connect to the big picture." Joanne visited the American Southwest one summer to study the culture of the Navajo Indians. The web in Figure 1.4 shows how she organized the knowledge and ideas she felt were important for her fifth-grade students to understand. Then, when she had her class list what they knew and what they wanted to learn about the Navajos, it was easy for her to help them group their ideas into the seven categories shown on the web in Figure 1.5.

For this unit, Joanne integrated reading and social studies and used a literature-based approach, so she created this literature web as a handout to provide

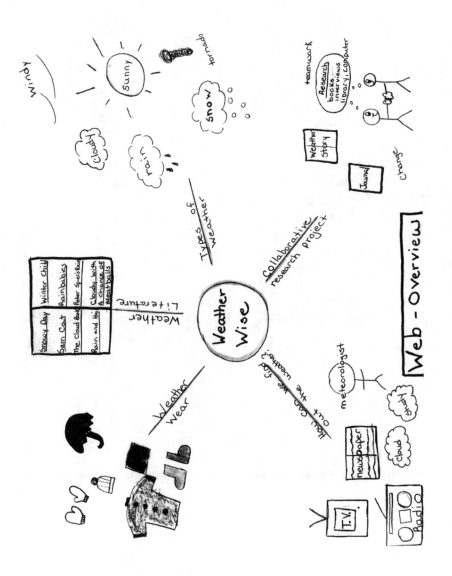

Figure 1.3 A planning web for a unit on the weather by Charlene Kempa.

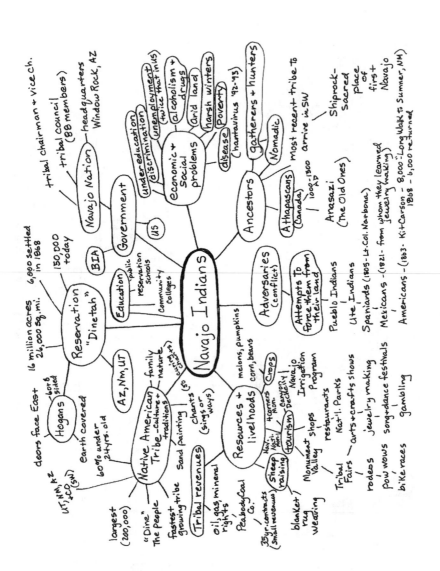

Figure 1.4 A web to guide a study of Navajo Indians and the Southwest.

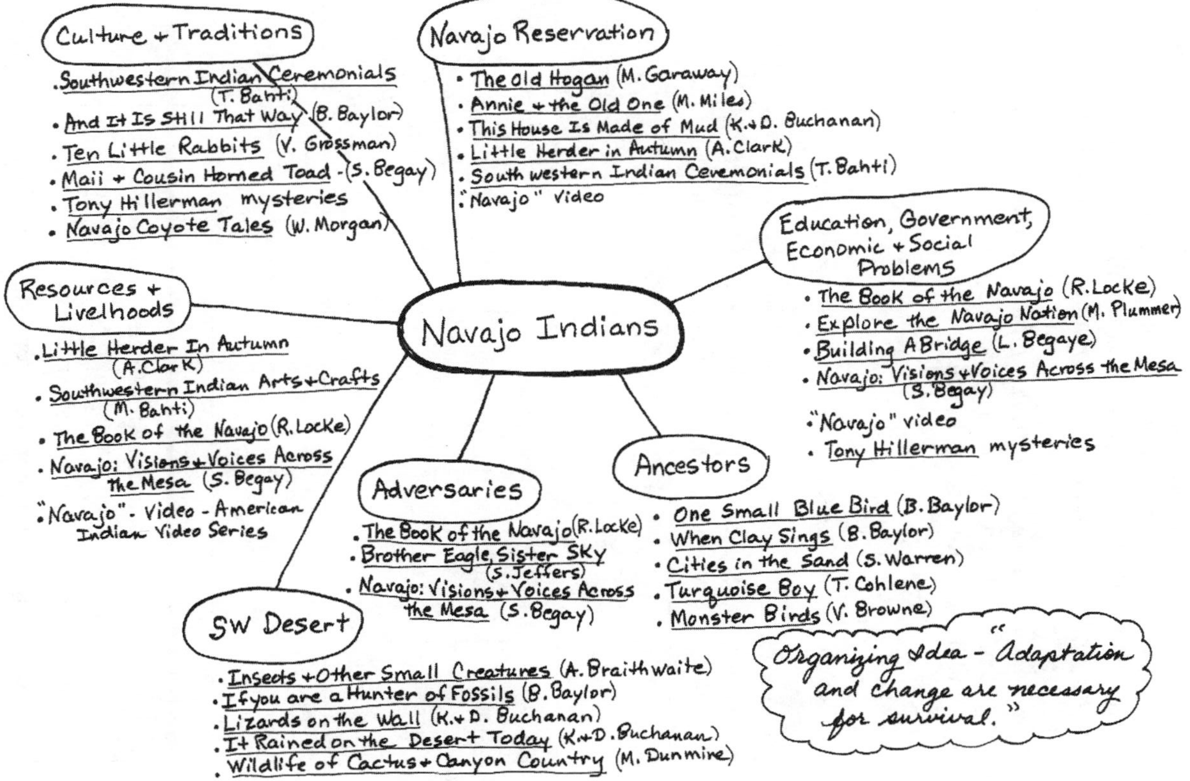
Culture + Traditions
.Southwestern Indian Ceremonials (T. Bahti)
• And It Is Still That Way (B. Baylor)
. Ten Little Rabbits (V. Grossman)
• Maii + Cousin Horned Toad - (S. Begay)
. Tony Hillerman mysteries
• Navajo Coyote Tales (W. Morgan)
Navajo Reservation
• The old Hogan (M. Garaway)
• Annie + the Old One (M. Miles)
• This House Is Made of Mud (K.+D. Buchanan)
• Little Herder in Autumn (A. Clark)
. South western Indian Ceremonials (T. Bahti)
"Navajo" video
Education, Government, Economic + Social Problems
• The Book of the Navajo (R. Locke)
. Explore the Navajo Nation (M. Plummer)
• Building A Bridge (L. Begaye)
• Navajo: Visions + Voices Across the Mesa (S. Begay)
"Navajo" video
• Tony Hillerman mysteries
Resources + Livelihoods
.Little Herder In Autumn (A. Clark)
• Southwestern Indian Arts + Crafts (M. Bahti)
• The Book of the Navajo (R. Locke)
• Navajo: Visions + Voices Across the Mesa (S. Begay)
"Navajo" - Video - American Indian Video Series
Navajo Indians
Adversaries
. The Book of the Navajo (R. Locke)
. Brother Eagle, Sister Sky (S. Jeffers)
. Navajo: Visions + Voices Across the Mesa (S. Begay)
Ancestors
• One Small Blue Bird (B. Baylor)
. When Clay Sings (B. Baylor)
. Cities in the Sand (S. Warren)
. Turquoise Boy (T. Cohlene)
. Monster Birds (V. Browne)
SW Desert
. Insects + Other Small Creatures (A. Braithwaite)
. If you are a Hunter of Fossils (B. Baylor)
. Lizards on the Wall (K.+D. Buchanan)
. It Rained on the Desert Today (K.+D. Buchanan)
. Wildlife of Cactus + Canyon Country (M. Dunmire)
"Organizing Idea - 'Adaptation and change are necessary for survival.'"

Figure 1.5 A literature web for the Southwest unit.

her students with titles of some of the literature she had collected and to use as a reading guide in pursuing each of the topics. In the web, Joanne included poetry, nonfiction, folktales, realistic fiction, and a video. Next Joanne and her students might create a web with the categories of *listening, speaking, reading,* and *writing* and with activities and projects listed for each category for students to complete to demonstrate their development as literate learners.

Deb: "I create my organizers on the computer and they are the materials I teach from." Deb believes picture books are not just for young readers and uses them with her middle school students in science and social studies. Deb orga-

A Model for Picture Book Use in Middle School Content Area

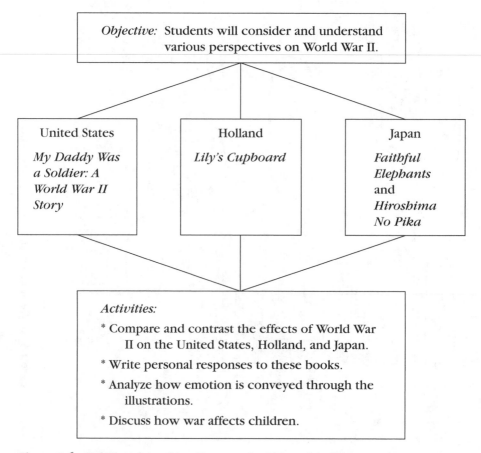

Figure 1.6 Deb Pease's teaching plan organized hierarchically.

nized her thinking about how she and her students would learn about World War II with the hierarchical organizer in Figure 1.6. She shares her organizers and webs with parents by including them in the class newsletter occasionally because they are simple, clear explanations of what she and her students are doing.

Many teachers who use webbing as a planning tool are enthusiastic about it because it is a nonlinear way of bringing structure and order to their thinking. Webbing allows them to add ideas as they occur, and it provides the *big* picture so that connections and insights can be seen more readily. Bulletin board webs make your plans visible and allow your class to *own* the topic and add ideas and information as they learn during the unit. Webs also offer concrete and organized ways to explain and describe curriculum to parents. Huck, Hepler, and Hickman (1993) and Norton (1995) provide further explanations of planning with webs.

Learning about Literature with Webs

In addition to using it for planning, some teachers use webbing in reading, science, and social studies to develop background knowledge or record brainstorming before reading. But fewer teachers recognize the potential of webbing to promote and support student response to literature. Webbing provides you and your students with a wonderful avenue for sharing and responding to literature (Cleland, 1981; Norton, 1992). It promotes thinking and learning about stories and enhances students' enjoyment and appreciation of literature. Webbing is a way to connect your students with stories and to encourage their interaction around these stories.

Webbing is an excellent strategy to use for fostering enjoyment and appreciation of literature and helping children become involved with literature as they interact with each other to learn. You can organize ideas for teaching a content-area unit and represent the elements, structure, or relationships in a story with a web, which will make children's understanding of the story easier and their responses richer. You can also help children organize their own ideas and information with webs.

Comments made by teachers who recently began to use webbing show their enthusiasm. Their descriptions of how they use webbing with literature show its potential as a tool for prompting literary response and learning about literature. These teachers use webbing with their students before, during, and after reading to prompt discussion and as a planning tool for writing:

Linda: "At first I thought it was an extremely disorganized way to write down information, but as I've used webbing and am more comfortable with it, I actually like it." Linda, a reading teacher, began webbing as a way of developing vocabulary and included her second-grade students actively in the webbing process. She noticed that in reading *Everett Anderson's Year,* by Lucille

Clifton, the children knew that *spring* meant season but that they did not know other meanings for the word. She wanted to build their vocabularies and expand their understanding of *spring* and other words in the story. Linda knew that for a huge proportion of the words in the English language there are multiple meanings and that lack of this knowledge hampers many readers and writers.

After talking about the story, Linda and her students chose several words for which they were unsure of the meanings. Working in pairs with dictionaries, they found several meanings for *spring* and the other words and decided to make bulletin board webs with this new knowledge (see Figure 1.7). Linda found webbing a handy tool for building vocabulary and structuring a bulletin board. It allowed her to include the contributions of all her students, and it made their vocabulary growth visible in the classroom. As a result of this webbing activity, Linda's second graders had broader vocabulary knowledge to support their responses to literature in the future.

"Kelly: "I use webs to encourage student participation in literature. When they really get into a book, that's when they really understand it."

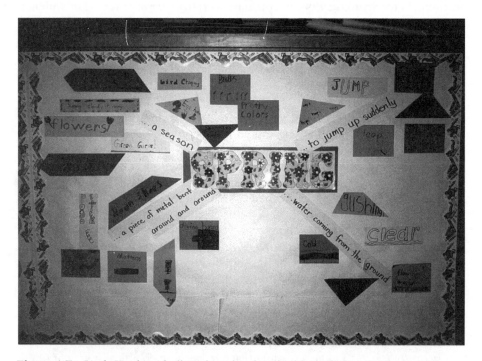

Figure 1.7   Linda Hopkins' bulletin board web to build vocabulary for the multiple meanings of *spring*.

Kelly, a fifth-grade teacher, uses webbing and grouping students in a variety of ways depending on her purpose and on the activity. She used one of her students' responses to a character in *The Talking Eggs,* by Robert San Souci, as a way of inviting everyone to participate in a character analysis. In the discussion following reading, James said, "Rose was really selfish." Kelly acknowledged the pertinence of this observation and said, "Let's explore James' idea some." The class offered evidence of selfishness, and Kelly said there were other ways to describe Rose as well. Then she invited the class to take part in an in-depth character analysis.

Kelly divided the class of twenty into four groups. She put able readers in two groups and developing readers in two other groups, so she and her consulting teacher could more easily monitor and work with the class. Each group chose a character to analyze on chart paper, and to ensure everyone's contribution within the group, Kelly gave each student a different colored marking pen. Groups made their webs by first deciding on four words to describe the character. After discussion among group members to get consensus about the supporting information, individual students wrote their *proof,* or incidents from the story, on the web. Then a spokesperson for the group shared the web with the class. The web in Figure 1.8 is a redrawn version of the character *Rose* done by one group.

By using ability groups, webbing, and colored markers, Kelly and her consulting teacher were able to help all the students better understand the various characters in the story and *get into* this piece of literature. The character webs helped Kelly's students see how folktales generally contain one-dimensional characters as well.

The Talking Eggs is actually a Cinderella story from the American South, and during this character webbing activity, one of Kelly's students commented on the story's similarity to the traditional Cinderella story. The response delighted Kelly and she used it as an opportunity to guide her students in a comparison of the two tales. After a retelling of the traditional tale by several students, Kelly constructed the skeleton of the web in Figure 1.9. Then the class decided what to compare between the tales, and Kelly wrote these terms in the inner circles: *characters, animals, rewards,* and so forth. Then Kelly recorded the students' ideas on the organizer.

This format is thought-provoking and requires students to support their opinions with ideas and information. It, or the Venn diagram (two intersecting circles of which you will find examples in later chapters), are excellent structures to use when you compare a book and its movie or video version. These organizers also work well when you and your students want to compare two main characters from different pieces of literature.

In addition, Kelly often has her students use the completed organizer as a blueprint for writing a comparative paragraph or essay. She finds that webbing

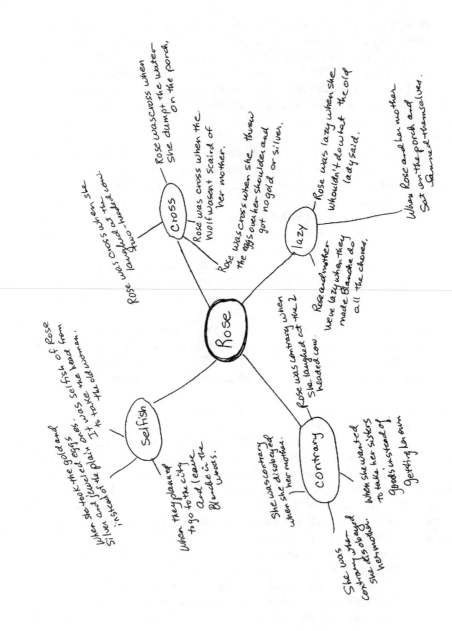

Figure 1.8 A character web for Rose in *The Talking Eggs*, by Robert San Souci, created by Kelly Haight's students.

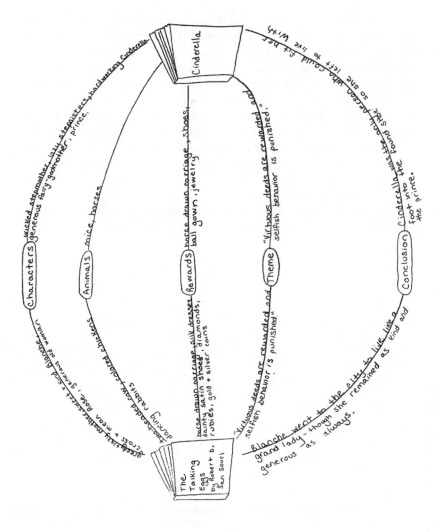

Figure 1.9 An organizer used by Kelly Haight's fifth graders to compare Cinderella tales.

The following text appears within the figure:

Cinderella

Characters: wicked stepmother, lazy stepsisters, hardworking Cinderella, generous fairy godmother, prince.

Animals: mice, horses

Rewards: horse drawn carriage, shoes, ball gown, jewelry

Theme: "Virtuous deeds are rewarded and selfish behavior is punished."

Conclusion: Cinderella was the only person who could fit her foot into the found shoe so she left to live like a prince.

The Talking Eggs by Robert D. San Souci

Characters: greedy, mean mother + mean Rose, generous Blanche, old woman

Animals: two-headed cow, multicolored chickens, rabbits

Rewards: horse drawn carriage, silk dresses, dainty satin shoes, diamonds, rubies, gold + silver coins

Theme: "Virtuous deeds are rewarded and selfish behavior is punished."

Conclusion: Blanche went to the city to live like a grand lady—though she remained as kind and generous as always.

gives struggling writers a structure and provides an outline and organization for their writing.

Michele: "I like the idea of webbing with stories. I feel the benefits are many because it is a great visual way to learn." Michele used a sequence organizer to build concept and word knowledge with her second graders after reading *Thunder Cake,* by Patricia Polacco. In the story, a young girl's Russian grandmother helps her overcome her fear of thunder by having the girl help her bake a cake as they anticipate an approaching storm. The class was studying weather in science, and Michele wanted to reinforce story vocabulary and the idea that light travels faster than sound. On chart paper, Michele wrote the words *storm clouds, lightning, thunder,* and *rain* inside clouds and added arrows to show the direction of events (see Figure 1.10). After talking about the story and reading it a second time, Michele and her class added special words from the story to describe thunderstorms and read them aloud together.

They hung the chart paper on a coat hanger with clothes pins and put the coat hanger on a rack in the classroom with other webs and graphic illustrations

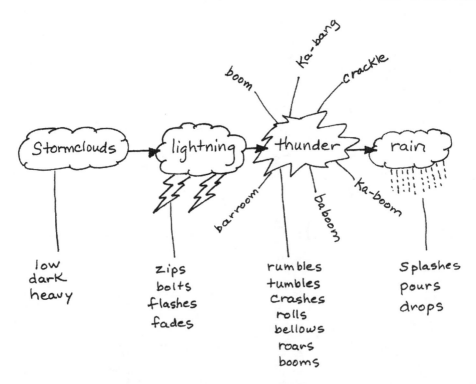

Figure 1.10 Developing science concepts and vocabulary in *Thunder Cake.*

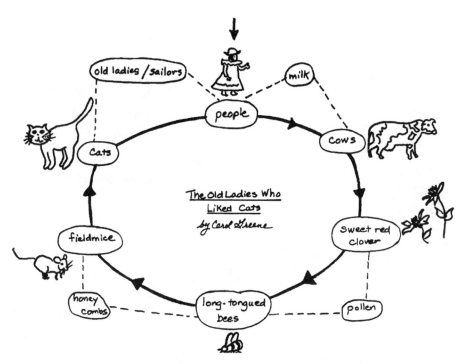

Figure 1.11 Pictures add interest to this cyclical organizer for *The Old Ladies Who Liked Cats,* by Carol Greene.

of stories they had read. Michele's children often return to this rack to reread webs and retell stories and to find out how to spell words when they are writing.

Another story the class just read was *The old Ladies Who Liked Cats,* by Carol Greene, and they created a cyclical organizer for it (see Figure 1.11). In this ecological folktale first told by Charles Darwin, the mutual interdependence and balance among plants and animals in an island community is disturbed when the old ladies are not allowed to let their cats out at night. Michele made the drawing during her students' discussion of the story, adding pictures to give her struggling readers cues about the print.

Chuck: "I think students better understand plot, characters, theme, setting, etc. when they see how they are connected." Chuck introduced *A River Ran Wild,* by Lynne Cherry, an environmental history of the Nashua River by providing his fourth-grade students with background information. He gave them each a web containing the literary elements *setting, characters,* and *problems* (see Figure 1.12), which he felt would give them a structure to better understand the actions of Marion Stoddart, the woman who organized the Nashua River Cleanup Committee and was responsible for the river's restoration. In

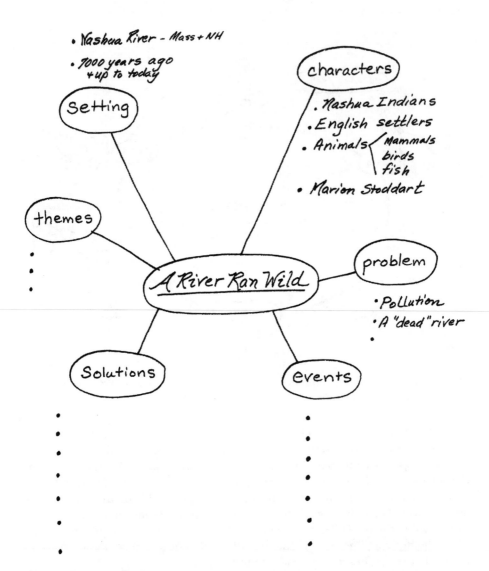

Figure 1.12   A literary web showing the story elements in *A River Ran Wild,* by Lynne Cherry.

small group discussion after reading, students used the webs to support their feelings and record their ideas about *events, solutions,* and *themes.* Groups then discussed their webs together to outline Marion Stoddart's actions and the resulting change in the river. During class sharing of webs, Chuck helped the class see from their webs the connections among characters, events, problems, and solutions. In further discussion about the story, Chuck helped his students make comparisons between the Nashua River and their local river.

Barry: "Identifying relationships among characters often helps my students see the conflict in stories." Barry used a feelings web (Galda, 1987) to encourage his fifth-grade students to identify and respond to the relationships among characters in *Bridge To Terabithia,* by Katherine Paterson. After reading and discussing this book, Barry had his students first respond individually in writing on their webs to the relationships Jess had with other characters (see Figure 1.13). Then they worked in pairs to chart on the blank outer lines the re-

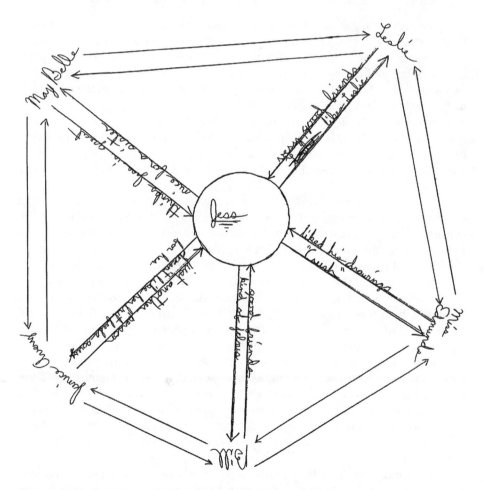

Figure 1.13 A feelings web for *Bridge to Terabithia,* by Katherine Paterson, created by fifth graders.

lationships among secondary characters before there was a class discussion of characters and conflict.

You can do the opposite by first having your students identify secondary characters' relationships on their own and then having them work in pairs to record the main characters' relationships. When you create a web such as this to develop interpretation and higher-level thinking, be sure to arrange each secondary character adjacent to another character she or he had interactions with in the story.

Assessment with Webs

Carolyn: "I have my students use webs to plan their own projects and I find it makes sense to assess what they've learned with webs too." Carolyn models webbing for her students until they are comfortable using it as a brainstorming and planning tool themselves. She often gives her students some of the categories to include when they plan their independent research but encourages them to be creative. To plan her research project, Karen, a third-grader, mapped out her own research project on manatees and included the two categories; *jobs or careers* and *literature,* that Carolyn suggested. At the conclusion of the study, one of the ways Carolyn assessed Karen's learning was with webbing. She asked Karen to create a web (see Figure 1.14) to show what she had learned about her topic.

It is important and interesting to note that Karen knew much more than what appeared on her web. The web was a vehicle that prompted Karen to recall and explain in much more detail what she had learned. In an individual conference with Carolyn in which Karen explained her web, Karen mentioned sharks and alligators as other possible dangers to manatees in addition to boat propellers. She said she could add *mammal, relatives* and *dugary,* as an example. In talking with Carolyn, Karen mentioned specific information on weight and size which was not on the web. She also told Carolyn about the ecological endangerment of manatees and the few books she found on the topic, which indicated to Carolyn a deeper understanding than was shown on the web.

You can also have your students write brief explanations of their webs. However, when you use webbing as an assessment tool, remember that the writing and organizing required on a web can constrain the task. For assessing learning, a web is most effective if you have your students explain orally the information and relationships the web does and does not show. Do not overlook, however, webs as one aspect of students' portfolios to demonstrate what they have learned.

Many examples of other types of webs appear in remaining chapters. These webs provide a place to begin your exploration of webbing as a flexible strategy for planning and teaching using children's literature. Many of the webs

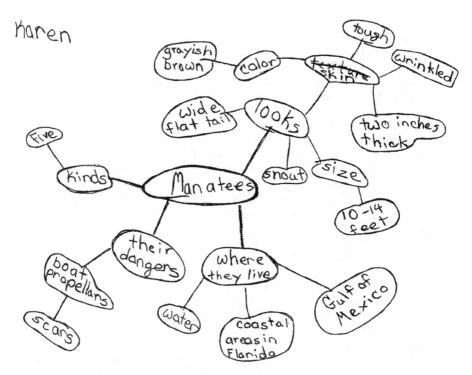

Figure 1.14 Karen Mele, a third grader, drew this web to show what she had learned.

or organizers that have been, and will be, presented in this book were created by teachers and/or students to encourage and share response, comprehension, literacy, and learning.

Conclusion

Webbing is a versatile strategy that supports planning, teaching, and assessment. Webbing is an excellent way to encourage response to literature while fostering enjoyment, appreciation, understanding, and learning. Webs represent visually the literary elements, structure, concepts, and relationships in literature. Through the process of webbing, students become involved with literature as they interact with each other to learn.

REFERENCES

Alvermann, D. E., Dillon, D. R., and O'Brien, D. G. (1987). *Using Discussion to Promote Reading Comprehension.* Newark, DE: International Reading Association.

Ausubel, D. P. (1968). *Educational Psychology: A Cognitive View.* New York: Holt Rinehart and Winston.

Bromley, K., Irwin-DeVitis, L., & Modlo, M. (1995). *Graphic Organizers: Visual Strategies for Active Learning K–8.* New York: Scholastic.

Cleland, C. (1981). Highlighting issues in children's literature through semantic webbing. *The Reading Teacher, 34*(6), 642–646.

Dunston, P. J. (1992). A critique of graphic organizer research. *Reading Research and Instruction, 31*(2), 57–65.

Flood, J., & Lapp, D. (1988). Conceptual mapping strategies for understanding information texts. *The Reading Teacher, 41*(8), 780–783.

Freedman, G., & Reynolds, E. (1980). Enriching basal reading lessons with semantic webbing. *The Reading Teacher, 33*(6), 677–684.

Galda, L. (1987). Teaching higher order reading skills with literature. In B. Cullinan (Ed.), *Children's Literature in the Reading Program* (pp. 54–58). Newark, DE: International Reading Association.

Heimlich, J. E., & Pittelman, S. D. (1986). *Semantic Mapping: Classroom Applications.* Newark, DE: International Reading Association.

Huck, C. C., Hepler, S., & Hickman. J. (1993). *Children's Literature in the Elementary School,* 5th ed. San Diego: Harcourt Brace Jovanovich.

Moore, D. W., & Readance, J. E. (1984). A quantitative and qualitative review of graphic organizer research. *Journal of Educational Research, 78,* 11–17.

Norton, D. E. (1995). *Through the Eyes of a Child: An Introduction to Children's Literature,* (4th ed.). Columbus, OH: Merrill..

Norton, D. E. (1992). *The Impact of Literature-Based Reading.* New York: Macmillan.

Novak, J. D., & Gowin, D. B. (1984). *Learning How to Learn.* Cambridge, UK: Cambridge University Press.

Pearson, P. D., & Johnson, D. D. (1978). *Teaching Reading Comprehension.* New York: Holt Rinehart & Winston.

Children's Literature

Cherry, L. (1992). *A River Ran Wild.* San Diego: Harcourt Brace Jovanovich.

Clifton, L. (1992). *Everett Anderson's Year.* New York: Holt (Henry).

Geisel, T. (1971). *The Lorax.* New York: Random House.

Greene, C. (1991). *The Old Ladies Who Liked Cats.* New York: Harper Collins.

Paterson, K. (1977). *Bridge to Terabithia.* New York: Harper & Row.

Polacco, P. (1990) *Thunder Cake.* New York: Scholastic.

San Souci, R. (1990). *The Talking Eggs: A Folktale from the American South.* New York: Scholastic

chapter 2

Identifying Literary Elements

This chapter explores the literary elements of each genre of literature. You will see how the representation of literary elements in a web helps your students understand the important components of that work and how the elements mesh to make a unique piece of literature.

What Is Genre?

Genre is a classification system for organizing literature. A genre is a family of stories or literary works that possess similar characteristics. The genres of literature we will consider are folktales, fantasy, realistic fiction, historical fiction, biography, poetry, and information books.

Often a piece of literature contains characteristics of two different genres and therefore crosses genre lines. Wolf and Gearhart (1994) tell us, "Indeed, the boundaries appear to be more porous than solid, as stories float between specific categories" (p. 441). An example of this is *The Salamander Room,* by Ann Mazer, the story of a young boy who wants to make a home for salamanders in his bedroom. The text contains information about food chains and ecology that is included in a mother-child conversation, yet the illustrations depict the fantasy that the boy conjures in his head as they talk. In the conversation, the mother nudges the boy to imagine and create, yet directs him subtly to do so in a way that is consistent with the laws of nature. On the reverse side of the title page, the Library of Congress categorizes the book as *fiction.* Since the illustrations and text seem contemporary, the genre of the story is realistic fiction. Yet clearly the *stuff* of this lovely, multilayered story is as much imaginary as it is factual, so some might consider it *informational fantasy,* a category that crosses genre lines.

Many picture books cross genre lines and contain characteristics of more than one genre. If you and your students are in doubt about what genre a particular story fits, ask yourselves "What characteristics connect it to a specific genre?" and "What are the author's and illustrator's purposes in creating the story?" You can also look at the category identified by the Library of Congress on the reverse side of the title page. In the case of picture books, examine pictures and text separately since illustrations often tell a different story than does the text. Then consider the total effect of story and illustrations before deciding on its genre. Remember that genre characteristics are not set in stone.

What Are Literary Elements?

Literary elements are the common components or similar structures of a particular genre of literature. Each genre has unique literary elements and characteristics. Many of the following elements can be found in each genre of literature:

- *Setting:* This the *when and where* of the story. It is the time, place, and situation in which the story occurs. The setting can be *integral,* or essential, to the story, or it can be a *backdrop,* or relatively unimportant, even unnecessary, to the story (Lukens, 1995).

- *Characters:* These are the beings, either people or animate objects, that carry the action. Main characters are often called *round* since they are well developed and they grow and change during the course of the story. Secondary characters are often called *flat* since they are not developed and the reader does not know them well.

- *Plot:* This is the *skeleton* of the story, the sequence of events or episodes that occur as a character or characters find solutions to problems or as they achieve goals. A basic view of plot is that a story has a beginning, a middle, and an end. Usually, a conflict is present, for example, person versus self, person versus person, person versus nature, or person versus society.

- *Theme:* The heart of the story or the glue that holds it together is often the most difficult for children to grasp. Themes can be *explicit,* stated literally, or *implicit,* unstated but understood. Younger children often grasp theme more easily when it is stated as a thought or sentence rather than as a word, for example, "Friends can be found in unexpected places." rather than *friendship.* It is important to remember that every story has multiple themes.

- *Point of view:* This is the storyteller, narrator, or individual who tells the story. *First person* is told with *I; omniscient* is told with *he* or *she,* and the narrator is all-knowing about details, thought, and actions; *limited omniscient* is told with *he* or *she* but tells the thought of only one character; and *objective* uses third person but allows readers to interpret and draw their own conclusions.

- *Style:* This is the *form* an author uses. Style is *how* something is said rather than *what* is said. It involves word choice and usage that convey ideas in distinctive ways. Lukens (1995) explains and gives examples of imagery, figurative language (personification, simile, metaphor, hyperbole, understatement, allusion, symbol, puns, wordplay), and devices of sound (onomatopoeia, alliteration, assonance, consonance, rhythm).

- *Tone:* This is the *attitude,* or stance, an author takes toward the subject and/ or the readers. It is communicated by word choice and usage. Tone can change within a story or be consistent throughout. It can be humorous, sentimental, condescending, didactic, reminiscent, resigned, cynical, reflective, uniform, straightforward, or any number of other ways that describe attitude. Again, Lukens (1995) provides examples from literature that clarify this literary element.

You and the children you teach will discover other elements that fit a genre of literature or may be characteristic of two particular books from one genre that you have read and want to compare.

Until recently, we thought that knowledge of literary elements was developmental, with older children and adults possessing a more elaborate concept of what constitutes a story than do younger children. To some extent this is true. A study by Lehr (1988), however, suggests that even kindergarten children have quite well-developed senses of story and can summarize plots, react to characters, and identify and match themes in related stories.

It is important to realize that not every story or selection possesses all the traditional literary elements. Information books and poetry are two genres that do not. As an example, *Mad as a Wet Hen! And Other Funny Idioms,* by Marvin Terban, is a collection of idioms, definitions, contemporary usage, and illustrations of their literal meanings. *A House Is a House for Me,* by Mary Ann Hoberman, is a poem about different kinds of houses in the environment. Neither book is a story in the usual sense, and neither book contains the usual main and secondary characters or explicitly stated problem. But both books contain many of the other literary elements already listed.

The theme of *Mad as a Wet Hen! And Other Funny Idioms* is that "Language is colorful and cannot always be taken literally." In this book, the narrator is the author; his tone is informative; and his style of writing is concise and to the point. The unstated problem is that many phrases in our language are often misunderstood and Terban attempts to clarify this misunderstanding. The theme of *A House Is a House for Me* is that everything in the environment has a place. In this poem, the setting is the world today; the goal is to identify a house for each of the live and inanimate objects; and the resolution is the identification of the houses. The poem is written from the point of view of an author with a creative eye, and the style involves a distinctive use of rhyme and repetition.

Research indicates that knowledge of story elements aids children's comprehension and memory of stories. Reutzel (1984) found that integrating story maps into a reading lesson helped readers attend to details and relationships among story elements. Reutzel and Fawson (1991) used a webbing strategy with predictable books to improve significantly the comprehension of below-average first graders. Reutzel (1985) also found that story mapping significantly improved fifth-grade students' comprehension.

Webbing also aids the story comprehension of students with learning disabilities. Sinatra and others (1985) reported that visually presenting story elements with semantic maps helped promote the comprehension of students with learning-disabilities and poor readers. Scanlon (1992) found that interactive semantic mapping aided the reading comprehension of students with learning disabilities. Idol (1987) used a group story-mapping strategy with third and fourth graders with learning disabilities and reading problems and reported improved comprehension.

Knowledge of story structure improves writing abilities as well. Fitzgerald and Teasley (1986) found that instruction focusing on forming a mental picture of a story's structure improved less able fourth-grade readers' organization and the overall quality of their compositions. Olson (1984) found that the writing of good book reports is easier when second- and fifth-grade children are aware of, and use, story structure as an aid in their writing. Sinatra and others (1986) taught students to make semantic maps after reading to provide organization for their written compositions. Sinatra and others (1990) also found that semantic maps provided a visual framework to aid in writing essays for students with limited knowledge of English. Bromley, Irwin-DeVitis, and Modlo (1995), authors of a professional book for K–8 teachers on graphic organizers, comment that they used graphic representations and webs to plan and guide their writing.

Schmitt and O'Brien (1986) raised two cautions about the use of story elements. First, teaching children the knowledge of structure is not necessary for comprehension of a story. In fact, we know that even young children who have no knowledge of story elements can recall and understand stories. But awareness of how story content is organized and interrelated may promote comprehension. Second, when structure is the focus in discussions of literature, we risk losing the most important aspect of the experience—appreciation and enjoyment of literature. We know that most readers can be helped to develop their sense of story not so much by direct instruction in story elements as by giving them many "opportunities to experience a rich variety of stories in an organized fashion using the grammar as a foundation" (Schmitt & O'Brien, 1986, p. 5). In this way, we enhance students' abilities to interact with characters and authors and thus better understand, appreciate, and enjoy stories.

Literary Elements in the Genres

Webs are used in a variety of ways to depict and to clarify the literary elements of stories and selections from children's literature. Cleland (1981) suggests webbing as a way to help children identify important issues and themes in children's books. Galda (1987) describes how webs help children better understand characters in literature. Bromley (1992) uses webs to depict literary elements and enhance reading comprehension. Norton (1993) explores the genre of historical fiction and webbing to encourage vocabulary development, literary discussions, and the development of instructional units. This text extends the possibilities for using webbing to all the traditional genres of literature.

Folktales

Folktales deal with the legends, superstitions, customs, and beliefs of ordinary people. *Why Mosquitoes Buzz in People's Ears,* by Verna Aardema, is an African folktale that was originally spoken and passed on from one generation to another. *The Paper Crane,* by Molly Bang, is a modern tale that is based on a

Japanese folktale about a magic crane. Folktales are timeless in their appeal, reflecting universal human feelings and desires. Folktales include four special kinds of stories:

- *Fairy tales* are stories that usually contain an imaginary being with some sort of special or magical power, such as the fairy godmother in "Cinderella."
- *Fables* are brief stories that illustrate a moral or lesson and include animals or inanimate objects that have been personified with human traits. Arnold Lobel's *Fables* is a collection of modern day fables. Each is a one-page story about a particular animal that concludes with a one-sentence statement or moral. Fables are attractive to both children and adults, perhaps because they are simple and concise lessons on human behavior.
- *Myths* are stories that answer questions about something people cannot explain. They describe a cosmic phenomenon, strange natural happenings on earth, the start of civilization, or the origins of a custom. They often include gods and goddesses, mystical universal forces, and magic.
- *Epics* are long folktales or collections of tales about legendary heroes who personify the best human traits and represent the ideals of a nation. Homer's *Illiad* and *Odyssey* are examples of epic poems.

Most folktales possess the elements already discussed in this text, but with slight modifications. Elements commonly found in folktales are:

- A brief introduction that identifies the setting, characters, and problem
- One-dimensional (flat) characters that possess an obvious trait (e.g., good, evil, envy)
- A problem, conflict, or goal
- A fast-paced plot with attempts to solve the problem or reach the goal
- A conclusion that quickly follows the climax
- The number *three* (e.g., three sons, three wishes, three attempts to win favor) (see Figure 2.1)
- A theme, lesson, or moral with universal appeal
- A style that uses the vocabulary and folkways of the common people

Folktales help children see that good often prevails over evil, that cleverness triumphs over strength and might, and that the plain and simple are often rewarded for their honesty and goodness. Folktales let children experience fast-paced action, sometimes violent and horrible acts but all in the guise of stories that contain elements of magic or fantasy and happened long ago. Through folktales, children learn about human problems, solutions, morals, and values, and they show children how different cultures have contributed to our society.

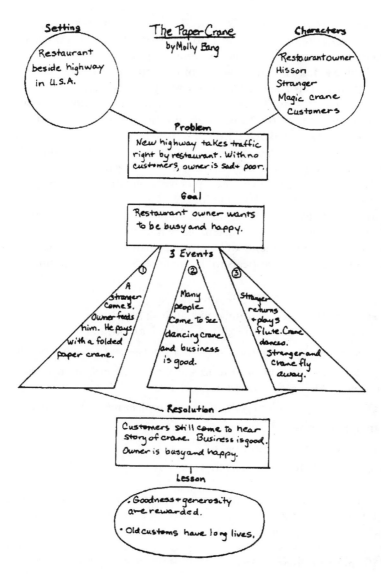

Figure 2.1 The literary elements of this modern day folktale include three important events.

Fantasy

Fantasy is fiction that contains an element of unreality. It twists or manipulates reality, often using fast-paced action, humor, magic, and imaginary events or characters. Maurice Sendak's *Where the Wild Things Are* is perhaps the most well-known modern example of picture-book fantasy for young children. *Just A*

Dream, The Wretched Stone, and indeed all of Chris Van Allsburg's books are popular examples of newer picture-book fantasies. Lois Lowry's *The Giver* is an example of fantasy that older readers enjoy. *Hey, Al,* by Arthur Yorinks, is an example of fantasy that concludes with a moral and is enjoyed by all ages.

Science fiction is a special kind of fantasy that is often set in other worlds and deals with the future. These stories are based on scientific facts but they explore the technology of the future and raise questions about the future of humanity. For example, Madeleine L'Engle's *A Wrinkle in Time* is created around the concept of the *tesseract,* a scientific term that means the fifth dimension. The story involves three children's travel by *tessering* through time to the planet Comatzoz and the help they receive from three imaginary characters named Mrs. Who, Mrs. Whatsit, and Mrs. Which.

In order for fantasy to be good, the impossible must be believable within the context of a logical and consistent story framework. In most fantasy, one or more of the common elements of literature is manipulated (see Figure 2.2), and because of these twists it appeals to the imagination. Fantasy includes:

- A setting that may be enchanted
- Characters that include humanlike animals, stereotypes of good and evil, heroes and heroines with magical powers, or extraterrestrial beings
- A problem, goal, or conflict, sometimes between forces of good and evil
- A plot that may include adventures of the characters, or, in science fiction, a heroic battle for the common good
- A climax, resolution of conflict, or accomplishment of the goal
- A theme or universal truth
- A point of view or a narrator
- A tone or style that is special in some way

Fantasy provides adventures into worlds of unreality for children. It helps children understand the difference between fiction and fact. It is often humorous and entertaining, and it allows children to use their imaginations and explore with characters who often have special powers. For these reasons, it is one of the most popular genres.

Realistic Fiction

Realistic fiction stories are true to life. They are set in a time period that children know and understand. They can be about people in other countries or in the United States. This genre includes realism in stories about animals, mysteries, sports, and adventures, as well as stories about those involved in the dilemmas and social issues of today's world. Topics include divorce, death, drugs, handicapping conditions, peer relationships, family problems, school failure, survival, and so on. The special elements of realistic fiction are:

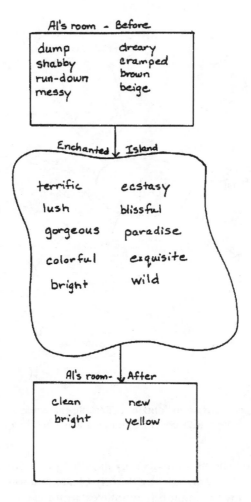

Al's room - Before

dump	dreary
shabby	cramped
run-down	brown
messy	beige

Enchanted ↓ Island

terrific	ecstasy
lush	blissful
gorgeous	paradise
colorful	exquisite
bright	wild

Al's room- ↓ After

clean	new
bright	yellow

Figure 2.2   In the fantasy *Hey, Al,* setting is
manipulated and moves from a cramped
apartment to an enchanted island in the sky
and back to the apartment.

- A setting that is real and believable
- Characters who reflect those found in everyday life (see Figure 2.3)
- A believable problem, goal, or conflict
- A plot that may not always end happily but that reflects reality and may contain humor
- A theme or universal truth
- A particular point of view or narrator
- A tone or style that is special in some way

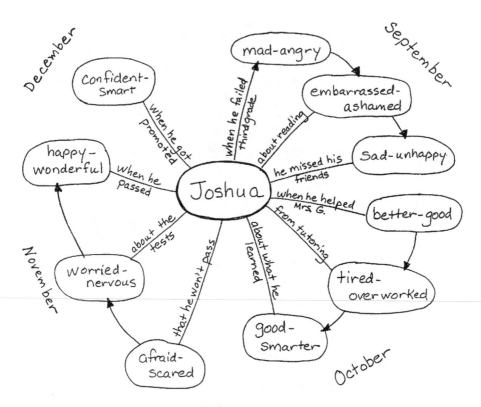

Figure 2.3   Good, realistic fiction contains believable characters like Joshua in this web showing his feelings as he is tutored by his third-grade teacher before he is promoted to fourth grade.

Realistic fiction shows students they have the power to change their lives. For example, *Dear Mr. Henshaw,* by Beverly Cleary, humorously helps middle-grade readers see how a young boy who lives with his mother and rarely sees his father copes with that situation while adjusting to a new school. In *Park's Quest,* Katherine Paterson sensitively portrays a young boy who desperately wants to know about his father, who was killed in Vietnam.

These stories help children know and learn about their world. They allow children to see that people are more alike than they are different. Realistic fiction can give children insight into their own problems and help them understand the feelings of others. It shows students that their emotions and experiences are not unique. Realistic fiction also helps students rehearse roles they may have in the future.

Historical Fiction

Historical fiction is based on facts and grounded in history but not restricted by it. It is realistic for the time period depicted and contains convincing dialogue between characters. Good historical fiction also contains accurate descriptions of settings and happenings that further children's knowledge of other times and places. *Weasel,* by Cynthia DeFelice, the story of a boy's experience with Indians in the Ohio wilderness in the early 1800s, is an example of this genre for older children. *Cassie's Journey: Going West in the 1860's* by Brett Harvey is an example of historical fiction for younger and middle readers. When authors of historical fiction take care to research their subjects, as these two authors have, the authenticity, quality, and realism of their stories are clearly apparent.

Historical fiction contains realistic and believable dialogue and accurate factual information as well as these elements:

- A setting that is authentic to a particular historical period (see Figure 2.4)
- Characters that act, speak, and have values that are true to the historical period
- A believable problem, goal, or conflict
- A plot or sequence of events
- A theme or universal truth that may include such things as loyalty, friendship, or courage
- A point of view or narrator
- A style or tone that is special in some way

Historical fiction enlivens the past for students. It makes content-area learning more interesting by providing related knowledge about people, places, and events in history. It also helps students become aware of their own heritage.

Biography

Biography is nonfiction that deals with the history of a person's life. Autobiographies are written by a person about his or her own life; biographies are written by writers who research and read about their subjects in order to portray the person's life the way it was accurately and interestingly. Evidence that information included in a biography is authentic makes it more believable.

Among the most accurate and entertaining biographies are those written by Jean Fritz. *And Then What Happened, Paul Revere?*, *What's the Big Idea, Benjamin Franklin?*, and *Why Don't You Get A Horse, Sam Adams?* are three of her books enjoyed by middle readers that represent realism and accuracy. Biography contains realistic, believable dialogue and accurate, factual information within these elements:

- An authentic setting where the main character lived or worked
- Characters (political heroes or heroines, sports figures, explorers, scientists, musicians, writers, actors or actresses, and so on) who act, speak, and have believable values

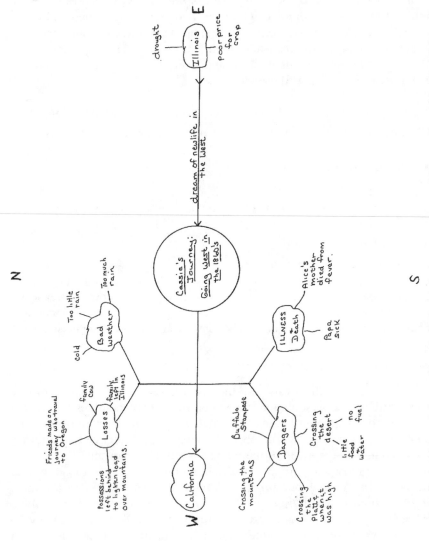

Figure 2.4 This web by Diane Mannix highlights setting, a critical feature of good historical fiction, in particular the hardships of westward travel for Cassie and her family.

- A believable problem or goal
- A plot or sequence of events substantiated by factual information that leads to an achievement or contribution
- A theme or universal truth
- A point of view or narrator
- A style or tone that is special in some way

Biography, like historical fiction, teaches children about other times, places, and people. Biographies such as *Anna Pavlova,* by Ellen Levine, provide role models who students can identify with and learn from (see Figure 2.5). Biographies may help students think about setting personal goals and aspirations as well. Books of this genre relate real happenings of real people to children, and so biography has a special allure.

Poetry

Poetry is an expression of a writer's inner thoughts and feelings and his or her relationship to the world and to others. Poets, more often than other writers perhaps, build sensory images through the use of *simile* ("shrill as a whistle"), *metaphor* ("the sun was an egg yolk"), *alliteration* ("leaping lizards lured me"), *onomatopoeia* ("slushing and slurping her slops"), or other techniques to produce a particular thought or feeling in the reader. Poetry uses sensuous and concise language that appeals to children's emotions and intellects by giving new or special meaning to everyday events, people, or places.

Because poems often contain rhyme, rhythm, and repetition, which enhance the message and impact, they should be read aloud to be enjoyed fully. Paul Fleischman's *Joyful Noise: Poems for Two Voices,* a collection of poetry about insects, can be read aloud chorally by two individuals or groups. Lee Bennett Hopkins's *More Surprises,* Jack Prelutsky's *Read Aloud Rhymes for the Very Young,* and Shel Silverstein's *Where the Sidewalk Ends* and *A Light in the Attic* are examples of collections of poems on a variety of topics that children enjoy hearing and that many teachers keep on hand for reading when they have a few minutes. Many of the elements of literature listed with the other genres can be found in poetry:

- A setting
- A character or characters
- A theme or universally understood message
- A point of view or narrator
- A special style or tone
- Creation of images (visual, auditory, or other senses)
- Use of rhyme, rhythm, and/or repetition

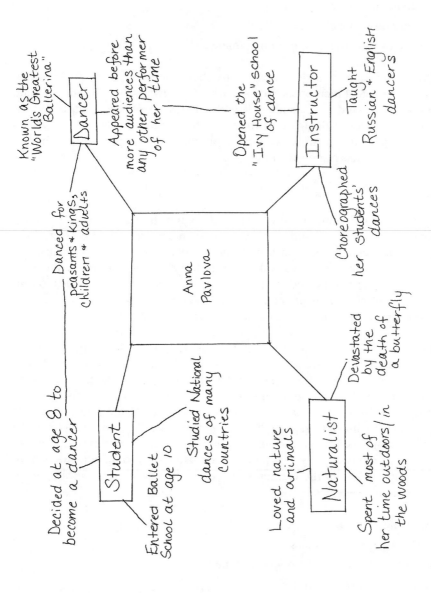

Figure 2.5 This web created by Karen Wandell of ballerina Anna Pavlova's life deepens children's understanding and appreciation of her as a real person.

Poetry allows children to experience the world in new and different ways. It provides opportunities to hear, see, and live in the everyday world with new insights. It also allows children to explore the world of the unknown and exercise their imaginations, while learning about and appreciating the rhyme and rhythm of language. The web in Figure 2.6 for *Night of the Whippoorwill,* by Nancy Larrick, identifies the special characteristics of her poetry and invites children to supply the titles of poems that fit those characteristics.

Information Books

Information books are nonfiction books written to inform and explain. For young children there are concept books on a variety of topics, from dinosaurs to word opposites. Alphabet books, like *David McPhail's Animals A to Z* or Tana Hoban's *A,B,See!* provide the very young with an introduction to the letters of the alphabet. Number books, like John Reiss's *Numbers* or Mitsumasa Anno's *Anno's Counting Book,* help teach and reinforce numeration. For older students, information books are written on all sorts of topics, from molecules and cats to drugs and the management of wildlife.

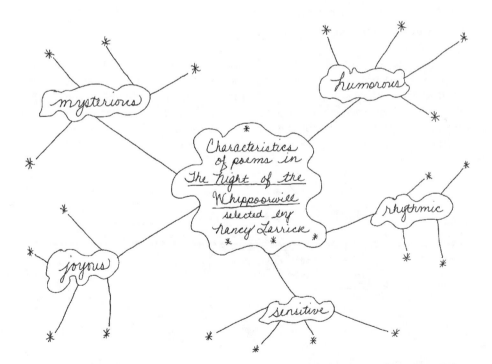

Figure 2.6 After hearing a poem read aloud, children can decide which characteristic it possesses and add the title at the asterisk on this web by Karen Wandell.

Two important things to consider when choosing an information book are how recently it was written and whether the information included is accurate. Often, the facts and concepts in older books are not up to date, especially if the topics are science, technology, or other areas where knowledge is expanding so rapidly that books quickly become outdated. One way to determine accuracy is to look at the author's credentials and/or the experiences that allow him or her to be an expert on the subject. Another way is to read several books on the topic to compare the information and concepts they contain for similarities and differences that could indicate accuracy or authenticity. Information books may contain some or all of these elements:

- An authentic setting from which the information is drawn
- Characters who explain the information or exhibit behaviors that share it in some way
- A central issue or problem
- A sequence of events or account of accurate and current factual evidence (see Figure 2.7) that clarifies or offers solutions to a problem
- A theme or main idea
- A point of view or narrator
- A tone or style that is distinctive

Information books provide children with knowledge and quench their thirst for answers to questions. Information books support content-area learning in science, social studies, and mathematics. They provide children with specific facts and information often not found in content texts, and the information they contain is often more current than that in content texts. Information books written about topics from the sciences, history, sociology, the arts, and the hu-

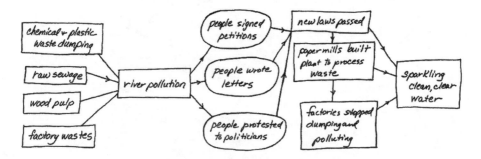

Figure 2.7   There is an abundance of accurate factual information and a thorough account of the Nashua River's history in Lynne Cherry's *The River Ran Wild.*

manities allow children to broaden their horizons as they learn about other people, places, and things.

 *Conclusion*

Each genre of literature possesses its own unique and characteristic literary elements. Some literary elements are common to all genres, and some are specific to one particular genre. By using webs, you can help children identify these elements and encourage rich responses to literature. Awareness and understanding of literary elements makes books more inviting, enjoyable, and comprehensible for children.

REFERENCES

Bromley, K., Irwin-DeVitis, L., & Modlo, M. (1995). *Graphic organizers: Visual strategies for active learning.* New York: Scholastic.

Bromley, K. (1992). *Language Arts: Exploring Connections.* Boston: Allyn and Bacon.

Cleland, C. (1981). Highlighting issues in children's literature through semantic webbing. *The Reading Teacher, 34*(6), 642–646.

Fitzgerald, J., & Teasley, A. B. (1986). Effects of instruction in narrative structure on children's writing. *Journal of Educational Psychology, 78*(6), 424–432.

Galda, L. (1987). Teaching higher order reading skills with literature. In B. Cullinan (Ed.), *Children's Literature in the Reading Program* (pp. 54–58, 89–96, 121–124). Newark, DE: International Reading Association.

Idol, L. (1987). Group story mapping: A comprehension strategy for both skilled and unskilled readers. *Journal of Learning Disabilities, 20*(4), 196–205.

Lehr, S. (1988). The child's developing sense of theme as a response to literature. *Reading Research Quarterly, 23*(3), 337–357.

Lukens, R. (1995). *A Critical Handbook of Children's Literature,* (5th ed.). Glenview, IL: Scott, Foresman.

Norton, D. E. (1993). Engaging children in literature. *The Reading Teacher, 46*(5), 432–441.

Olson, M. W. (1984). A dash of story grammar and . . . Presto! A book report. *The Reading Teacher, 37*(6), 458–461.

Reutzel, D. R. (1985). Story maps improve comprehension. *The Reading Teacher, 38*(4), 400–404.

———. (1984). Story mapping: An alternative approach to comprehension. *Reading World, 24*(2), 16–25.

Reutzel, D. R., & Fawson, P. (1991). Literature webbing predictable books: A Prediction strategy that helps below-average first graders. *Reading Research and Instruction, 30*(4), 20–30.

Scanlon, D. J. (1992). "Interactive semantic mapping: An interactive approach to enhancing LD students' content area comprehension. *Learning Disabilities: Research and Practice, 7*(3), 142–146.

Schmitt, M. C., & O'Brien, D. G. (1986). Story grammars: Some cautions about the trans-
lation of research into practice. *Reading Research and Instruction, 26*(1), 1–8.

Sinatra, R., Berg, D., & Dunn, R. (1985). Semantic mapping improves reading comprehension of learning disabled students. *Teaching Exceptional Children, 17*(4), 310–314.

Sinatra, R., Stahl-Gemake, J., & Morgan, N. (1986). Using semantic mapping after reading
to organize and write original discourse. *Journal of Reading, 30*(1), 4–13.

Sinatra, R., Beaudry, J. S., Stahl-Gemake, J., and Guastello, E. F. (1990). Combining visual
literacy, text understanding, and writing for culturally diverse students. *Journal of
Reading, 33*(8), 612–617.

Wolf, S. A., & Gearhart, M. (1994) . Writing what you read: Narrative assessment as a
learning event. *Language Arts, 71*(6), 425–445.

Children's Literature

Aardema, V. (1975). *Why Mosquitoes Buzz in People's Ears.* New York: Dial.

Anno, M. (1977). *Anno's Counting Book.* New York: Crowell.

Bang, M. (1985). *The Paper Crane.* New York: Greenwillow.

Cherry, L. (1992). *A River Ran Wild.* San Diego: Harcourt Brace Jovanovich.

Cleary, B (1983). *Dear Mr. Henshaw.* New York: Morrow Junior Books.

DeFelice, C. (1990). *Weasel.* New York: Avon.

Fleischman, P. (1988). *Joyful Noise: Poems for Two Voices.* New York: Harper & Row.

Fritz, J. (1973). *And Then What Happened, Paul Revere?* New York: Coward, McCann.

———. (1974). *Why Don't You Get A Horse, Sam Adams?* New York: Coward, McCann.

———. (1976). *What's the Big Idea, Benjamin Franklin?* New York: Coward, McCann.

Harvey, B. (1988). *Cassie's Journey: Going West in the 1860's.* New York: Holiday House.

Hoban, T. (1982). *A,B,See!* New York: Greenwillow.

Hoberman, M. A. (1984). *A House Is a House for Me.* New York: Viking Penguin.

Hopkins, L. B. (1987). *More Surprises.* New York: Harper & Row.

Larrick, N. (1992). *Night of the Whippoorwill.* New York: Philomel.

Levine, E. (1995). *Anna Pavlova: Genius of the Dance.* New York: Scholastic.

L'Engle, M. (1962). *A Wrinkle in Time.* New York: Farrar, Straus & Giroux.

Lowry, L. (1993). *The Giver.* Boston: Houghton Mifflin.

Mazer, A. (1993). *The Salamander Room.* New York: Scholastic.

McPhail, D. (1988). *David McPhail's Animals A to Z.* New York: Scholastic.

Paterson, K. (1988). *Park's Quest.* New York: Dutton.

Prelutsky, J. (1986). *Read Aloud Rhymes for the Very Young.* New York: Knopf.

Reiss, J. (1971). *Numbers.* New York: Bradbury.

Sendak, M. (1963). *Where the Wild Things Are.* New York: Harper & Row.

Shreve, S. (1984). *The Flunking of Joshua T. Bates.* New York: Scholastic.

Silverstein, S. (1974). *Where the Sidewalk Ends.* New York: Harper & Row.

———. (1981). *A Light in the Attic.* New York: Harper & Row.

Terban, M. (1987). *Mad as a Wet Hen! And Other Funny Idioms.* New York: Clarion.

Van Allsburg, C. (1991). *The Wretched Stone.* Boston: Houghton Mifflin.

Van Allsburg, C. (1990). *Just a Dream.* Boston: Houghton Mifflin.

Yorinks, A. (1986). *Hey, Al.* New York: Farrar, Straus & Giroux.

chapter 3

Selecting Quality Literature

No discussion of children's literature is complete without considering the characteristics of quality literature. This chapter looks at what makes quality stories and how quality illustrations are created. The chapter presents three book selection tips for students and discusses the important place multicultural literature should have in every classroom.

What Is Quality Literature?

A visit to a library, bookstore, supermarket, or drug store with an eye to the children's books available in each will alert you to the range of quality in children's books. Of course, quality is a highly personal matter and is not often defined the same way by any two people. Several attributes often come to mind, however, when we think of quality in children's books:

- *Excellence:* An excellent book is one that is outstanding or exceptional in some way. For example, a book may be superior for its literary and/or artistic style, use of language, originality, and importance of ideas.
- *Permanence:* This refers to the length of time a particular book has endured as a well-loved piece of literature. In order for a book to stand the test of time, it must be memorable and of universal interest. Books that are lasting favorites with children are often books of excellent quality.
- *Distinctiveness:* A distinctive book is an unusual book, one that you respond to and experience in a unique way. It has the power to connect forcefully with you or make a link in some way with your experiences, attitudes, beliefs, or knowledge. With a newly published book it is impossible to know for sure if the book has permanence, but you may be able to make a guess based on your feelings about the book's excellence, distinctiveness, and your personal response to it.

Keep in mind, though, that books you consider good *and* some you may not consider examples of quality literature still have a place in your classroom. Children enjoy many popular titles that will probably not stand the test of time but that they nonetheless enjoy reading, and therefore will read. You can read to them from quality literature and make it available in your classroom. Sharing your enjoyment of a particular book and the reasons for that enjoyment is one way of encouraging students to read quality books themselves.

When selecting literature for your literacy program, it is important to remember to choose a variety of quality literature from every genre. There are other criteria to consider in choosing literature such as developmental appropriateness, appeal to students, and cultural and social authenticity (Cooper, 1993).

While younger children may not be able to articulate quite as clearly as can older students about what is distinctive and appeals to them in a particular book, there are clues to be discovered by observing what they read. Younger children often want a particular book read over and over to them, which Holdaway (1983) says is a child's way of telling us what is good for him or her: "A good book is one that a child will turn to again and again" (p. 3). Butler (1983) believes that "A good children's book is a book which is an experience for a child, an enjoyable experience, a literary experience" (p. 3). So we know that distinctiveness and personal response is a critical component in judging what a good book is, especially for younger readers. Huck (1983) says: "I think children do not find the good books unless somebody helps them. That somebody can be a librarian, it can be an enthusiastic teacher, it can be a parent" (p. 3).

Adults are probably more sensitive than are children to characteristics of excellence, permanence, and distinctiveness in children's literature because they have had broader and richer experiences with books and life in general. Children are probably more sensitive to the way a book appeals to them personally, and young children often show this preference by continually turning to favorite books. Often these books are so repetitive or predictable that they are not adult favorites. But it is from rereading them over and over again that children begin to learn language patterns, vocabulary, and the elements of story, among other things.

To provide teachers with titles of popular books children choose to read, each year the International Reading Association (IRA) publishes a list of 100 books, called *Children's Choices,* in the October issue of *The Reading Teacher.* From the 4000 or so books published yearly for children the IRA and Children's Book Council (CBC) choose 500 books, as examples of good books for recreational reading and teaching reading. These selections are then tested in five school districts around the country, and children vote for their favorites. In addition to the list, a graded and annotated bibliography of the 100 most popular books is published every year.

Why Choose Multicultural Literature?

In a relatively brief period of time, the racial and ethnic makeup of our country has dramatically changed. Statisticians predict that the majority of the school-age population in the United States by the next century will be African Americans, Asian Americans, Latinos, and Native Americans (Ramirez & Ramirez, 1994).

Since our world is becoming increasingly diverse, we need to understand and appreciate others' similarities and differences. To this end, multicultural literature can serve your students well. Norton (1991) tells us it has an important place in the curriculum. "The study of multicultural literature is a powerful means for literacy educators to help students develop an appreciation and understanding of their literary and cultural heritage" (p. 38).

When your students read European, Asian, African, Native American, or Hispanic literature, they learn about the values and beliefs of diverse people. (Examples of these books are found in Chapters 7 and 8 and are noted with an asterisk [*].) Reading folktales, fairy tales, fables, and myths of the past helps your students see how these stories are integral to different cultures. Reading information books, biographies, and realistic fiction from diverse authors and cultures gives students knowledge, role models, and affirmation of themselves. In addition to increasing the cultural awareness of all students, multicultural literature builds self-esteem and empowers students of diverse backgrounds.

You and your students will find that reading works from other cultures enriches the curriculum, develops geographic literacy, and is personally rewarding as well. For example, books like *Amazing Grace,* by Mary Hoffman and Caroline Binch, and *Flossie and the Fox,* by Patricia McKissack, give all students, not just young girls with African American or Black ancestry, main characters to identify with who are strong, clever, single-minded, and persevering. Folktale collections like *Legends of the Sun and Moon,* by Eric and Tessa Hadley, provide students with alternative explanations from many cultures for the existence of sun, moon, and stars.

As with any literature, you should carefully select and share multicultural literature with your students. Quality literature that has multiracial or multiethnic characters and deals with relevant multicultural topics and issues enriches the curriculum and learning for all your students.

What Makes a Quality Story?

You can help children learn to understand and appreciate quality by identifying a favorite book and focusing on their personal responses. You can also teach young children about the criteria of excellence, permanence, and distinctiveness in their favorite books. Help them ask and answer questions about a favorite book:

- Why did you enjoy it?
- What did it remind you of?
- What things make it excellent or outstanding?
- What things make it distinctive or special?
- Is it worth remembering? Why or why not?
- Would other children like and appreciate it?
- Does it have a theme that everyone can understand?

You can also encourage students to judge quality in story by discussing specific story elements with them. When children are aware of these elements, they can more easily respond to a book in terms of them.

Not all genres possess the same literary elements, as you know from reading Chapter 2. For instance, poetry may or may not possess characters or a setting and may best be judged by answering the questions just listed. To help children evaluate information books, ask questions like:

- How accurate is the information?
- How current is the book?
- What are the author's credentials?
- Did the author or illustrator do any research in order to write or illustrate this book?

Questions like these also encourage children to evaluate historical fiction and biography. For further discussions of specific genres, see Norton (1995) and Sutherland and Arbuthnot (1991).

The following list is a guide for discussing the elements of quality in story with children. You can help them ask other questions about specific genres by looking back to the discussion in Chapter 2 of the elements of these genres.

Setting
- Where and when does the story take place?
- Is it appropriate to the story?

Characters
- Who are they and how are they developed?
- Do they seem real and convincing?
- How do they grow and change during the story?

Plot
- What happens in the story?
- What are the events? Do they keep you interested?
- What is the conflict or problem? Does the solution make sense?

Theme
- What is the main message or *heart* of the story?
- What is the *glue* that holds the story together?
- What did you learn from the story?

Point of View
- Who tells the story?
- How does the narrator tell about characters and events? Is it effective?

Style

■ Is the writing special in some way?

■ How does the author use words to express ideas?

Tone

■ What is the author's attitude?

■ What special feelings does the book give you?

Whether for an adult or a child, good literature possesses unique language that truly delights the senses and develops the knowledge of those who read it or hear it read. Literature shows children and adults how others live and have lived, and as we understand the lives of others, we develop a better understanding of ourselves and the people in our own world.

Learning to appreciate and love literature should be a positive and enriching part of a child's school experience. Learning to love reading and to enjoy literature as a child can be the start of a lifelong habit that brings pleasure and knowledge (Sutherland & Arbuthnot, 1991). Children are not born with a preference for quality literature, and many will not receive encouragement or experience the joy of reading at home. For these children, the reading beliefs and behaviors you exhibit, as well as your use of literature in the curriculum, are critical. When you use and read books of high literary quality and give children the opportunity to read books of their choice, it helps them develop a taste for quality. Children can then begin to compare and contrast different traits in books and become appreciative readers of quality books.

There are a number of awards that provide recognition for outstanding quality in children's literature. The Newbery Medal was named for John Newbery, the first English publisher of books for children, and is given yearly to the book considered the most distinguished contribution to literature for children. The Caldecott Medal was named for Randolph Caldecott, an English illustrator, and is given yearly to the most distinguished picture book for children. The CBC publishes two listings: Outstanding Science Trade Books for Children and Notable Children's Trade Books in the Field of Social Studies. Lists of books that have received some of these awards are found in Appendix B.

What Makes Quality Illustrations?

When you teach your students to recognize quality illustrations, you help them develop both their artistic and literary appreciation. We know that quality illustrations, as well as a quality story, contribute to a book's excellence, permanence, and distinctiveness. Every teacher has observed a child at one time or another who is completely mesmerized by the pictures an illustrator has created to tell a story. Spellbound attention, wide-eyed wonder, eager page turning, exclamations of delight and appreciation, and sometimes even disinterest in print characterize these events. Pictures that have the power to connect with a reader and communicate messages in these ways possess some aspect of quality, whether the illustrations enhance the content of the story for the reader, elicit children's feelings and responses, or both (see Figure 3.1).

Four major factors affect the ways in which children perceive and evaluate illustrations in picture books (Cianciolo, 1990). First, a child's age and stage of cognitive and social development impact on what he or she perceives. Second, the way adults have prepared a child for an experience with a picture book is critical to the child's perception. Third, the child's emotional and psychological state at the time the book is read is important. Fourth, exposure to a book or the number of times a child has looked at the pictures affects his or her interpretation and evaluation. All these factors account for differences in children's perceptions and responses and the many ways in which pictures in books function for children.

Good pictures have the power to communicate with children and encourage their personal responses to a story. Sometimes pictures tell a story on their

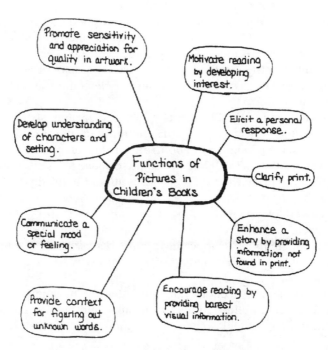

Figure 3.1   Illustrations and artwork in children's books serve several functions.

own and allow children to understand that story without reading the text, such as the pictures in *King Bidgood's in the Bathtub,* by Audrey Wood. In books like *The Magic Schoolbus at the Waterworks,* by Joanna Cole, pictures enrich the printed story and actually contain a second story. In other books, like *Owl Moon* by Jane Yolen, the pictures reflect most, but not all, of the story; that is, the text is more complete than are the pictures.

While building children's awareness of quality in pictures, you can, at the same time, develop their *visual-verbal literacy.* This is a term Stewig (1988) uses to mean the ability to decode messages in pictures and encode these ideas in coherent oral language. While many children can easily tell which illustrations they prefer, most have trouble expressing why they like them. Stewig compares this to the adult who says, "I don't know anything about art, but I know what I like." Lack of background on which to make evaluations and lack of language with which to express preferences handicap children and adults alike. But children and adults can learn to identify aspects of quality in pictures they prefer and put a value on them when they are given opportunities to engage in these activities.

Caldecott Medal and Honor books are especially good for developing visual-verbal literacy, as these books are judged and awarded this distinction on the quality of their illustrations (see Appendix B). This is not to say that children cannot learn to read pictures from other children's books, a basal reader, or a content text, but the Caldecott books are a valuable and dependable source of excellent illustrations. Although many picture books appear appropriate only for younger children, the thinking skills involved in visual-verbal literacy make pictures from these books challenging for upper elementary and middle school students as well.

Traditionally, there are six aspects of art—color, line, shape, texture, arrangement, and total effect—that contribute to its impact. Consider these six aspects when making judgments about the quality of pictures in children's books. It is also good to help children become sensitive to these aspects of good art as they begin to make their own decisions about the quality of the pictures in the books they read.

Do not overlook the possibility of enlisting the help of the school art teacher in developing children's understanding and appreciation of how six aspects of art combine to make appealing picture books. An art teacher can help deepen your children's understanding of and sensitivity to what makes quality picture books.

As you read the next sections remember that the most important thing to consider is whether the illustrations fit the story and help to communicate a message. Illustrations should convey information, ideas, mood, or feelings to the reader.

Color

When you talk with your students about the colors an illustrator uses, ask them:

- What colors do you see?
- Are the colors bright, soft, or something else?
- Where and when are colors used?
- Do the colors match the mood or content of the story?

To help sensitize children to color and how an illustrator uses it effectively, show them a book like *Arrow to the Sun,* by Gerald McDermott, which is done in bright yellows, oranges, and other colors in contrast to black. Or use *Why Mosquitoes Buzz in People's Ears,* by Verna Aardema and illustrated by Leo and Diane Dillon, which uses pastel shades in contrast to white and black backgrounds. Or use *Frog and Toad Are Friends,* by Arnold Lobel, in which only soft shades of green and brown appear (see Figure 3.2). The comparison web in Figure 3.3 shows how color and the other five aspects of art are used in *Arrow to the Sun,* by Gerald McDermott, and in *Frog and Toad Are Friends,* by Arnold Lobel.

When your students can describe how one illustrator uses colors, you can show them the work of other illustrators who use colors in different ways. Then children begin to see similarities and differences as they learn to compare the way different illustrators use color. Comparing books that contrast with each other is often easier than evaluating a single book.

Ask children why they think McDermott did not use shades of green and brown for *Arrow* or why *Frog and Toad* was not done in bright primary colors. And ask why *Arrow* begins with shades of yellow, orange, and rust, and as the story progresses adds other bright colors, such as pink, green, and blue. It is questions like these that help children see how color enhances the content and mood of a story.

Figure 3.2   Lobel uses shades of green and brown, the colors of real frogs and toads, in this "Frog and Toad" books. (Picture by David Caramore, Grade 2).

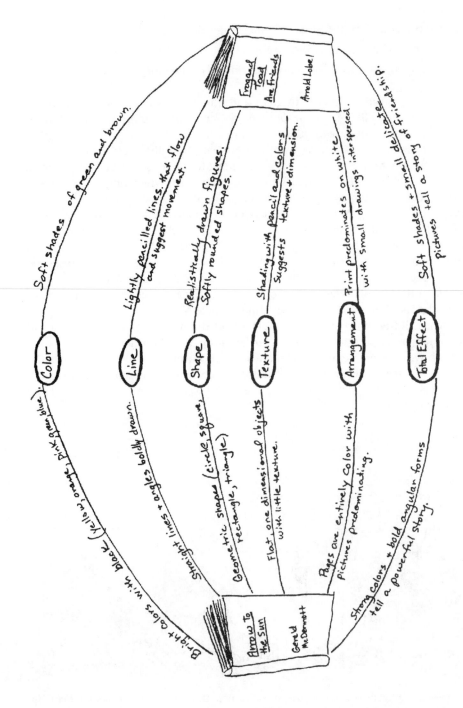

Figure 3.3 Creating a web like this one can help children compare the artwork in two different books.

Frog and Toad Are Friends — Arnold Lobel

Arrow To the Sun — Gerald McDermott

Color
Soft shades of green and brown.
(Yellow, orange, pink, green, blue.)
Bright colors with black.

Line
Lightly pencilled lines that flow and suggest movement.
Straight lines + angles boldly drawn.

Shape
Realistically drawn figures. Softly rounded shapes.
Geometric shapes (circle, square, rectangle, triangle)

Texture
Shading with pencil and colors suggests texture + dimension.
Flat one dimensional objects with little texture.

Arrangement
Print predominates on white with small drawings interspersed.
Pages are entirely color with pictures predominating.

Total Effect
Soft shades + small delicate pictures tell a story of friendship.
Strong colors + bold angular forms tell a powerful story.

Line

To help your children understand how illustrators use line, ask questions that help them identify how line is used in individual books. Then they can compare books that contain contrasting uses of line. Ask questions like:

- Where do you see lines?
- Are the lines thick or thin? Dark or light?
- Do the lines do something special for the picture?

You might begin with black and white illustrations that use line in obvious ways. Shel Silverstein's books *The Missing Piece* and *A Light in the Attic* show the use of simple, humorous drawings using only black lines on the white background. Some illustrators do one-dimensional, cartoon-style drawings and add color as Dr. Seuss (T. Geisel) has done in *Oh! The Places You'll Go.* In *Castle,* David Macaulay uses black lines to create texture and depth in drawings of a medieval castle (see Figure 3.4). Other illustrators add dimensionality and texture with fine lines that cross. This technique is called crosshatching and can be seen in *Mufaro's Beautiful Daughters: An African Tale* by John Steptoe (see Figure 3.5).

K.KARCHER

Figure 3.4 Black line drawings are a perfect medium for communicating the architect's or engineer's perspective in the information book, *Castle,* by David Macaulay. (Drawing by Katie Karcher, Grade 12).

Figure 3.5   An example of crosshatching in *Mufaro's Beautiful Daughters* by John Steptoe. (Drawing by Daniel Ray, Grade 12).

You can also show your children how illustrators use line in other ways for special effects. In *Python's Party,* Brian Wildsmith uses both thick and thin lines to add texture. The thicker, crayonlike lines show the heavy foliage of the jungle, and the thinner, pen-and-ink lines show the wiry hair of a goat and the softer fur of a fox. In *Owl Moon,* illustrated by John Schoenherr, the soft, delicate lines and shades of blue he uses capture the mood and feeling of a cold winter night.

Again ask your children some questions that require their evaluating how an illustrator uses line. Ask them if they think Wildsmith's *Python's Party* would be as interesting if it were done with Dr. Seuss's cartoon-style drawings. Or ask them how well they think Shel Silverstein's use of line would fit *Why Mosquitoes Buzz in People's Ears* or *Owl Moon.*

Promoting discussions with questions like these sensitizes children to how artists use line to communicate and achieve special effects. Once they become aware of this aspect of artwork, children can identify it in almost any illustration and then speculate on how line adds distinctiveness to the content or mood of the story.

Shape

You can prompt discussions about shape with these questions:

- What shapes do you see?
- Are shapes distinct or subtle? Simple or ornate? Realistic or abstract? Free-flowing or rigid?
- Do they match the story or help it in some way?

Even young children can identify the variety of shapes that illustrators use. Initially, you can help children identify distinct shapes—circles, squares, rectangles, and triangles—such as those in *Arrow to the Sun.* Ask children why they think McDermott used these geometric shapes and whether they match the story or help it in some way. In contrast, a book that contains subtle shapes is *Dawn,* in which Uri Shulevitz uses soft, fuzzy shapes to communicate the quiet and subdued mood of a peaceful place and time (see Figure 3.6). In *Round Trip,* Ann Jonas uses black and white shapes, reversing them as foreground or background to tell the story that requires first reading in the normal way and then turning the book upside down and reading it in reverse to finish (see Figure 3.7).

Some illustrators create collages that use realistic shapes. In *The Paper Crane,* Molly Bang uses paper cutouts and other materials to tell the story of a paper crane that comes alive and changes the fortunes of an old man. In *The Snowy Day* and other works, Ezra Jack Keats uses oils and collage to tell simple stories about the life of Peter, a young black child. Eric Carle's artwork in *Pancakes, Pancakes!* shows use of paint, collage, and a touch of the abstract to create simple, bold shapes for animals and people.

You can introduce children to other examples of how artists use shape. Graeme Base's *Animalia,* an animal alphabet book with a surrealistic look, contains a myriad of ornately detailed animals and objects on each page that all begin with the same letter of the alphabet. Mitsumasa Anno uses abstract shapes as an appropriate complement to the content of *Anno's Alphabet: An Adventure in Imagination.* Chris Van Allsburg, in *The Polar Express,* uses realistic

Figure 3.6 Water colors lend themselves well to Uri Shulevitz's pictures of the dawn's reflection in a lake. (Picture by Michelle Reynolds, Grade 3).

shapes and forms in muted pastels to tell a story about the meaning of Christmas. To help children understand the way these artists use shape, ask why they think Base's detailed shapes fit his subject or how Anno's abstract shapes allow the reader to pretend and imagine more easily than photographs might allow.

Texture

Discussions of texture can begin with questions like:

- Do the surfaces of things look different from each other?
- Do objects look like they feel a certain way? Rough, smooth, furry, jagged, solid, heavy, airy, or light?
- What makes the objects look the way they do?

To help children appreciate and understand how an illustrator creates the visual sensation of feeling or texture, first show them pictures that contain little or no texture. A book like *The Missing Piece,* by Shel Silverstein, with its simple outline drawings, shows children art in which there is no texture.

Then you can share pictures in which the illustrator manipulates color, line, or shape to create texture or a pattern that suggests texture. In *Owl Moon,* John Schoenherr uses many fine lines to give the bark on the trees a rough look and the owl's feathers a soft, full, ruffled look. In *The Snail's Spell,* by Joanne

Figure 3.7 Distinct black and white shapes from recognizable pictures when *Round Trip,* by Ann Jonas, is held upside down as well. (Picture by Derrick Ryan Brundege, Grade 4).

Ryder, Lynne Cherry uses many fine lines and shades of colors to create a real-looking turtle with a plated shell, a toad with rough, bumpy skin, furry chipmunks, and a snail with soft skin and a smooth shell (see Figure 3.8). Shades of color combined with geometric patterns in *Arrow to the Sun* give depth to pictured objects. In *Python's Party,* Brian Wildsmith expertly combines layers of brilliant color, fine lines, and smudged, indistinct shapes to create scenes of the jungle and wild animals that are effectively textured. With pencil drawings in tones of black, gray, and white, Chris Van Allsburg achieves wonderful texture and realism in *Jumanji* that include hairy monkeys, an exploding volcano, and a snake and chair upholstery that share the same bold pattern.

The mediums of collage and woodcut also allow an illustrator to give the sensation of texture. Ezra Jack Keats, Leo Lionni, Eric Carle, and Molly Bang all use collage to achieve dimensionality and visual differences in objects. Lionni uses collages composed of crayoned shapes, torn newspaper, wallpaper, and tissue paper overlays with color to provide texture in *Frederick* and *Alexander and the Wind-Up Mouse.* Marcia Brown in *Once a Mouse* uses woodcuts in subdued colors to portray texture. Ed Emberley in *Drummer Hoff* uses simple, three-color stylized woodcuts. Figure 3.9 shows Ezra Jack Keats' use of collage in *The Snowy Day.*

Arrangement

A few questions can elicit talk about how illustrations and print are arranged:

- Where do you find the print on the pages?
- Where do you find the pictures on the pages?
- Do you think the print and pictures go together in a special way for some reason?

Sometimes the arrangement of pictures and text in a book seems to have no rhyme or reason, but often with close observation, your children will discover a special design or composition to a book. Caldecott Medal books such as *Arrow to the Sun* by Gerald McDermott in Figure 3.10 and Caldecott Honor books are especially good to use to help build your children's knowledge of arrangement or composition. These books are chosen specifically for excellence in artwork, and arrangement is often carefully orchestrated.

Maurice Sendak's *Where the Wild Things Are,* one of the most popular and best-selling books for younger children, has an arrangement of print and pictures that enhances the story. Print is found on a white background on the left side of each double page from the beginning of the story, when Max is at home in his bedroom, until he sails "in and out of weeks and almost over a year to where the wild things are." Initially, pictures occur on the right side of each double page, with the first picture quite small, but they increase in size as the story progresses. By the time Max is ready to sail away, the picture is so large it

Figure 3.8 Soft natural colors and fine lines depict the world of a snail in a garden in *The Snail's Spell*, written by Joanne Ryder and illustrated by Lynne Cherry. (Picture by Kimberly Clark, Grade 12).

Figure 3.9   Ezra Jack Keats uses collage with a variety of patterns and textures in *The Snowy Day.* (Picture by Rachel Daddezio, Grade 2).

covers the entire right page and a third of the left page. When Max reaches the land of the wild things and while he is there among the monsters, the print appears across the bottom third of both double pages and pictures occur across the upper two-thirds of both facing pages. After Max makes friends and is proclaimed king, the "wild rumpus" appears on three entire double facing pages with no print. When Max sails back home, the print again appears on the left-hand side of each page and pictures gradually shrink until he finds a hot dinner waiting on the table in his room.

Figure 3.10 Bright colors and geometric shapes similar to the artwork of native Americans of the Southwest fill entire pages and predominate over the text of Gerald McDermott's *Arrow to the Sun*. (Picture by David Law, Grade 4).

Sendak uses the size and placement of pictures and the placement of print as the story progresses to heighten the reader's involvement in the journey that results in Max's confrontation with and conquest of the wild things. Sendak carefully arranges text and pictures to convey sequence of events and mood in this fantasy.

As you help children notice the way a few good books are designed, they will see the design and composition in other books they read. Understanding how authors and illustrators arrange print and pictures can help children appreciate and articulate their reasons for preferring one book over another.

Total Effect

Prompt discussion of the impact a book has on your children with these questions:

- How do color, line, shape, texture, print, type, pictures, end papers, and cover fit together?
- Are they all related in some special way? How?
- Do all the artistic aspects blend together to create a special design or composition?

Giving your children opportunities to examine and compare the work of different illustrators encourages awareness of color, line, and shape and of how they are manipulated to achieve texture and total effect. With this insight, children will better understand the impact illustrations have on the content and mood of stories in picture books.

The total effect or impact a book has on a child is determined first by the way illustrations and format complement the story and second by how the reader is able to relate to the whole package. Sometimes the effect a book has is clear from the look of wonder or smile of satisfaction on a child's face. Sometimes effect can be measured by the repeated requests for reading of a particular book. Sometimes effect is seen in the number and type of questions asked or observations made.

We can teach children about the elements that contribute to the effect or impact of a book. Again, good examples of the total effect of content interwoven with the aspects of art discussed previously are most often found in Caldecott Medal and Honor books where examples of quality in artistic media and styles are also to be found.

Artistic Media and Styles

Media

Media are the materials and processes an artist uses to create pictures. Illustrators of children's books employ a wide range of media, sometimes one type of medium is used alone and sometimes several are used in combination in the same picture book. Teaching children to recognize media and their uses in literature helps develop artistic appreciation and enjoyment of literature. Brief descriptions of several types of media follow along with examples of well-known picture books and their illustrators:

- *Collage:* The use of materials such as cut or torn paper, cloth, and string glued to a flat surface to make a picture. Leo Lionni, in *An Extraordinary Egg,* a story about three frogs who befriend an alligator that hatches from an egg, uses collage and paint as well.

- *Drawings:* This medium is the making of pictures or sketches using pencil, pen and ink, charcoal, colored pencil, crayons, colored markers, pastels or colored chalk, or wash, which is ink that is thinned with water. Chris Van Allsburg used pencil in *Jumanji,* while Stephen Gammell used colored pencils in *Song and Dance Man,* by Karen Ackerman.

- *Painting:* This is the use of pigment (powder) and liquid or paste mixed together and spread on paper or canvas. Watercolors look soft, delicate, and often transparent. Tempera is not as transparent as watercolor and can be seen in Maurice Sendak's *Where the Wild Things Are.* Oils are opaque and result when pigment is mixed with linseed oil. Acrylics use a plastic base and are opaque and brilliant. Gouache is powder mixed with a white base. It provides the rich colors in *Music, Music For Everyone* by Vera Williams.

- *Photography:* The use of photos, such as those in *Lincoln: A Photobiography* by Russell Freedman.

- *Printmaking:* When a picture is carved from a block of wood or linoleum and the surface is inked and printed. Marcia Brown's *Once A Mouse* is an example.

- *Scratchboard:* When designs are scratched onto the surface of a smooth white board that has been painted with black ink. Brian Pinkney's work in *The Dream Keeper and Other Poems* by Langston Hughes is an example.

- *Mixed media:* When illustrators use two or more media or invents their own combinations. Ed Young combined watercolor and pastel drawings in *Lon Po Po: A Red-Riding Hood Story from China.* Faith Ringgold's striking multimedia technique is described at the conclusion of *Tar Beach.*

Style

Style is the form of expression an artist uses to create pictures. Style is the product of the artist's imagination, skill, and chosen medium. Although each artist has an individual style, artwork in general is often grouped by similarities in style. An illustrator's style may blend facets of more than one of these styles and may not fit neatly into one category. Helping your children recognize style also develops their artistic appreciation and enjoyment of literature.

In picture books, artistic style ranges from realistic to abstract. Pictures done in a *realistic,* or representational, style are true to life and provide accurate depictions of objects and scenes. Lifelike drawings, paintings, cartoon-style drawings, photographs, and drawing media are all examples of realism. Pictures done in an abstract style are the opposite of realistic.

Abstract illustrations are less tangible than are realistic pictures. Often the form and surface qualities of objects are emphasized and reality is distorted. Abstraction may be *impressionistic,* showing what the eye sees before the brain recognizes objects. Pictures in this style emphasize light and give fleeting impressions of natural objects. The art in *Dawn,* by Uri Shulevitz, is an example. Or abstraction may be *expressionistic,* communicating a central message through graphic representations with few details. *Music, Music For Everyone,* by Vera Williams, is an example. *Surrealistic* art presents fantasy images and dreams with an unusual use of color and unlikely happenings as in *The Eleventh Hour: A Curious Mystery,* by Grahame Base.

Other styles found in picture books include: *primitive* (in which the art is called folk art and depicts a particular culture or the time period of the story), *cartoon-style* (uses line drawings and color as Dr. Seuss [T. Geisel] did in *Oh, The Places You'll Go*).

Illustrators often use a particular style and medium for which they become well known. Even young children recognize the unique style characteristics of their favorite author/illustrators. For example, Jan Brett's careful representations in detailed pictures with striking borders show the activities of the townspeople and give a hint of what is to come on the next pages of *Berlioz the Bear.* These characteristics of her style are also found in *Town Mouse Country Mouse* and in most of her other work.

David Macaulay's style ranges from realistic to abstract in *Black and White* and was recognized with the Caldecott Medal in 1991. In four separate stories within this book, Macaulay uses realism, impressionism, cartoons, and his own unique style to show how artists can mix styles successfully within one picture book to achieve a special effect.

It is the unique use of both media and style together that results in quality in illustrations. Artists use the materials and processes that comprise media and their own particular style or form of expression to create illustrations that enhance print and help elicit children's feelings and responses to literature. We can help children examine and identify both media and style to see how these factors contribute to quality in illustrations as well. For a more in-depth treatment of both media and style you may want to read Frezzolini (1992), Lynch-Brown and Tomlinson (1993), Russell (1994), and/or Kiefer (1995).

Selection Tips for Kids

While an artists' use of media and style often creates illustrations that captivate children's interests and help them select a book, the difficulty of the print they will read is also an important factor for children to consider. Mary, an elementary school media specialist, realizes the impact of a teacher's recommendations on what students select to read. She routinely reads the books she orders and talks with her classes about her opinions of these books. Mary also gives daily *booktalks,* described in Chapter 4, to each of her classes because she has learned that books she describes even briefly are also those her students eagerly choose to read.

Mary realizes the importance of developing a community of readers within each of her classes. She initiates conversations about books her students are reading and eagerly takes part in book discussions with them. Because she also recognizes the powerful impact that peers have on each other's reading habits, Mary regularly encourages conversations in which her students share with each other their personal reactions to and opinions of books, authors, and illustrators.

Mary also believes, however, that many students lack a simple strategy for selecting a book. She often saw her students signing books out of the library that seemed too difficult for them. In casual conversations with these students when they returned books, Mary realized that many students were not reading them. Through observation and talks with students, Mary has come to believe that book selection is one of the keys to reading satisfaction. When the right book finds the right student, she says the result is electrifying.

Here are three book selection strategies to help your students find the right book:

- *Can it be for me?:* Mary uses this strategy (Sharp, 1992) with older students and reports good success. She teaches her students that there are twelve aspects of a book to consider before signing it out of the library (see Figure 3.11). By checking each of the twelve criteria first, a student examines the book fairly closely and knows quickly that he is very interested or that the book is not for him. Mary posts this mnemonic device in the library on large chart paper where her students can readily refer to it. You and your students can also make laminated bookmarks from tagboard for each student with this mnemonic printed on it.

- *Five-finger test:* This strategy works well with younger students and with easy-to-read books. Have the child choose a page in the middle of the book to read aloud. Have the child hold down one finger each time he encounters a word he cannot pronounce. If he reads an entire page with fewer than five words missed, the book is probably readable with some help. But if more than five words are missed, the child will need help to read it.

- *Two-fist test:* For older students reading more difficult books, this test works the same way as does the five-finger test. With two pages of text, the student can miss ten words and will need help reading the book. If he misses fewer than ten words, he may be able to read the book on his own or with some help.

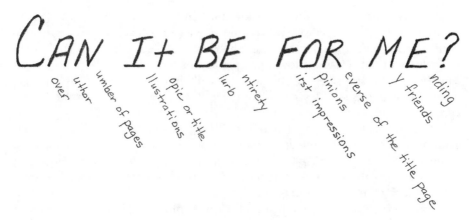

Figure 3.11   Mary Bonner, a library media specialist, uses this book selection strategy with older readers.

Of course, these book selection strategies are only guides. Do not forget that younger students can often read more difficult books than you might expect. Interest and background knowledge can make otherwise difficult books easier. Many picture books have difficult vocabulary, but their highly predictable nature makes them easy to read. Of course, with the help of a parent, sibling, or caregiver, any student can read a book that on first inspection may seem too difficult, so do not limit your students' book selections by these criteria.

Once your students find a good book to read, it is much easier to find another good book that may get them "hooked on books." Finding other books by the same author is the first thing to suggest. Next have your students look for other books on the same topic or from the same genre, but do not forget the role you play in helping students select quality literature. Your world knowledge and reading experiences are much broader than is true for your students, so you can draw from a wide range of books to suggest to kids.

Conclusion

Quality literature possesses excellence, permanence, and distinctiveness. Teaching children about what makes a quality story and how color, line, shape, texture, arrangement, and total effect contribute to quality in illustrations, develops their artistic and literary appreciation. Teaching children about media and style helps them better understand and enjoy the literature they read. Today, multicultural literature has an important place in every classroom.

REFERENCES

Butler, D. (1983). In *What's A Good Book?* Weston, CT: Weston Woods.
Cianciolo, P. J. (1990). *Picturebooks for Children* (3rd ed.). Chicago: American Library Association.
Cooper, J. D. (1993). *Literacy: Helping Children Construct Meaning* (2nd ed.). Boston: Houghton Mifflin.
Frezzolini, S. (1992). Glossary of terms in art and design of children's books. *Children's Book Council Features.* July–Dec.
Holdaway, D. (1983). In *What's A Good Book?* Weston, CT: Weston Woods.
Huck, C. S. (1983). In *What's A Good Book?* Weston, CT: Weston Woods.
Huck, C. S., Hepler, S., & Hickman, J. (1993). *Children's literature in the elementary school* (4th ed.). San Diego: Harcourt Brace.
Kiefer, B. (1995). *The Potential of Picturebooks.* Englewood Cliffs, NJ: Prentice Hall.
Lynch-Brown, C., & Tomlinson, C. (1993). *Children's Literature.* Boston: Allyn and Bacon.
Norton, D. (1991). Teaching multicultural literature in the reading curriculum. *The Reading Teacher, 44*(1), 28–39.
Norton, D. E. (1995). *Through the Eyes of a Child: An Introduction to Children's Literature, 4th ed.* Columbus, OH: Merrill.
Ramirez, G. & Ramirez, J. (1994). *Multiethnic Children's Literature.* Albany, NY: Delmar.
Russell, D. L. (1994). *Literature for Children, 2nd ed.* New York: Longman.
Sharp, P. (1992). I need a good book . . . fast! *School Library Media Activities Monthly, 8*(8), pp. 30–31.
Stewig, J. W. (1988). *Children and Literature* (2nd ed.). Boston: Houghton Mifflin.
Sutherland, Z., & Arbuthnot, M. H. (1991). *Children and Books* (8th ed.). Glenview, IL: Scott, Foresman.

Children's Literature

Aardema, V. (1975). *Why Mosquitoes Buzz in People's Ears.* New York: Scholastic.
Ackerman, K. (1988). *Song and Dance Man.* New York: Scholastic.
Anno, M. (1975). *Anno's Alphabet: An Adventure in Imagination.* New York: Harper & Row.
Bang, M. (1985). *The Paper Crane.* New York: Scholastic.
Base, G. (1988). *The Eleventh Hour: A Curious Mystery.* New York: Harry N. Abrams.
Base, G. (1987). *Animalia.* London: Harry N. Abrams.
Brett, J. (1994). *Town Mouse Country Mouse.* New York: Putnam.
———. (1991). *Berlioz the Bear.* New York: Putnam.
Brown, M. (1982) *Once a Mouse.* New York: Macmillan.
Carle, E. (1990). *Pancakes, Pancakes!* New York: Scholastic.

Cole, J. (1986). *The Magic Schoolbus at the Waterworks.* New York: Scholastic.

Emberley, E., & Emberley, B. (1967). *Drummer Hoff.* Englewood Cliffs, NJ: Prentice-Hall.

Freedman, R. (1987). *Lincoln: A Photobiography.* New York: Clarion.

Hadley, E., & Hadley, T. (1983). *Legends of the Sun and Moon.* Cambridge, UK: Cambridge University Press.

Hoffman, M., & Binch, C. (1991). *Amazing Grace.* New York: Scholastic.

Hughes, L. (1994). *The Dream Keeper and Other Poems.* New York: Knopf.

Jonas, A. (1983). *Round Trip.* New York: Greenwillow.

Keats, E. J. (1962). *The Snowy Day.* New York: Scholastic.

Lionni, L. (1994). *An Extraordinary Egg.* New York: Knopf.

———. (1967). *Frederick.* New York: Pantheon.

———. (1970). *Alexander and the Wind-Up Mouse.* New York: Pantheon.

Lobel, A. (1971). *Frog and Toad Are Friends.* New York: Scholastic.

Macaulay, D. (1991). *Black and White.* Boston: Houghton Mifflin.

———. (1977). *Castle.* New York: Houghton Mifflin.

McDermott, G. (1974). *Arrow to the Sun.* New York: Viking.

McKissock, P. (1986). *Flossie and the Fox.* New York: Scholastic.

Ringgold, F. (1991). *Tar Beach.* New York: Scholastic.

Ryder, J. (1988). *The Snail's Spell.* New York: Penguin.

Sendak, M. (1963). *Where the Wild Things Are.* New York: Harper & Row.

Seuss, Dr. (1990). *Oh, the Places You'll Go!.* New York: Random House.

Shulevitz, U. (1974). *Dawn.* New York: Farrar, Straus & Giroux.

Silverstein, S. (1976). *The Missing Piece.* New York: Harper & Row.

———. (1981). *A Light in the Attic.* New York: Harper & Row.

Steptoe, J. (1987). *Mufaro's Beautiful Daughters: An African Tale.* New York: Scholastic.

Van Allsburg, C. (1981). *Jumanji.* Boston: Houghton Mifflin.

———. (1982). *Ben's Dream.* New York: Houghton Mifflin.

———. (1985). *The Polar Express.* Boston: Houghton Mifflin.

Wildsmith, B. (1974). *Python's Party.* New York: Franklin Watts.

Williams, V. (1984). *Music, Music for Everyone.* New York: Greenwillow.

Wood, A. (1985). *King Bidgood's in the Bathtub.* New York: Harcourt Brace Jovanovitch.

Yolen, J. (1987). *Owl Moon.* New York: Scholastic.

Young, E. (1989). *Lon Po Po: A Red-Riding Hood Story from China.* New York: Philomel.

chapter 4

Sharing Literature

This chapter explores several ways you can share literature with your children. It gives ideas for the use of webbing to support oral reading, storytelling, booktalking, and a literate classroom environment. The suggestions are meant as a starting point for using webs to make literature sharing more effective and to stimulate your children's understanding, enjoyment, and appreciation of literature.

Why Read Aloud?

Reading aloud to children has many benefits. When you read aloud to your children, you provide them with a model of good reading that they can imitate. Besides being pleasurable, enjoyable, soothing, and energizing, reading aloud:

- Builds general knowledge
- Expands vocabulary
- Develops concepts of print
- Reveals different language patterns
- Reveals different writing styles
- Encourages visual imagery
- Boosts comprehension
- Extends knowledge of literary elements
- Broadens genre knowledge
- Improves listening skills
- Fosters curiosity and imagination
- Promotes motivation to read and to learn
- Builds ease with the English language
- Inspires writing
- Increases achievement

Research findings strongly favor reading aloud. Reading to children is the single most important activity for building the knowledge required for later literacy (Anderson, Hiebert, Scott, & Wilkerson, 1985). In a longitudinal study, storybook reading by parents to their young children before beginning school was the single most important factor leading to the children's later success in school (Wells, 1986). It seems common sense, then, that teachers at all grade levels should set aside time for reading aloud.

In a survey of 537 teachers of K–6, the most frequently occurring read-aloud practices showed *a teacher who reads for 10 to 20 minutes a day from a trade book that is not connected to a unit of study and spends less than 5 minutes in discussion, including talk before and after the reading*

(Hoffman, Roser, & Battle, 1993). This is a troubling picture in light of what we know about the benefits of reading aloud. These researchers also examined the characteristics of model read-aloud programs and made the following suggestions:

- Set aside a special time and place for a daily read-aloud.
- Select quality literature.
- Share literature related to other literature.
- Discuss literature in lively, invitational, thought-provoking ways.
- Group children in ways that maximize their responses.
- Offer a variety of opportunities for response and extension.
- Reread selected pieces.

During daily read-aloud times, here are several ways to promote children's enjoyment, appreciation, and learning. Seven guidelines for making your read-alouds more effective follow.

Seven Tips for Read-Alouds

1. *Choose literature you enjoy.* When you relish a story or poem, you communicate that enjoyment to the children. When you select literature you enjoy, oral reading of the selection is also probably fueled by genuine feeling, and is therefore smoother and more animated than it is when you read a story you do not particularly like. Sharing your enthusiasm and love of literature through good oral reading also provides a role model for your children. Be sure to seek new stories and poems so that your repertoire grows and is current. Share new books along with old favorites and read a range of selections from every genre. A blend of old and new titles representing all types of literature is a treat for both you and your children.

Talk with the library media specialist when you need books on special topics. References such as those listed below will also give you titles and descriptions of good books to read aloud;

- *Children's Books in Print.* New York: R.R. Bowker (Annual).
- *The Bookfinder: A Guide to Children's Literature about the Needs and Problems of Youth Aged 2 and Up* by (Ed.) S. Dreyer. Circle Pines, MN: American Guidance Service.
- *Adventuring with Books: A Booklist for Pre K–Grade 6* by Julie Jenson & Nancy Roser (Urbana, IL: National Council of Teachers of English, 1993).
- *Children's Literature: An Issues Approach,* 3rd Ed. by Masha Rudman (New York: Longman, 1995).

- *The New Read-Aloud Handbook* by Jim Trelease (New York: Penguin, 1993).

- *Kaleidoscope: A Multicultural Booklist for Grades K–8* by Rudine Sims Bishop, Ed. (Urbana, IL: National Council of Teachers of English, 1994).

- *Books Kids Will Sit Still For* by Judy Freeman (R.R. Bowker, 1990).

- *Hey! Listen to This: Stories to Read Aloud* by Jim Trelease (New York: Penguin, 1992).

- *High Interest, Easy Reading: A Booklist for Junior and Senior High School Students, 6th Ed.* by William McBride, Ed. (Urbana, IL: National Council of Teachers of English, 1990).

- *Multiethnic Children's Literature* by Gonzalo Ramirez and Jan Ramirez (Albany, NY: Delmar, 1994).

2. *Read it first.* This makes the story and language familiar. When you read the story or poem first before sharing it with children, you avoid surprise or embarrassment over a concept or word that is offensive. If you are uncomfortable with language or ideas in a book, either omit those particular sections or do not read the book at all. If the use of questionable material is justifiable, inquire about school policy on censorship, and consider obtaining parental permission before sharing the material.

3. *Practice.* Especially if reading aloud is a new experience, practice before reading to a group is a must. Using inappropriate phrasing or stumbling over words creates potential comprehension problems for the children and also dampens their interest. Fluent reading is not only more comfortable to hear, it also demonstrates a model of good oral reading for children. Practice in front of a mirror to discover how to use your eyes, voice, and facial expressions effectively. To create mood, heighten suspense, and generally read with better expression, you should vary your intonation, juncture, stress, and pacing.

Familiarity with a story ensures its enjoyment by all. Reading a book or story first helps you determine an author's style and tone, make mental notes about how to interpret various characters, and identify critical points in the story so you know where to stop and start for best effect. As you gain experience and confidence in reading orally, you may find that skimming or previewing suffices. An exception to this is poetry, which should *always* be practiced before being read aloud since it is written for the ear as well as the mind.

4. *Be sure children can see and hear you.* Position yourself front and center so that the children face you or can comfortably turn to see and hear you. Stand or sit on a chair or desk so you are comfortable and can enjoy the reading. When you read to a small group, sit on a low chair and hold the book close to or at the children's eye level. Minimize distractions so that every child enjoys and appreciates what is read.

5. *Share story pictures.* If you read a picture book, master the art of reading from the side so that children can see pictures at all times, or read the text first

and then show the pictures. You can also show the pictures first to prepare for the text and then show no pictures while you read. If you choose to do this, let the children look at the pictures as they reread the book. Or use a combination of methods. Since so much of a picture book's appeal is the pictures, sit or stand close enough to children that they can see the pictures. Even older children enjoy seeing the few illustrations in books written for them. Walk the book around the room for everyone to see these smaller drawings since this additional visual input enriches and broadens responses. The audience and story determine how best to share text and pictures.

6. *Watch for children's responses.* Try to *read* the audience as you read orally to them, watching for signs that your children are involved or do not understand. Watch for spontaneous responses such as a smile, grimace, rapt attention, or other changes in facial expression that coincide with characters' actions, story mood, or plot. These responses signal emotional involvement with the story and are the basis for interpreting and evaluating literature. Accept, encourage, and extend these observed responses with questions and discussion when the situation is right. An observed response or remark a child makes, such as a comment about a setting that sounds like his grandmother's house or a value judgment about how one should act in the real world compared to a character's actions often triggers discussion. The responses you note and extend are often critical to the development of deeper and more insightful responses.

7. *Revisit the story.* Both during and following reading, be sure to allow time for discussion to encourage your children's responses to what they have heard and to extend their comprehension. Time for discussion and talk allows children to share their interpretations, analyze the story, and construct story meanings together. Discussion can help clarify concepts, vocabulary, and issues that your children are not familiar with or do not understand.

After you read a book aloud, children enjoy rereading it again even though they have just heard it. Let them examine pictures closely. Make the book available by including it in a display with other books by the same author and illustrator or other books on the same topic.

Working with some books in depth and reading the same story aloud on several occasions broadens and deepens student response. Just as adults reread favorite poems or novels, so do children enjoy hearing stories read to them more than once. Deeper insights into characters and events develop when children are already familiar with plot structure. Also, an author's particular style is sometimes not evident or appreciated until the second or third reading.

If you follow these seven guidelines and children are not listening or are disruptive while you read, ask yourself some questions. Do you like the story? Is it well written, interesting, and fast-paced enough to maintain attention? Can children understand it? Were you familiar with the story before you read it? Did you practice it? Is your voice well modulated, and do you use appropriate facial expressions? Are conditions in the classroom conducive to listening? If your answers are yes, perhaps you need to talk with children about how to listen effectively or to place disruptive children close to you and the book.

Using Webs to Share Books

As Kelly, a fifth-grade teacher, began to read *Roll of Thunder, Hear My Cry,* by Mildred Taylor, she wrote in her literature response journal: "Since all the characters were introduced in Chapter 1, I was afraid my students would be confused, but we found that making a web helped us organize who was who." The web of main characters Kelly made as she read this book orally appears in Figure 4.1. Making a web like this is a good way to help your students understand and remember the characters and their relationships. As you meet a character in the story, add the character to the web in its proper place.

Now, look at some classrooms where teachers do not use webbing, but could use it to share literature more effectively.

- In a first-grade classroom, a group of children participate with their teacher to tell the story *The Grey Lady and the Strawberry Snatcher,* by Molly Bang. They look closely at the pictures and talk together to identify what is happening.

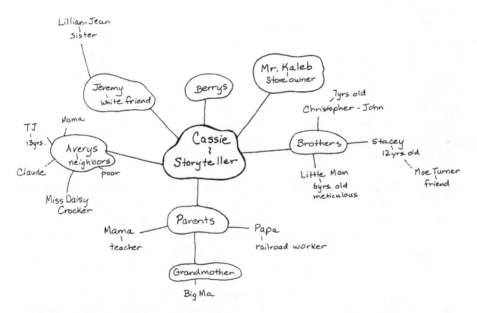

Figure 4.1 As Kelly read aloud the first few chapters of *Roll of Thunder, Hear My Cry,* by Mildred Taylor, she created this web to help her fifth graders identify characters.

■ A class of third-graders sit quietly as their teacher reads *Abraham Lincoln,* by Ingri and Edgar D'Aulaire. She stops occasionally to make comments and ask questions, and students offer observations and opinions.

■ In a sixth-grade classroom, a teacher reads poems from *Navajo: Visions and Voices across the Mesa,* by Shonto Begay, stopping after each poem to either reread it or talk with students about the sounds, images, repetitive language, figures of speech, and especially moving poems they hear.

In each of these situations, students became involved with literature as they responded to what they heard and saw. How might these teachers use webbing to share literature more effectively and promote their students' understanding and enjoyment?

The first-grade teacher might create two simple webs, such as those in Figure 4.2, to introduce the characters before the children look at the book. After reading the story together, the children can add other descriptive words to the webs and then share these webs in a retelling of the story to the class. The webs extend and reinforce vocabulary and allow a book that is too small for whole-class sharing to be enjoyed by everyone together.

Before reading to her third-grade class, this teacher could create a web such as the one in Figure 4.3. She could use it to introduce the story, and the children could add important occurrences to the web at each stop on Abe's journey from the wilderness to the White House. A web like this one can help students remember and clarify the major events in Lincoln's life that helped him become president. If the book is read in conjunction with a social studies unit on the Civil War, for example, children can add other information to the web as they integrate what they learn from their content text with the knowledge they gain from literature.

The sixth-grade teacher might share the elements *sensory images, visual images, touches your heart,* and so on from the web in Figure 4.4 before reading Begay's poetry. Then she and her students could add the titles of poems that fit each category. Students might add other important categories to the web, too. This web could serve as a visible reminder of what students liked about the poetry and as a blueprint for writing a book report.

There are many other ways of using webbing as you share literature. You can use webbing:

Before Reading: Webs can help you assess and organize the knowledge children have about a certain topic. Creating webs before reading or listening provides a framework into which children can put new information and ideas that come from what they hear. Webbing allows for new information to be attached to known information and thus ensures comprehension and learning. Webbing before reading also plays a role in developing interest in the book to be read (as in Figure 4.2). In many cases, the more students know about a plot, theme, setting,

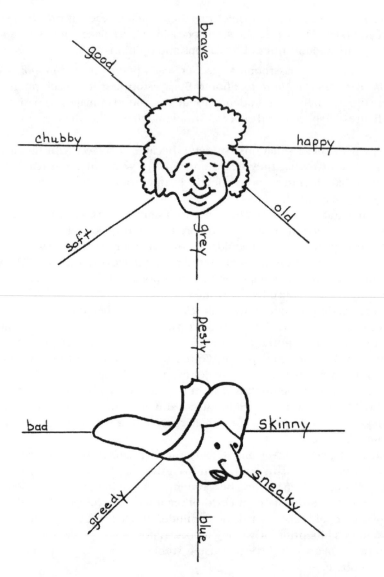

Figure 4.2   These vocabulary webs from *The Grey Lady and the Strawberry Snatcher,* by Molly Bang, introduce the story, and children can add words after the read-aloud as well.

or the characters, the better the chances are they will want to hear the book, listen carefully as it is read, and understand and remember what they have heard.

During Reading: Use webbing in a number of ways as you read aloud to your children. Creation of a vocabulary or a key words web can focus attention on new vocabulary as it occurs in a story or reinforce it after the story has been read. Students can identify important words and classify them in different sections of a web. As students hear a story, they can make a web to represent the relationships among concepts or ideas in the selection, chapter, or story (as in Figure 4.1). As a web is constructed, students have opportunities to discuss events and emotions, for example, that can help ensure that they understand what is happening in a story. Then, as they continue to listen to a story, what they hear tends to make more sense to them.

After Reading: Use webbing after reading as a way of summarizing and highlighting important concepts and information (as in Figure 4.3). Webs that contain the elements of literature, sequence of events, characters' feelings, causes and effects, and so on give students visual diagrams of critical story compo-

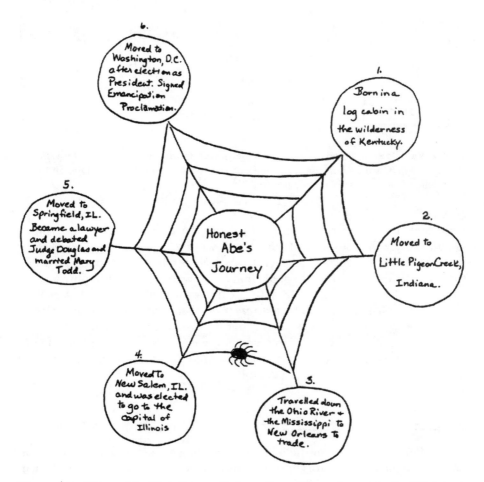

Figure 4.3 This web by Chris Czarnecki shows the setting and events in the D'Aulaires' story *Abraham Lincoln.*

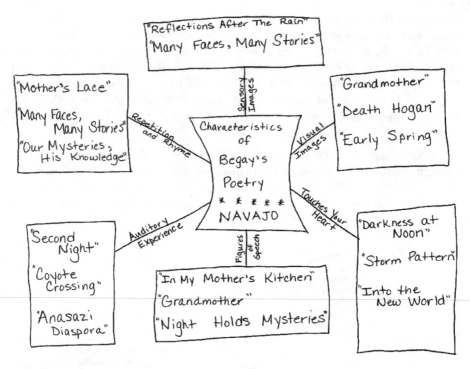

Figure 4.4   Presenting part of Karen Wandell's web for the poems in *Navajo: Visions and Voices across the Mesa,* by Shonto Begay, sets the stage for the read-aloud and students can add information as they listen.

nents and allow them to reflect on what they have heard. Making interpretations and evaluating stories and the author's writing style is thus made easier for students. Following reading, students can predict what will happen next in a story and make a web of these predictions. This web can establish purposes for listening and focus listening during the next day's read-aloud session as well.

Before you ask your students to web on their own, you should first use webbing in a variety of ways before, during, and after read-alouds. Your students may need to be comfortable creating webs, first with you and then in small groups with peers, before you ask them to finish a partially created web or make their own webs independently.

Why Use Storytelling?

Storytelling shares many of the benefits of reading aloud. Perhaps most important among these is that storytelling stimulates the imagination, instills a love of language, improves listening skills, inspires writing, develops vocabulary, promotes comprehension, and motivates reading. A look back at the list of reading aloud benefits reveals that there is only one benefit, *builds concepts of print,* that is not a direct result of storytelling.

When you give your children opportunities to retell stories they have heard or search for their own stories to tell, the benefits of storytelling are accentuated (Hamilton & Weiss, 1990). Children who tell stories reap many rewards. For them, storytelling:

- Improves self-esteem
- Builds confidence and poise in speaking to a group
- Stimulates inventive thinking and improvisation
- Improves expressive language skills
- Improves class cooperation
- Fosters learning in general

When children tell folk and fairy tales, the easiest kind of stories to tell, they learn about the world and build an appreciation of other cultures. They develop literary knowledge and a frame of reference for their own moral and ethical development.

You will learn a great deal about your children from listening to them tell stories. Their storytelling will give you insights into their personalities, language development, thinking, creativity, learning styles, and interpersonal relationships both inside and outside school. When shy or usually quiet children tell stories or use props and puppets in their storytelling, they can become characters and step temporarily into other personalities. Many teachers see children bloom through storytelling and discover their students' otherwise hidden qualities.

Some teachers who enjoy reading and read often to children are afraid of storytelling. But contrary to popular belief, you do not need special talents or skills to be a storyteller. If you stop to think about it, you practice storytelling every time you tell someone about something you have seen or done. Storytelling is just retelling a story, whether an actual event or a tale once told by someone else and now written down.

Storytelling provides a different forum for sharing literature than does reading aloud. When telling a story, you can use your hands and body in ways that are not possible if you are holding a book. A storyteller also can use drama and props to add interest and power to a story, and unlike a reader, can hold the audience's attention with uninterrupted eye contact. Storytellers can make print come alive for children by removing the print from the interaction that occurs between the reader and the story. For these reasons, telling stories has a special place in the sharing of literature and makes it an alluring avenue to explore with your students.

Five Tips for Storytelling

When you tell a story, there are several things that make it easier and ensure that you are effective. First, choose a story you enjoy. Then, read and practice it until you are familiar with it and your presentation is smooth. Vary your voice and pacing for maximum effect and arrange the setting so children can see you and hear you. Remember, you do not need to memorize a story or tell it word for word. Here are five tips for storytelling;

1. *Choose a story with a clear plot and strong characters.* A story with a clearly defined plot that builds steadily to a climax is best. Focus on folktales at first since they are short and contain fast-paced action and characters with one basic trait. Folktales that are *linear,* beginning in one setting and ending in another, or *circular,* concluding where they begin, are often the easiest to tell.

2. *Learn the story.* Read the entire story aloud several times. Then close the book, introduce the characters and setting, and tell the actions in the sequence in which they happen. Your portrayal will be more vivid if you imagine what your characters look like, how they might act, and how each feels about other characters. If the story uses repetitions or unique wording, memorize these to help retain the original style and flavor.

3. *Practice.* It may take a few hours to learn a folktale and somewhat longer to learn a narrative tale. Space your practice out over two to three weeks rather than trying to learn the story all at once. Use a mirror and then practice on a friend, or use a tape recorder. A video camera is even more helpful since you can see the effect of your body language as well as that of your voice.

4. *Slow down.* The single most helpful suggestion for beginning storytellers may be to slow down. The listener better comprehends the spoken word and the speaker produces with more clarity when pace slows. Often just taking two or three deep breaths before you begin will help regulate your breathing and pace your delivery.

5. *Use your voice and body naturally.* Observe yourself in a mirror during storytelling. Do your head, eyes, hands, and arms move to emphasize points? For example, it helps children visualize the story when you raise a hand to shade your eyes as you look into the distance and say, for example, "He looked up the road and he looked down the road." Let your hands establish some of the story emphasis by moving them naturally to strengthen points, depict actions, and add interest.

These five tips are also appropriate for your students who strive to become storytellers. Be sure to encourage them to participate as you tell the story by supplying words, sounds, or repetitive phrases occasionally. In this way you actively involve children in storytelling, building their confidence and making it easier for them to tell their own stories effectively.

Hamilton and Weiss's *Children Tell Stories: A Teaching Guide* (1990) is filled with practical ideas for classroom storytelling. They suggest simple folktales and fables from around the world as children begin storytelling and provide the text of 25 stories. These stories are each a page or less in length and are arranged in order of difficulty beginning with the simplest. A few of the titles and places of origin are:

- "How the Rabbit Lost His Tail" (Native American)
- "The Rat Princess" (Japanese folktale)
- "The Miser" (Middle Eastern folktale)
- "The Country Mouse and the City Mouse" (Greek fable—Aesop)
- "How Brother Rabbit Fooled Whale and Elephant" (African–American folktale)
- "The Baker's Daughter" (English folktale)

The book includes plans for a six-week storytelling unit that is adaptable to all grade levels with hints and handouts for replication, such as suggestions for learning a story, techniques for telling a story, interview questions for families, ideas for parents, and self-evaluation sheets for students. It is a wonderful resource for an introduction to storytelling.

Storytelling with Webs

Telling a story from the pictures in a book will help you feel more comfortable as a storyteller. For example, a pre-kindergarten teacher believed strongly in daily read-aloud periods and began reading to her class on the first day of school in September. But she found that the children were not ready, interested, or able to sit still and listen to even the simplest of books. So she began by telling the story in her own words and using the pictures to support her storytelling. She found this was successful and used it to prepare her children for listening to formal read-alouds later. When her children were able to listen, one of the books she read was *Whale in the Sky,* by Anne Siberell, a folktale about the origin of the totem pole. She then created the picture web of events in Figure 4.5 to aid their recall of what they had heard and to support their retellings of the story.

You can also use a web to enhance telling a story. A standard literary web or plot web provides all the necessary elements to include as you relate the story to a group of children. Use puppets, flannel board figures, or other visuals to introduce a story, maintain interest, strengthen a point, or otherwise enrich your children's understanding and appreciation of stories.

Webs can help children of all ages become storytellers. When telling stories themselves, children gain confidence by first reading a book, then creating a web of important ideas and information either by drawing pictures or using written words and phrases, and finally telling the story by referring to the web. Webs can help ensure that the storytelling is organized and inclusive. Often, a few ideas included on the web will trigger children's memories, and they will be able to relate rich and elaborate stories.

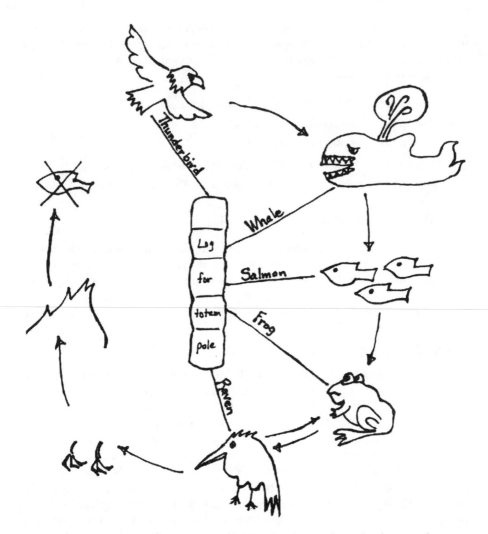

Figure 4.5   This picture web supports children's story retelling after hearing the Northwest Indian folktale *Whale In the Sky,* by Ann Siberell.

Booktalking with Webs

You can encourage your students to read quality literature that supports their content area units of study by giving *booktalks,* short presentations designed to help someone learn about a book and be inspired to read it. Booktalks are enthusiastic personal pitches to sell books, using a combination of verbal and visual modes in no prescribed format. You may or may not have read the books you talk about and introduce to your class. Of course, the most successful booktalks are those done on books you have read and genuinely like. The rationale for booktalks is twofold. First, many children are immediately interested in a book their teacher suggests or has read and likes. Second, you can share many books quickly with a class through booktalks and can pique student interest in reading.

One sixth-grade teacher found that booktalks paid dividends in student interest and increased the amount of actual reading they did. She asked the school library media specialist to identify a number of books to accompany her class's social studies unit on ancient Egyptian civilization. She then spent several minutes each day introducing a few of these books to her class in short booktalks using some of the booktalk ideas listed below:

- Use a web to discuss the literary elements of the story.
- Introduce an author and tell about his or her special expertise with the topic.
- Use a theme and share several books on a topic.
- Show a picture that relates to the book in some way.
- Draw a web, picture, or map that fits the story.
- Share a real object that is relevant to the story.
- Use a puppet to introduce the plot or characters.
- Read a first paragraph or interesting part.
- Make a web of key vocabulary words.
- Create an acrostic with the title or character's name.
- Roleplay one of the characters.
- Read information on the book's flap orally.

Once you have modeled booktalks, your students can do their own. But children should give booktalks only on books they have read. They will know these books well and can talk easily about them. A web is one method of telling a little about a book to sell it. With a web, such as the one in Figure 4.6 made by a fourth-grade student, a booktalk can be organized and presented in a somewhat structured and related way. Webbing gives students practice in representing key information and relationships in a concise visual display. As students become comfortable using webs to structure their presentations, they become more adept at using webs to structure their writing as well.

Conclusion

When you share literature through reading aloud, storytelling, or booktalking, to be most effective there are some basic guidelines to keep in mind. Webs can enhance children's understanding and enjoyment of literature whether they lis-

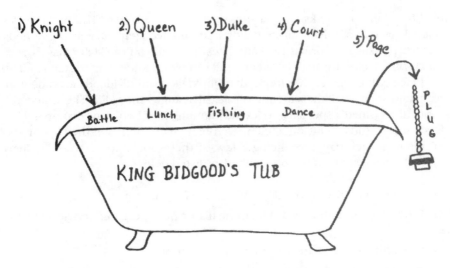

Figure 4.6 This web, containing both important vocabulary and sequence of events, was the basis for a booktalk a student gave on Audrey Wood's story *King Bidgood's in the Bathtub*.

ten to stories or tell their own. You and your children can use webs in many ways to promote listening and reading.

REFERENCES

Anderson, R. C., Hiebert, E. H., Scott, J. A., & Wilkerson, I. A. (1985). *Becoming a Nation of Readers: The Report of the Commission on Reading*. Washington, DC: National Institute of Education.

Hamilton, M., & Weiss, M. (1990). *Children Tell Stories: A Teaching Guide*. Katonah, NY: Richard C. Owen.

Hoffman, J. V., Roser, N. L., & Battle, J. (1993). Reading Aloud in Classrooms: From the Modal Toward a "Model." *The Reading Teacher, 46*(6), pp. 496–503.

Wells, G. (1986). *The Meaning Makers: Children Learning Language and Using Language to Learn*. Portsmouth, NH: Heinemann.

Children's Literature

Bang, M. (1980). *The Grey Lady and the Strawberry Snatcher*. New York: Four Winds.

Begay, S. (1995). *Navajo: Visions and Voices across the Mesa*. New York: Scholastic.

D'Aulaire, I., & D'Aulaire, E. (1957). *Abraham Lincoln*. Garden City, NY: Doubleday.

Siberell, A. (1982). *Whale in the Sky*. New York: Dutton.

Taylor, M. (1976). *Roll of Thunder Hear My Cry*. New York: Dial.

Wood, A. (1985). *King Bidgood's in the Bathtub*. San Diego: Harcourt Brace Jovanovitch.

chapter 5

Responding to Literature

This chapter explores differences in children's responses to literature. It discusses ways in which webbing can aid in the creation of a literate environment, in reading stories interactively with children, and in engaging them in drama. You will see how webs can help structure responses and serve as springboards for different kinds of responses.

How Do Responses Differ?

Both research and theory tell us that response to literature grows from the personal interactions we have with print and that interactions are different for everyone (Purves, Rogers, & Soter, 1990; Rosenblatt, 1985; Sutherland & Arbuthnot, 1991). Both children and adults bring different experiences, values, beliefs, and knowledge to print. As we read, we make different meanings when we interact with print at different times and even in different places. Rosenblatt (1991) suggests that there are two predominant ways of responding to literature. If your purpose for reading is to acquire and remember information, you read from an *efferent* (from the Latin for "carry away") stance. If, on the other hand, you pay attention to what you are thinking, feeling, and experiencing as you read, then you have adopted an *aesthetic* stance toward print. In Figure 5.1, the picture Jessica drew after hearing *Where the Wild Things Are,* by Maurice Sendak, shows how she identified with Max's taming of the monsters and how she related aesthetically to the story.

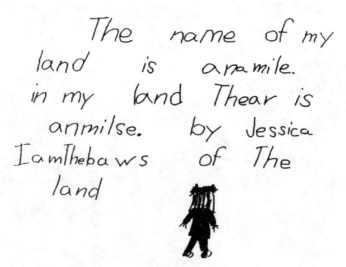

The name of my
land is a ra mile.
in my land Thear is
anmilse. by Jessica
I am Theba ws of The
land

Figure 5.1   A young child relates to Max's power in *Where the Wild Things Are,* by Maurice Sendak, by drawing a queen with a veil and writing that she wants to be "baws" of the land.

Rosenblatt suggests thinking of these two forms of response on a continuum and remembering that in every reading there is a mix of both types of response. For example, children who read *All the Places to Love,* by Patricia MacLachlan, may feel the beauty, comfort, and serenity of nature more than they are able to remember in sequence the places visited in the story, for example, plowed fields, river, blueberry barren, barn, and marsh. Just as with adults, what one child identifies with, feels, and remembers is often quite different than what another sees as most important or memorable. Each child brings his own special background and experiences to literature and so potentially has a different literary transaction and response to a story or poem.

Rapt attention, a question, an observation, a comment or an opinion, a recalled memory, or a demand to hear a story or poem again are all evidence of an aesthetic response to literature. As children talk, draw, write, dramatize, dance, or retell a story or poem, it can be recaptured and relived first and then discussed from an efferent stance.

Included in an efferent response and perhaps extending a bit beyond it is the *critical* response to literature. This is a stance toward print that requires the reader to analyze, examine, and evaluate both what and how the author says things and helps the reader make meaning. You can help your children acquire a critical response by drawing their attention to character development, the effect of setting on mood and message, use of stylistic devices, similarity in themes across books, and so on.

Rosenblatt (1991) warns teachers to be clear about not simply using literature for the efferent purpose of teaching information, however. For example, she says when American history is studied, a novel about colonial life is valuable but primarily as an aesthetic experience, a sharing of what it would have been like to live in those days, rather than a way of teaching incidental information. Only after a book is experienced and an aesthetic response is elicited is it appropriate or effective to examine the story critically for the information and understandings it may hold.

While children's responses to literature are essentially individual and personal and are shaped by their experiences and perceptions, there are other factors, such as the environment and the people in it, that influence what children read and how they respond. Both teacher and children influence each other's reading and response (Hickman, 1984). Children model their responses for each other, sharing favorite parts of stories or appealing passages, drawing pictures, making puppet plays, designing game boards, and otherwise rethinking and representing stories in different ways for each other. Children in a class form a community of readers who show each other how to act like readers and respond personally to the books they read.

Teachers also play a critical role in developing children's responses to literature. Teachers who read, enjoy what they read, and share this with children become models that children can imitate. These teachers regularly read aloud to children and read children's books independently as well. They let children see them reading and tell the children about the books they read. They ask children for their opinions of certain characters or authors and tell children why certain books are favorites. These teachers make time each day for silent reading and make sure there is a variety of materials at a range of grade levels available for children to read, and they encourage activities that foster responses. They are skillful discussion leaders, guiding talk about books and characters so that children arrive at new meanings. In all of these ways and many more, teachers can foster children's responses to literature. Figure 5.2 contains twenty activities that encourage divergent understanding, thinking, and language use in children's responses to literature.

Creating a Literate Environment with Webs

The atmosphere you create in your classroom encourages or inhibits your children's responses to literature. For example, as you talk with your children about why you love a book like *Stellaluna,* by Janell Cannon, whose pictures and story blend fiction and information in a way that touches your heart and teaches you at the same time, your children will realize that their observations and feelings about books are also important. And when you organize and arrange the physical environment of your classroom and school, you will find many ways to involve children with literature and help them feel comfortable about sharing their responses to and opinions about the books they read. Maryann, a special education teacher, made a bulletin board using the web in Figure 5.3 to provide her students with a ready resource for their book discussions and writing. Maryann wanted her students to be familiar with the literary elements, and she encouraged them to refer to the bulletin board to name and use these elements of story structure.

It is important to create an environment that is rich in print. To do this, it is necessary to make books and other printed materials available in your classroom and to allow time for your children to read. Some teachers find that establishing a classroom library is the first step. The library can include books you own, books you periodically borrow from the public library, magazines, comics, and the newspaper. Public libraries often have a wider range of books than school libraries do and will allow classroom teachers to borrow them for longer than is usual.

Locate your library in one corner or part of the room—perhaps with a filmstrip projector, tape recorder, and materials for drawing and writing (such as different types of paper, pencils, crayons, and felt-tip pens)—and call it the literacy center, reading corner, or reading-writing area. There are many children's books available on tape or filmstrip that beginning or reluctant readers enjoy. Locating writing materials in the same area as books helps children make the connection between reading and writing and allows them to use books as models in their own writing.

W rite a sequel, poem, book review, travelogue, letter to the editor, journal entry, or advertisement for the book.

A nalyze the growth of a character, the author's style, or the role of setting in the story.

Y odel, sing a song, create music, or write song lyrics related to the story.

S uggest a more interesting title or chapter titles.

T alk to a buddy about what you think is special, excellent, or distinctive about the story.

O rganize a "jackdaw" or collection of objects to symbolize the story, and make a display of them.

R oleplay or dramatize your favorite character, scene, or sequel.

E at a special food or dish you have made that a character might have eaten.

S urvey your class or grade level to find out who has read the book or another book by the same author or illustrator and graph the results.

P romote the book by making a book jacket or vest for yourself out of a paper bag and by decorating it to advertise the story.

O ffer to listen to a buddy read a chapter or story and talk about what you heard.

N ote ways the story might be different if the main character's gender, race, age, religion, or language were different.

D raw a web, map, picture, or banner to represent the story using pens, pencils, paints, or the computer.

T ell two or more buddies about the story by comparing it to another story with the same theme, setting, or problem.

O bserve closely the dedication, book flaps, and illustrations to see what you can learn about the author and illustrator, and list your ideas.

A rrange a collage about the story from pictures and words cut from magazines and scraps of fabric or other materials.

B uild something from straws, toothpicks, pasta, or other objects to show what you learned from the story.

O perate a tape recorder as you read your favorite part of the story, and replay it to hear how you sound.

O btain three sayings or quotations that give the story's message.

K eep an imaginary diary such as one the main character might have kept.

Figure 5.2 Twenty ways to respond to a book.

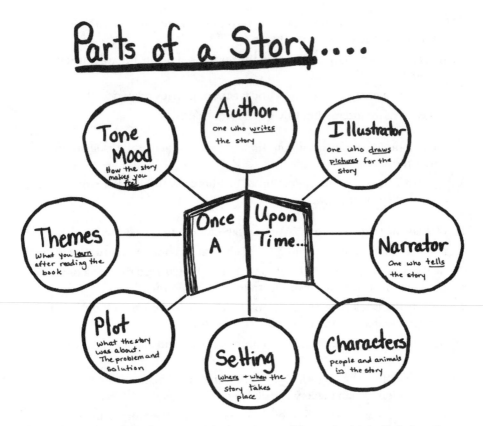

Figure 5.3 Maryann Parker, a special education teacher, made this bulletin board to help her resource room students name and use the literary elements.

When you give children time to read and write, you will find that they love to make their own books. Many resources provide information on bookmaking. In *How to Make Books with Children*, Joy Evans and Jo Ellen Moore provide easy-to-follow instructions and a variety of designs for making books.

Most children are eager to read what their peers have written, so if there is a large bulletin board in your classroom on which to display every child's writing, not just the few you identify as the best, its presence will enhance self-esteem and ownership of writing as well as promote your children's reading of each other's work. To this end, do not forget to include the books students have written in the classroom library.

A monthly book club can provide your classroom library and students with inexpensive paperback books. Each month companies like The Trumpet Club (PO Box 604, Holmes, PA, 19043) or Scholastic Books (730 Broadway, NY, 10003) will send order forms and brochures advertising books they have for sale. If children order books and you send in their orders, you are eligible for credits that can be used toward free books for your classroom. In this way, you build the reading habit and encourage children to own their own books while you increase your classroom library.

Webbing can be helpful in the creation of a literate environment. When you and your students create webs before, during, or after reading to represent the structure or elements in a particular book, try to use large chart paper and a felt marker rather than the blackboard. A web created on the blackboard is often lost when it is erased, but a web created on chart paper, can be posted near the reading-writing area to encourage children to retell and discuss the story. Using webs in this way promotes story enjoyment and comprehension as well as oral language development.

Merri, a first-grade teacher, often uses webbing in her classroom. For example, she regularly features the work of an author or illustrator as a focus for reading aloud, interactive book sharing, and creative dramatics. Jane Yolen is one of Merri's favorite authors and when she discovered that Yolen would be present at a local conference, Merri made arrangements for her school to host a visit from Yolen following the conference. In preparation for the visit, Merri read four of Yolen's books to her children, and together they made a web to represent the books and the children's responses to them (see Figure 5.4). Merri had

Figure 5.4 Merri Earl and Jane Yolen and the web of Yolen's work that Merri and her children put on a bulletin board.

created a literate environment for her students that supported their learning about literature, language development, and literacy growth.

Webbing is also an effective tool to use with cooperative learning since webs can easily be co-created. There are many benefits to having students work with partners or in small groups as they read, retell, draw, and write. Children talk, question, argue, defend, build social skills, share knowledge, and learn from each other. For example, Figure 5.5 shows a web made by two first-grade boys to map out a story they created about Frog and Toad. Donna, their teacher, used webbing almost daily with the class in one way or another and had just read *Frog and Toad Together,* by Arnold Lobel. She then had *cooperative partners* plan sequels to the story to tell the class. From the web they had created, these boys told their story of Frog and Toad getting ready for Easter. The text of their story follows.

Frog and Tade estre Pinick
Frog and Tode wrae getting.
rede for estre thay wint to bed.
erley the nxst marnig thay loke.
but thay did not hav eggs.
wat wile we do sed toad i dant no.
we will salv it but toad dinint.
fele good wat will i do now
I will mall the estre buney a llder
so he roght the leter the
estrbune get the leter so the
nxt nit the strebuy wint to the
hose and gave teme eggs
But that onley savt one prblum
toad was not well
so he toce care of toad.
he gave him chikn sup and jello
thn toad wint to bed erly
and got up the nxt mornig and felt betr
Then toad and frog wint to the estre pinick

Their story contained two problems and solutions for both problems, something Donna felt neither boy might have created independently. So webbing fostered interactions between the boys and inspired them to use their literacy to grow and stretch.

Many teachers, like Donna, who demonstrate and model webbing for their students, report that their children begin to use webbing independently without being directed to. These teachers regularly use webbing with their classes to brainstorm, organize, and represent ideas. When children have a model to

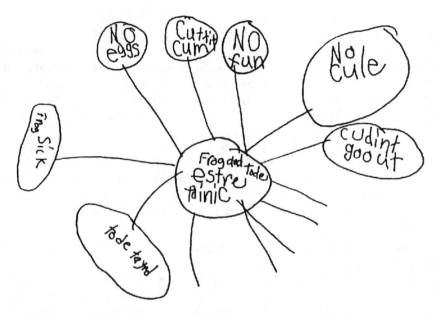

Figure 5.5 David and Todd respond to stories about Frog and Toad with their own web for a new story called "Frog and Toad's Easter Picnic."

imitate and materials to use, you will be surprised at their spontaneous use of webbing for a variety of purposes. One second-grade teacher found her students webbing on newsprint with markers to plan a story they wanted to write.

Webs are also useful for sharing literature in thematic units. One third-grade teacher uses a web structure on her bulletin board with the theme "Books About . . ." as the core idea. She changes this topic to promote interest in books that are related to her content-area units of study, the seasons, or holidays. Each web strand is an actual book jacket borrowed from the school library media specialist's file or a book jacket made by a child. She also occasionally uses the web structure as a record of good books children have read. As children finish books, they write short advertisements and illustrations for them, and each of these becomes a strand in a "We Recommend . . ." theme web.

Interactive Story Reading with Webs

In literate classroom environments, teachers foster the freedom to respond to books. These teachers make children feel that their opinions will be accepted and valued no matter whether they match those of the teacher or other students. They give children the freedom to agree or disagree as long as they can support their opinions with rational ideas and information. When the classroom atmosphere is open for discussion and the airing of opinions, children will feel free to offer their thoughts and responses to books as they interact with each other.

In this environment, it is important that you see students as participants in the story-reading process. By encouraging students to participate when stories are read, you promote a personal emotional response, the processing of information, and direct involvement that can have a positive effect on enjoyment and comprehension. There are several ways to promote interactive story reading.

1. *Begin by constructing a web to represent what students already know.* Your students usually have some knowledge of the setting, theme, genre, or characters of the story. When they recall and record this information on a web, it is preparation for becoming involved in the story and for understanding it. In this way, you enhance comprehension by cooperatively constructing meaning into which new information fits.

2. *Respond personally to the story and share your responses and interpretations freely.* Encourage your children to do the same. For example, when you let your children know how a story makes you feel, what you did or did not like about it and why, what you think the author meant, and the kinds of pictures the story helps you create in your mind, you provide children with a model of personal response to imitate and value.

3. *Encourage involvement with the story by fostering student predictions.* Making a guess or hypothesis about what may happen next in a story involves students in the story and ensures their comprehension. A sixth-grade teacher who read aloud to her class from Natalie Babbitt's *Tuck Everlasting* found that at the end of each chapter her students enjoyed making predictions about what might happen to Winnie Foster and how the Tuck's problem might be solved. Even young children can participate in and reap benefits from story reading in this way. A first-grade teacher reports that she uses prediction and webbing so much in her read-aloud sessions that her children now routinely hypothesize and predict as they read stories in the basal text and selections from their science books. Both teachers routinely represent their students' predictions in webs that provide records so that predictions can be revisited and checked for accuracy.

4. *Make story reading a shared venture between you and your students.* Stop occasionally at appropriate points to look closely at a picture and discuss it or to share a feeling, observation, or interpretation. This significantly enriches story enjoyment and comprehension for many children. You can:

- Ask Why...?, What do you think...?, and How...? These questions foster personal interpretations and evaluations, and children will sometimes use literal information to respond, making it unnecessary to ask literal questions.

- Restate what children have said and probe for an elaboration.

- Offer positive feedback or praise for opinions no matter whether you agree with them.

- Add or give information yourself to extend student response or knowledge related to the story.
- Provide clues or cues to tease children's understanding or perceptions of a story.
- Clarify uncertainties by relating examples of something children know to what they have trouble grasping.
- Listen and encourage student-student dialogues.
- Encourage children to add new information to a web as they read a story and discover facts and ideas that are appropriate.

Some teachers who do not like to interrupt their story sharing or reading will read the entire story through once, and then during a rereading encourage children to discuss the story, interact more fully with each other, and perhaps generate a web. No matter whether you encourage cooperative interactions and use webbing during a first or second reading, remember that cooperatively constructing meaning with a web can enhance children's enjoyment and appreciation of literature.

When you provide opportunities to hear, read, talk about, write, and respond in a variety of personal ways to literature, you help children develop responses to their full potential. In addition, when you give them time to respond through talk, writing, art, drama, and other means, you help them know and enjoy literature.

Discussion and Webbing

Talk and discussion develop a community of readers and writers in the classroom. As you and your students share memories, questions, opinions, interpretations, and analyses of a story you've read together, you develop a shared meaning of the story. Discussion during and after reading allows for collaboration and co-construction of meaning. This type of activity is more real and authentic than is having students individually complete workbook pages or answer written questions for grading. In discussing stories, you will discover that there is much to be learned from your students and they will discover that they can learn much from each other.

Peterson and Eeds (1990) maintain that *grand literature* produces *grand conversations.* They also believe that an aesthetic response is basic to any exploration of literature and that even the youngest children are capable of understanding and responding to story structure. Grand conversations that are built on aesthetic responses can occur in a whole-class setting or in small response groups as teacher and students co-produce meaning together. You and your students should remember two simple rules for effective dialogue (p. 22):

- Respect the interpretations of others and help in their development whenever possible.

- Remain open to many possibilities for interpretation of a story, and value spontaneity, which fosters insights.

Many teachers who use literature response groups find that journal entries make excellent prompts for discussion. In their journals, students can record their personal responses to a story or write responses to story-specific, teacher-directed questions, such as, "What were the unusual goings-on in this chapter?," "How did the setting contribute to the mood or influence the main character?," or "What are the meanings of these vocabulary words as used in this chapter?" Students can also write predictions about what will happen next or any question they have about the story. When volunteers share their journal entries with their literature response group, the discussion and talk that ensues is natural and often leads the group to new understanding of and insights about the story.

A webbing activity that fosters discussion and can be used across grade levels and curriculum areas is the *discussion web* (Alvermann, 1991). This activity encourages students to work cooperatively as they look at both sides of an issue before drawing conclusions. The web in Figure 5.6 shows the type of questions you might fashion. In this case it relates to the ethical issue of whether Nathan, the 14 year-old main character in *Weasel,* by Cynthia DeFelice, should kill an Indian named Weasel. Any question like this one that has no right or wrong answer and involves multiple viewpoints or opinions is possible.

One way to use a discussion web is to have each student first think about the question and then pair with another student to take turns filling in the web by listing ideas on both sides of the question. Partners can in turn pair with a different set or sets of partners to refine their thinking and work toward consensus. The four or six can decide which ideas best support their conclusions and choose a spokesperson from their group who jots down the ideas that best support the conclusion. Each spokesperson shares these with the class in a whole-group discussion.

The discussion web prevents a small number of vocal students or the teacher from dominating discussion and gives all students an opportunity to contribute opinions. It allows students to give an opinion in a relatively risk-free environment with a peer first and then in a small group. The discussion web helps develop tolerance for different points of view and can be used before or after reading or before writing. Some teachers have students write their opinions as well or write an essay based on the conclusion and opinions shared in their group.

Whether you use literature response groups, journals, whole-group discussion, cooperative discussion web groups, or other strategies that involve discussion, you will want to have some means of assessing student responses to literature. By observing and examining the processes your students use and the products they create, you can determine their responses to the literature they

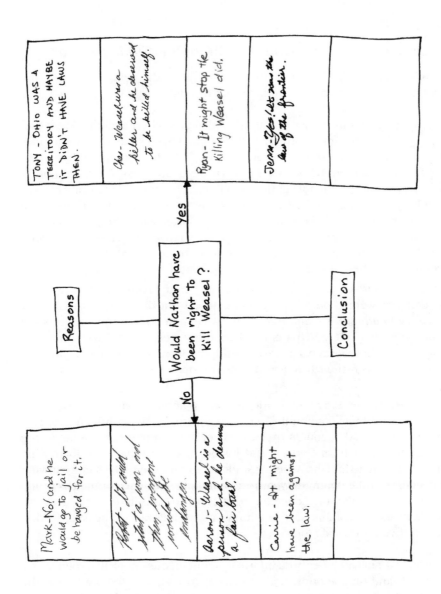

Figure 5.6 A discussion web with student responses.

Reasons

Would Nathan have been right to Kill Weasel?

Yes

Tony - Ohio was a territory and maybe it didn't have laws then.

Char - Weasel was a killer and he deserved to be killed himself.

Ryan- It might stop the killing Weasel did.

Jenn- Yes, it's now the law of the frontier.

No

Mark-No! and he would go to jail or be hanged for it.

Robert- It could start a war and then prevent more bloodshed.

Aaron- Weasel is a prisoner and he deserves a fair trial.

Carrie - It might have been against the law.

Conclusion

95

hear or read. A child's involvement in discussion, dramatization, or a variety of writing activities can give good insights into that child's response to literature. Use the checklist in Figure 5.7 or one like it to record your children's responses and guide your instruction.

How Does Webbing Guide Drama?

Webbing helped the teachers and students in each of the next three classroom descriptions plan their response to literature through creative dramatics.

■ Excitement was in the air in a third-grade class where children were preparing a play about an ant colony. The children had been studying communities of all kinds and the ant culture intrigued them. They had observed their classroom ant colony for several weeks. They had read and reported to each other on every trade book about ants in the local libraries. They had made a web on a bulletin board and recorded everything they were learning on it. It was from this web that they wrote their play. Two other classes and the parents of the children involved had been invited and were seated in the classroom eagerly awaiting the production. A video camera was set up to record the play, and the classroom atmosphere was alive with anticipation.

■ The same sort of electricity was crackling in a pre-first-grade classroom where children were about to use puppets to act out the song picturebook, *I Know an Old Lady Who Swallowed a Fly,* by Glen Rounds. The teacher used a sequenced picture web to help her children know when it was their turn to act out the song. The children had made puppets from scraps of felt glued to potholders to which their teacher had sewn loops of elastic on the backs for their hands.

■ In a sixth-grade classroom, students were planning a video documentary on the history of their community, which is located at the confluence of two rivers. They had read accounts by local historians of important events in the past, biographies of local leaders, and historical fiction that described what might have happened. Plans were for students to film themselves interviewing older residents of the community, historic buildings, evidence of the river's impact on the community, and collections of art and artifacts in the local museum. The students used webbing as a prewriting strategy before drafting each section of the narrative for their documentary.

Creative drama includes both informal, spontaneous drama like roleplaying farm animals and their actions. It also includes formal, scripted drama like the ant colony play. It may include an audience, as with the ant colony play and the documentary that would ultimately have an audience. Or it may not include an

Figure 5.7 Inventory for response to literature.

 B Beginning, D Developing, I Independent

_____ Enjoys pictures in books
_____ Enjoys stories and books
_____ Chooses reading as a free-time activity
_____ Shares reading experiences with others
_____ Takes part in drama related to stories
_____ Communicates ideas about stories in writing
_____ Reads a variety of genres
_____ Names favorite author/s
_____ Names favorite illustrator/s
_____ Prefers certain types of books
_____ Responds with smiles, laughter, or other emotions
_____ Relates personal experiences to stories
_____ Uses both pictures and print to make meaning
_____ Makes meaning from a sequence of events or actions
_____ Asks questions and seeks meaning related to stories
_____ Retells stories just read
_____ Makes predictions about story events
_____ Makes interpretations about stories
_____ Compares story with similar stories or works of same author
_____ Searches for meaning in print by locating information to clarify or verify an idea
_____ Participates in whole-class discussions about books
_____ Participates in small-group discussions about books
_____ States an opinion and supports it with ideas
_____ Modifies an opinion in light of new information
_____ Listens and values other opinions or alternative views
_____ Uses literary elements in discussing stories
      _____ Setting
      _____ Characters
      _____ Plot
      _____ Theme
      _____ Point of View
      _____ Style
      _____ Tone
_____ Understands layers of meaning in stories
_____ Understands symbolism and metaphor in appropriate stories
_____ Identifies special uses of language and stylistic devices

audience, as with the pre-first-grade children who were all involved. Spoken language is sometimes improvised, as with the ant play, and sometimes written language is read interpretively, as with the narrative that accompanied the historical documentary. Stewig and Buege (1994) describe many other ways to use improvised literature-based drama to help children attain important social, intellectual, and emotional goals.

Drama has special benefits for children who are struggling to learn English. Children who are not native English speakers find satisfaction and pleasure in creative dramatics. Drama offers a vehicle through which these children can express their ideas using body language while they build self-confidence and competence. Body movement has a strong relationship to second-language acquisition because it provides a powerful, concrete learning base (Isenberg, 1991). Bilingual children are different from English-speaking children chiefly in vocabulary, and creative dramatics allows for the building of this vocabulary.

You can use webbing to plan and organize several forms of creative drama as you promote your students' personal response, understanding, and appreciation of literature.

Pantomime

When children use gestures and actions silently to communicate meaning, they are engaged in pantomime or mime. While children do not speak during pantomime, it does require purposeful talk to plan and carry out this form of drama. When they pantomime, children learn how nonverbal language demonstrates feelings and thoughts. They see how important gestures and the face are in communicating meaning.

Children love to act out stories. For example, when Nancy's third graders heard the story *The Snail's Spell,* by Joanne Ryder, they made a web of the snail's characteristics and then imitated the boy as he pretended to be a snail in a garden. The children also made webs of other animals' traits and pantomimed their movements. Jeff imagined he was a cougar and made a web (see Figure 5.8), wrote and revised a poem based on the web (see Figure 5.9), and drew a picture to accompany the poem (see Figure 5.10).

A sixth-grade class, in which wildlife and the environment were the focus of a month-long study, ended their unit with a pantomime festival or *mime fest.* The students made webs to explain terms such as *water cycle, biodegradable, hibernation,* and *shelters.* Each web, done on a piece of paper, was then folded and put into a hat so students could take turns picking from the hat and acting out the term for the rest of the class to guess. These students were mentally and physically involved with literature as they used pantomime.

Charades

Charades is a game in which the audience guesses a title, quotation, or name that is acted out for them. Actors not only represent whole words, but also

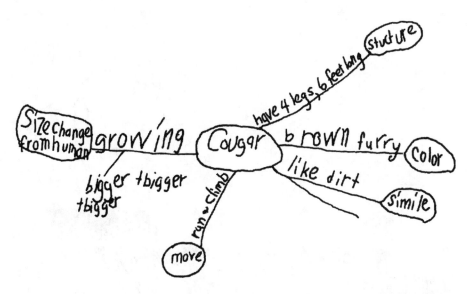

Figure 5.8 After webbing the snail's characteristics, Jeff Long made a web about a cougar and pantomimed its behavior.

```
The Cougar's Spell
By Jeffrey R. Long

        Imagine
      you are furry
and have strong bones inside you.
        Imagine
      you are brown,
    the color of coffee.
        Imagine
     you are growing,
         bigger
          and
         bigger
          and
         bigger.
        Imagine
   You are six feet long,
  lying under a green tree,
    all furry and brown.
        Imagine
you have four powerful legs now.
     You seldom walk.
        Instead,
  you run, and climb trees,
   and make your own tracks.
  It is easy to move this way,
   and it feels fast and cool.
```

Figure 5.9 From the web in Figure 5.8, Jeff created this story on the computer.

Figure 5.10   The picture that accompanied Jeff's story.

syllables in words, small words, and letters of the alphabet. Charades is a good way to involve both presenter and audience since actors try to represent words with actions and the audience tries to find words for what they see.

In a fourth-grade class where the science topic was electricity, students read biographies of famous Americans. One student chose *The Double Life of Pocohantas,* by Jean Fritz, and performed a charade of the book title after first making a web to show how she would do the charade. Each student did a charade for their book title, and the class guessed the title. In this way, webbing supported these students' charades.

Roleplay

In roleplay, children become characters and take on their characters' role. They dramatize the characters by speaking and acting as the character might speak and act. Roleplay is a powerful tool at all age levels since it does not require reading and since students can often do it their seats. For example, children can roleplay a scene, event, or the entire story *after* they have heard it read. Or students can roleplay *before* they hear parts of a story as a way of predicting and experiencing potential interactions of characters (Flynn & Carr, 1994).

When students step into the shoes of a character, they will find it easier to empathize with and understand the character. When you use roleplay, urge your children to close their eyes as they:

- Visualize the way the character looks.
- Feel the emotions the character feels.
- Decide how the character might act.

Shannon's middle school special education students helped her create the relationship web of characters in Figure 5.11 after listening to the story *Seventh*

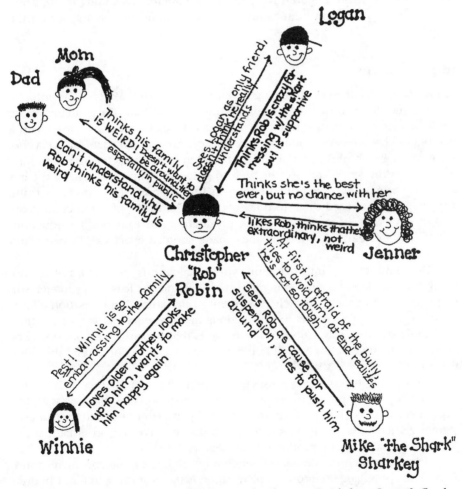

Figure 5.11 A relationship web like this one by Shannon Smith from *Seventh Grade Wierdo,* by Lee Wardlaw, helps students empathize with characters as well as roleplay, improvise, or otherwise dramatize literature.

Grade Wierdo, by Lee Wardlaw. Discussing the main character, Christopher "Rob" Robin, and how he felt about Mike, Logan, Winnie, and his parents as they made the web helped Shannon's students empathize before they roleplayed their favorite scenes from the story. Shannon felt that this roleplaying helped her students understand the story and articulate its themes better.

A third-grade class heard *Pedro's Journal,* by Pam Conrad, and parts of *Columbus: His Enterprise,* by Hans Koning, which their teacher read to them. They learned that Columbus took hundreds of Arawak Indians to Spain as slaves and murdered or drove to suicide, hundreds of thousands of them, about half the population of Hispaniola. Then the class talked about how the Arawak Indians of Hispaniola and Columbus, his brothers, and sailors may have looked, acted, and felt before children roleplayed the interactions among them. Their roleplaying helped them better understand Columbus and his impact on the New World.

Improvisation

Improvisation is drama with dialogue but with no script. Material for improvisation comes from stories your children know or have read. They can improvise entire stories or parts of a story. To involve your class, choose a story with a number of characters or modify a story so there are enough parts for everyone. Then make a web of the characters, numbering each character in order of appearance in the story, and use the web to guide the improvisation. In the ant colony improvisation mentioned earlier in this chapter, some students made stick puppets and used them to portray their parts in the play. Other students took care of back-stage aspects of the production, for example, introduction, music, set, and curtain. The web they made showed every child's name and responsibility.

One advantage of improvisation is that dialogue is ad-libbed, not memorized. Memorizing and presenting scripted dialogue, at least for younger students, may simply dampen their enjoyment of literature. Improvisation allows children to interpret characters and actions in more personal ways than they might in a scripted play. Another advantage is that the original work does not need to be followed closely. Children can shorten, change, or extend the original story.

Improvisation provides young children with a sense of story as it fosters their literacy development (Martinez, 1993). It also provides children with the experience necessary to perform more formal plays later in which they deliver memorized lines, wear costumes, make props, and take part in tasks that are part of a formal dramatic production (see Figure 5.12).

If your goal in using drama is to encourage children to personally respond, enjoy, and appreciate literature, improvisation is the best thing to use. Children get close to literature and are intimately involved with it through improvisation. They understand the feelings, emotions, and actions of characters when they act out a story and use the voices of the characters.

Readers Theater

When your students perform a work of literature by reading it orally, this is called readers theater. Readers generally sit on stools, chairs, or the floor facing the audience and hold the material they will read. The audience imagines the action and characters, and there are usually no props or costumes. Performances are done without a narrator or with one who provides the setting and action. Performers learn how to use gestures and their voices. They must change tone, pitch, volume, and rate of delivery to communicate meaning.

All types of literature, even nonfiction, lends itself to readers theater. Nonfiction has the added benefit of bringing interesting, up-to-date, and informative material to social studies, science, and health (Young & Vardell, 1993).

Figure 5.12 Both teacher and students can easily transform an improvisation into a formal play with these eight ideas.

1. *Choose a story with many characters and lots of action and dialogue.* Include additional characters if necessary, for example, five trees rather than one, but make certain that every student has at least two or three lines of dialogue.
2. *Read the story several times until everyone is familiar with it.* Analyze characters and roleplay so everyone understands the story.
3. *Write down the dialogue.* If the story is divided into sections, groups or individuals can transcribe different parts of the story, and the job is easier.
4. *List or make a sequence web of the main events of the story.* Each event can become a scene in the show, or events can be combined.
5. *Try it and edit.* Aim for a fifteen- to thirty-minute play depending on the age of the students. Omit scenes or events that are redundant and action or dialogue that is not important.
6. *Cast the show.* Ask for volunteers and have students try out by reading parts. You and a committee of students can make decisions. Do not forget a narrator who can provide transitions.
7. *Rehearse the play.* Practice so students learn to speak loudly and clearly as they face the audience.
8. *Keep props and costumes simple.* The students and the art teacher will have creative ideas for costumes and props that are not elaborate. The suggestion of a character's physical attributes using color, a special hat, or an object to carry will often suffice.

You can use readers theater with children as young as first grade. The only prerequisite is that children need to be able to read independently so they do not struggle with word recognition, fluency, or expression. The story or poetry should offer action and excitement so children can dramatize it easily. To help your children understand the story before they perform it in readers theater, web the literary elements or sequence of events with them first. Webbing reinforces their comprehension of the story.

Choral Speaking

When your children read or recite a poem or piece of rhymed prose together, the performance is called choral speaking. An entire class can speak together, or the class can be divided in half with the halves responding to each other. Paul Fleischman's poetry, *Joyful Noise: Poems for Two Voices* has parts for readers and is a perfect vehicle for choral speaking. It can be read by children as young as third grade. You can include solos, duets, quartets, or other types of groupings that make sense to you. Typically there are four kinds of choral speaking:

- *Refrain:* The leader speaks most of the lines, and the group repeats the refrain.
- *Line-at-a-time:* One student or a small group of students speaks a line or two, then another speaks a line or two, and so on.
- *Antiphonal:* Two or more groups of speakers alternate. Sometimes females and males are grouped together or voices are grouped according to pitch. Alternate groups or combine them for effect.
- *Unison:* An entire group speaks lines together with no subgrouping.

Combining choral speaking with an improvisation can be interesting. For example, one group of third-graders studying the weather had read Judi Barrett's *Cloudy with a Chance of Meatballs* and decided to share the book with the class. They acted out the story, adding poems about foods that fell from the sky. The poems grew from a web they had made of all the possible foods that might fall from the sky. Some of the poems were spoken in unison and some by pairs of children who took turns speaking lines. Each student found a poem about a different food and made a copy for the person they recited with so that no memorization was needed. The class loved this creative sharing of this humorous book.

Videotaping

The video documentary mentioned earlier in this chapter that was created by the sixth graders is an example of students' dramatic involvement with content-area literature. Videotaping a show such as this was wonderful motivation for them to read and interact with each other about what they read to create webs and to collect snapshots to weave into the videotaped history of their community.

Videotaping has many possibilities for involving students in literature and learning. Some teachers have found that their students enjoy videotaping reenactments of books or stories they have read. Improvised dialogue and narration coupled with costumes and rudimentary props make it a creative experience. Other teachers find that creating and videotaping a documentary motivates students to read historical fiction, biography, and other content-area materials.

Puppets

The hand puppets the prekindergarteners used in their enactment of the song/picturebook about Old MacDonald are only one of a variety of puppets children enjoy using. Puppets made from paper and sticks, paper bags, socks, cardboard cylinders, boxes, tagboard and straws, gloves, and mittens are easy ways to help children respond to what they read or hear.

After hearing folktales of the Northwestern Indians, two third-grade girls created a web from which they made up their own folktale and then used simple stick puppets to dramatize their story. They tied a cord across the corner of the classroom from the crank handle of a window to the knob of a closet door and draped a sheet over it. They knelt behind the sheet and improvised dialogue and actions to accompany their story. Stick puppets are simple to make, and even older students enjoy them as a way of sharing stories.

Puppets provide shy children with a way of expressing themselves and give all children a chance to be creative in their responses and interpretations. Use puppets to support storytelling, roleplay, or improvisation.

Art and Music

Encouraging children's artistic and musical connections to the books they read allows them a rich range of response. The school art teacher can teach you and your children much about artistic media and styles, and your children can experiment themselves by working in the media of their favorite illustrators. For young children, drawing pictures after listening to a story is a good way to encourage a response to literature. We know that a picture can stimulate oral language and that often children have very involved stories to tell about pictures they have drawn. Creating webs serves the same function. With the support of a web, even young children tell stories with a beginning, a middle, and an end that are thoughtfully connected. The drawing and scribbling young children do signals emergent literacy and is a precursor to the development of formal writing. So you not only enhance response to literature when you allow children to draw, but you also aid the development of expressive skills in general.

The school music teacher can also help you and your children learn about the kind of music and musical instruments that relate to the time periods and settings of books. The music teacher can teach your students songs or suggest tapes or records that relate to particular pieces of literature.

A fourth-grade teacher enlisted the help of the music teacher, who taught the students several pioneer songs that were included in their enactment of a play based on one of Laura Ingalls Wilder's books about the prairie. Most improvisations or plays are more enjoyable and creatively performed with the addition of music. Do not overlook the fact that there is much good music that the music teacher can suggest or provide to authenticate or accompany your reading or your children's reading of literature. It is often through music that children's creative senses are touched.

When these kinds of crossovers happen, you can integrate your curriculum and enrich your children's responses to books at the same time. Music and art allow for a fuller range of enjoyment and understanding of literature.

Conclusion

Responses to literature grow from interactions with print and are highly personal. They occur when children bring various meanings and background knowledge to print as they create a new personal experience from reading. Responses range from the aesthetic to the efferent and critical and depend on some level of understanding. You can promote rich responses by encouraging children to use webs to interact with each other and with stories. You can also use webbing to create a literate environment, support interactive story reading, guide discussion, and support dramatization.

REFERENCES

Alvermann, D. E. (1991). The discussion web: A graphic aid for learning across the curriculum. *The Reading Teacher, 45*(2), 92–99.

Evans, J., & Moore, J. E. (1985). *How to Make Books with Children.* Monterey, CA: Evan-Moor.

Flynn, R. M., & Carr, G. A. (1994). Exploring classroom literature through drama: A specialist and teacher collaborate. *Language Arts, 71*(1), 38–43.

Isenberg, J. (1991). Creative drama and play in the early childhood classroom. *Educating Disadvantaged and Minority Children, 1*(6), pp. 4–6.

Martinez, M. (1993). Motivating dramatic story reenactments. *The Reading Teacher, 46*(8), 682–688.

Peterson, R., & Eeds, M. (1990). *Grand Conversations: Literature Groups in Action.* New York: Scholastic.

Purves, A., Rogers, T., & Soter, A. (1990). *How Porcupines Make Love II: Teaching a Response-Centered Literature Curriculum.* New York: Longman.

Rosenblatt, L. M. (1985). The transactional theory of the literary work: Implications for research. In C. R. Cooper (Ed.), *Researching Response to Literature and the Teaching of Literature: Points of Departure* (pp. 33–53). Norwood, NJ: Ablex.

Rosenblatt, L. M. (1991). Literature—S.O.S.! *Language Arts, 68*(6), 444–448.

Stewig, J. W., & Buege, C. (1994). *Dramatizing Literature in Whole Lanaguage Classrooms,* 2nd ed. New York: Teachers College Press.

Sutherland, Z., & Arbuthnot, M. H. (1991). *Children and Books,* 8th ed. Glenview, IL: Scott, Foresman.

Young, T. A., & Vardell, S. (1993). Weaving readers theatre and nonfiction into the curriculum. *The Reading Teacher, 46*(5), 396–406.

Children's Literature

Babbitt, N. (1978). *Tuck Everlasting.* New York: Farrar, Straus & Giroux.

Barrett, J. (1978). *Cloudy with a Chance of Meatballs.* New York: Macmillan.

Cannon, J. (1993). *Stellaluna.* New York: Scholastic.

Conrad, P. (1991). *Pedro's Journal.* New York: Scholastic.

DeFelice, C. (1990). *Weasel.* New York: Avon.

Fleischman, P. (1988). *Joyful Noise: Poems for Two Voices.* New York: Harper & Row.

Fritz, J. (1983). *The Double Life of Pocohantas.* New York: Putnam.

Koning, H. (1976). *Columbus: His Enterprise.* New York: Monthly Review Press.

Lobel, A. (1972). *Frog and Toad Together.* New York: Scholastic.

MacLachlan, P. (1994). *All the Places to Love.* New York: Harper Collins.

Rounds, G. (1990). *I Know an Old Lady Who Swallowed a Fly.* New York: Holiday House.

Ryder, J. (1988). *The Snail's Spell.* New York: Penguin.

Sendak, M. (1963). *Where the Wild Things Are.* New York: Harper & Row.

Wardlaw, L. (1992). *Seventh Grade Wierdo.* New York: Scholastic

chapter 6

Writing as Response

This chapter addresses webbing as it supports writing and a written response to literature. Webbing supports the writing process by acting as a tool for planning, organizing, drafting, and revising. It also supports students as they read literature since it is a strategy for writing notes, reports, stories, and journals and for sharing personal literary response. You and your students can create webs on paper or with computer software programs.

How Does Webbing Aid the Writing Process?

- *Justin:* "A web gets me started in my writing and it helps with ideas."
- *Lindsey:* "It helps me know what I'm going to write."
- *Schyler:* "It helps me sort my ideas and put them on a piece of paper."
- *Pradepta:* "It helps me because sometimes I forget what I wanted to write."
- *Dan:* "Because sometimes I go back and make sure I have everything I wanted to write."

These are answers from third-grade writers to the question "How does a web help you in your writing?" These students had observed their teacher, Pat, as she used webbing in a variety of ways, but they also used webbing routinely themselves. Pat often created webs to organize information and ideas in science and social studies. She demonstrated webbing as a tool for brainstorming. She modeled it as a vehicle for planning compositions. She showed the children how to refer to their webs as they drafted so their work would reflect many ideas, much information, and good organization. As a result of Pat's systematic and intentional use of webbing as a teaching tool, her students regularly used webbing to record their ideas and plan their writing. It is interesting to note that Pradepta and Dan say they refer to their webs during drafting as an aid to memory. Webs help all these students structure their thinking and guide their writing.

Many teachers who use a process approach to the teaching of writing discover webbing. These teachers find that webbing supports student writers in every aspect of the writing process, especially those students for whom writing does not come easily.

In classrooms where a process approach to writing is used, good teachers encourage their students to rehearse and plan what they will write before drafting. They urge students to refer to the plan they have made actively, whether it is a web, notes, or an outline, as they draft their writing. These teachers recognize and promote the recursive nature of the writing process. They invite students to reread and revise, and to help their peers do the same, with an eye to communicating the message effectively. In these classrooms, students also have opportunities to publish their work or share it with a real audience.

If students are to write well, it is commonly accepted that they need exposure to good literature models. The best writing for children is found in quality literature written especially for them. To help students become good writers, surround them with the best books and stories, help them see themselves as authors by becoming authors, and make the reading-writing connection real for them. Several experts elaborate on the links between reading and writing:

- "The reading-writing connections that matter most belong to the quiet moments when a writer is snuggled up, reading a book" (Calkins, 1994, p. 266).
- "Writing is learned by writing, by reading, and by perceiving oneself as a writer" (Smith, 1982, p. 199).
- "All children need literature. Children who are authors need it even more" (Graves, 1983, p. 67).

For some students, making the jump from reading good literature to writing good prose comes easily. For others, however, one does not necessarily follow the other. These students need help bridging the gap and making the connection between reading and writing.

As a teacher, you can help your students read with a writer's eye—to explore the impact, look, and sound of good writing. You can introduce them to authors and make sure they understand that authors are real people. You can provide them with a variety of materials, plenty of time, positive reinforcement, and encouragement to write. You can write yourself and share your problems and successes with them. Teachers can also guide students to use strategies like webbing that make writing easier and more pleasurable.

Planning with Webs

Webbing is one way of making the reading-writing connection real for children. It does for older students what drawing a picture does for very young children. When a young child draws a picture, it is a stimulus for talking about a topic. The picture serves as a springboard for oral composition by providing the child with content to talk about. The picture is the child's way of rehearsing and planning what to say when he shares his picture with his peers. As children become more verbal and gain writing skills, the drawings they use to stimulate their writing become more sophisticated. Webs function in the same way for older students. They allow students to represent and organize graphically some rather sophisticated ideas and relationships and then write or talk about what they have drawn.

By creating a web from what is read or heard, students rehearse and plan for what they will talk or write about. After reading a story, students can sequence the events in a web format and use the structure to retell the story or write a summary of it. In this way, responses to literature grow from webbing. Younger children can help you create a web, while older students can learn to create their own webs with your guidance.

In one school, two teachers collaborated on a project to stimulate and develop their students' writing. A fifth-grade class adopted a class of second-graders and taught them how to write letters and keep buddy journals. One of the things the fifth-graders were eager to do was write stories and make books for the younger students. Betty, the fifth-grade teacher, had seen a web on chart paper in the second-grade classroom (see Figure 6.1) that Penny had made with her children after they heard *If You Give a Mouse a Cookie,* by Laura Numeroff. The web gave Betty an idea for helping some of her reluctant and struggling writers.

Betty borrowed the web, shared it with her students, and showed them how to use it as a model for writing their own stories for the second-graders. First, Betty read *If You Give a Mouse a Cookie* to her students, and together they webbed the elements of the story (see Figure 6.2). Then Betty helped her students create a new web by changing the setting and action. They changed the setting to the mouse's home and made a new web for the action to reflect the chain of events that might occur when a boy visits a mouse's home and the mouse gives the boy a piece of cheese. In this way, they used webbing to plan a new story. Figures 6.3 and 6.4 show a web and original story that grew from this lesson.

The structure of predictable stories like *If You Give a Mouse a Cookie* provides a blueprint for writing as well as a way of developing reading behaviors. Predictable stories contain repetitive language patterns or familiar sequences that make it easy for children to anticipate and supply appropriate language as they read the stories or hear them read. Betty shared other predictable books with her students:

- *Brown Bear, Brown Bear, What Do You See?,* by Bill Martin (repetitive words, phrases, and questions)
- *Five Little Monkeys Jumping on the Bed,* by Eileen Christelow (familiar sequences)
- *The Big Fat Worm,* by Nancy VanLaan (repetitive story patterns)
- *The Cat That Mack Ate,* by Rose Robart (cumulative tale)
- *Good-Night Owl,* by Pat Hutchins (predictable plot)
- *This Old Man,* by Carol Jones (familiar rhymes and song lyrics)

Betty suggested that her students could rewrite these stories. They could web them as they had webbed *If You Give a Mouse a Cookie,* modify the webs

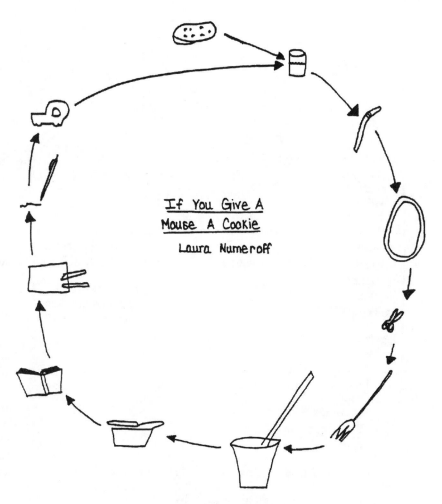

Figure 6.1 A second-grade teacher's picture web for *If You Give a Mouse a Cookie*.

by changing one or two aspects of their structure, and then write sequels or new stories. In fact, she told them, with webs to help them, they could write interesting sequels to any story they knew the second-graders had read and liked. With this preparation, a few books to read and use as models, and some unlined paper on which to draw their webs, her students excitedly started their book-writing project.

Two weeks later, Betty's class had completed cloth-cover books that contained some of the best writing Betty had seen her students do. Penny's class ea-

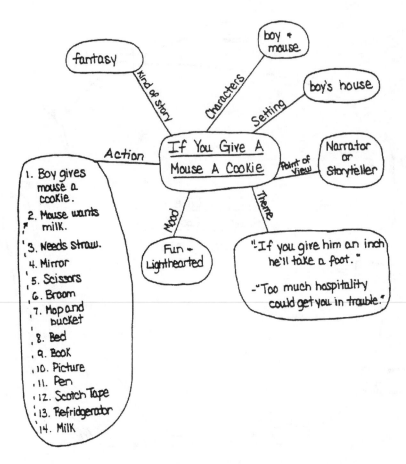

Figure 6.2   A fifth grader's web of *If You Give a Mouse a Cookie*.

gerly listened as a few fifth-graders each day read their books aloud before they donated them to the second-grade classroom library.

This scenario shows one way to use webs to help support your students' rehearsal and planning for writing. This example shows how a visual display of the elements of a story and the important information from that story can be a springboard for retelling, rewriting, and creative writing. Your explorations with webbing and other genres of literature can be equally effective. By using literature as a model, you can help your students write better reports, information books, realistic fiction, and so on.

Organizing with Webs

In addition to helping students identify what to include in their writing, webbing helps with organization. One of the things writers do when they organize information is to decide on order to include ideas in the writing. Organizing is an important part of rehearsal and planning and a step that is often overlooked. It is easy to assume that children will intuitively know how to order their ideas in the most effective sequence, which is not always the case.

We can show children how to include their ideas in webs and then sequence the ideas in an order that makes sense. The following section shows how this idea worked with fourth graders.

Some of Lisa's fourth-grade students who were reading biographies had questions about the authors. They wondered how the authors knew everything they included in the stories they wrote about other people's lives. Lisa thought this might be a good time to introduce biographical writing and the autobiography in particular. She read them *Broderick,* by Edward Ormondroyd, a short biographical fantasy about a mouse's life, and *A Weed Is a Flower: The Life of*

Figure 6.3 A fifth grader's web for a modified verson of *If You Give a Mouse a Cookie.*

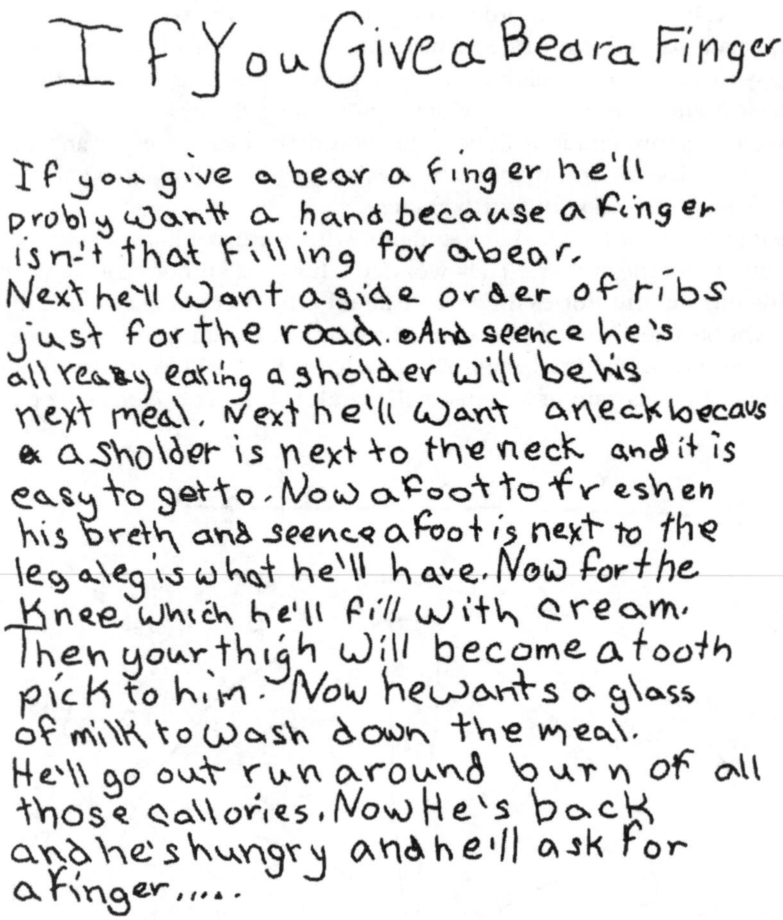

I f You Give a Bear a Finger

If you give a bear a finger he'll
probly want a hand because a finger
isn't that filling for a bear.
Next he'll want a side order of ribs
just for the road. And seence he's
allready eating a sholder will be his
next meal. Next he'll want a neck becaus
a sholder is next to the neck and it is
easy to get to. Now a foot to freshen
his breth and seence a foot is next to the
leg a leg is what he'll have. Now for the
knee which he'll fill with cream.
Then your thigh will become a tooth
pick to him. Now he wants a glass
of milk to wash down the meal.
He'll go out run around burn of all
those callories. Now He's back
and he's hungry and he'll ask for
a finger.....

Figure 6.4   A story written by a fifth grader from the web in Figure 6.3.

George Washington Carver, by Aliki Brandenberg. She helped the students make webs of the important events and people in the lives of Broderick and Carver. Then the class as a whole made a web of the kinds of things they could include in their own autobiographies. They suggested topics such as birth, family, friends, future, hobbies, school, best memories, fears, and favorites. Throughout the creation of this web, there was discussion of how students might obtain some of the information they needed. Talking to parents, looking at birth certificates, and thinking about major events in their lives and their hopes for the future were all part of the planning.

By this time, the students were eager to make webs to guide the writing of their own autobiographies. Tina was intrigued with the idea of a spider web and included such topics as *favorites, birth, family,* and *future* in her web (see Figure 6.5).

Lisa encouraged her students to take their webs home and talk with family members to see what else they might want to include and to get any information they needed. The next day the class talked about how sequence and order can affect a written piece. Lisa told her students that each strand on the web they had made could be a separate paragraph or section in their autobiography. She then helped them sequence and number the strands on Broderick's and George Washington Carver's webs in the order the authors had used.

Next, Lisa read opening paragraphs of two biographies to the class. She chose two books by Jean Fritz, *What's the Big Idea, Benjamin Franklin?* and *Where Do You Think You're Going, Christopher Columbus?* The biography of Benjamin Franklin begins by describing the street on which he was born in Boston and includes few details about his birth. In her biography of Christopher Columbus, the author begins with a description of Genoa and then talks about Columbus's birth. In this way, Lisa showed her students that they could rearrange the order of the strands or paragraphs in their autobiographies to add interest and to achieve a different effect.

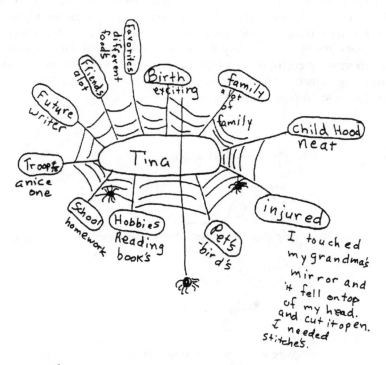

Figure 6.5 Tina's web for her autobiography.

After this look at order and form in four biographies and some discussion of ideas for organizing their own life stories, Lisa had her students tentatively number the strands in their webs to indicate the order in which they would include their ideas. She helped them understand that this order could be changed but that, by having an overall organization in mind before writing, the composing would be easier and the finished product might be more interesting to read, as well as being better written. Her students then began using their webs to help write their autobiographies.

Figure 6.6 shows the cover of Tina's book, which Tina describes as fascinating. In Figure 6.7 Tina demonstrates the importance she places on her web by including it as the first chapter. Several children, like Tina, listed facts and ideas on their webs under each strand topic, so they would not forget to include the information when they began writing.

Notetaking and Reporting with Webs

Webbing can be equally useful for students as they read and respond to information books. Webs can serve as a tool for notetaking and writing reports. One of the biggest problems with assigning written reports is that students often copy information directly from reference books, using words they cannot pronounce and do not know the meaning of. The resulting reports are disconnected bits of information copied from a number of sources, which the students themselves often do not understand. One way to alleviate this problem is to emphasize that a good report is a piece of writing that uses the writer's own voice to communicate ideas and information. Webbing provides a good strategy for helping students begin to learn how to do this.

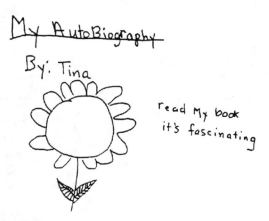

Figure 6.6 The title page for Tina's autobiography.

Context

page 1 My web
page 2 My birth
page 3 My childhood
page 4 My family
page 5 My injury
page 6 My pet
page 7 My future
page 8 My picture
page 9 My friends
page 10 My troop

Figure 6.7 The Table of
Contents for Tina's book.

Renée, a third-grade teacher, found that webbing is a good way of helping her students begin to write in September, especially those students who have writing difficulties. Renée and her students create webs of information to which they add connecting words so the web becomes a blueprint for drafting a piece.

First, Renée and her students decided to read biographies of famous people and then write a report on each person's life to present to another third-grade class. To demonstrate webbing as a report-writing tool, Renée read *Chicken Sunday,* by Patricia Polacco, to her class. Then, as the class talked together about the things in Eula Mae Walker's life that were significant, Renée organized their ideas on a web using the overhead projector (see Figure 6.8). This allowed everyone to see the webbing process and identify the important aspects of Eula's life. After the children supplied the information, Renée showed them how to add words to connect web strands, for example, *is a, of, because,* and *which is why.* When connecting words like these are added, the web becomes a blueprint for writing a report. Students with difficulties in writing need only copy the web strands and connecting words in order to write full sentences. Of course, this much structure is not necessary for all students and may even inhibit the creativity of some, so it is best to use it when you first begin webbing and only with those students it will benefit.

Nancy, another third-grade teacher, found that a good way to begin a report, once each student had a topic, was to have them brainstorm a web with strands for all the ideas they thought they might want to include in their reports. By beginning with a web of possible ideas, her children could then go

CHICKEN SUNDAY

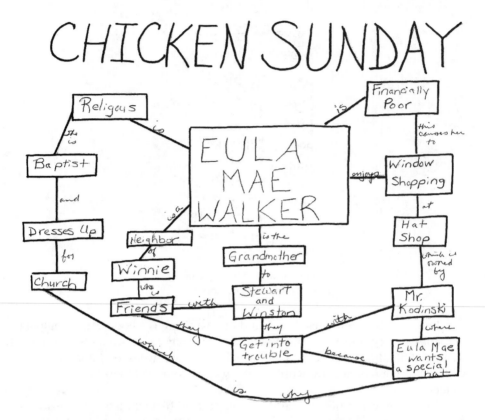

Figure 6.8   A character web created by Renée Jahelka with connecting words that can act as a blueprint for writing.

about their reading and information gathering with a purpose. She showed them how to paraphrase and add specific information to their webs; she modeled for them how they could add strands and delete strands that did not seem important or were included in other strands.

Webs serve as blueprints for first reports by allowing children to construct visual displays of their topics. As students become more skillful writers and begin to deal with more information, show them how to use a heavy marker to brainstorm and a pencil to add information as they read from various information and reference books. You also will undoubtedly want to help them use such strategies as data charts, three-inch by five-inch notecards, and outlines to prepare their reports.

Story Writing with Webs

When her third-grade students were familiar with story structure and could use webs independently to gather information and write reports, their teacher,

Nancy, had them use webbing to write original stories that contained factual information. Nancy agreed with the thinking of Wolf and Gearhart (1994) that "Stories follow patterns, and an understanding of genre aids the student's ability to analyze stories and to write fresh tales that follow or veer from traditional patterns" (p. 441). Nancy also read daily to her students from a variety of genres to provide them with models of story structure and good language.

Nancy's students first chose an animal to read about and gather information on (see Figure 6.9). She then used the structure *problem, events, solution* to establish a chain of events. Working from the web and the story-map outline, Shelly, a student who typically avoided writing and found it tedious, wrote a fact-based fantasy about *Katie Koala* (see Figure 6.10).

Keep in mind that webbing may not be necessary for all of your students all of the time. At first, it can provide a concrete way to rehearse, plan, organize, and make decisions about writing. Using webs can not only help students improve the content of their writing but also can have an impact on the form and structure of what students write. Some will use webs at first and quickly understand how to include or gather information so that they may move to another system of making notes or outlines for themselves. Others will be comfortable

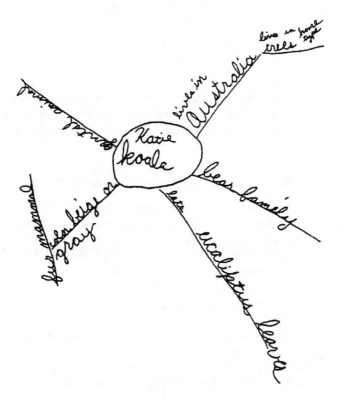

Figure 6.9   Shelly's web of information about Koala bears.

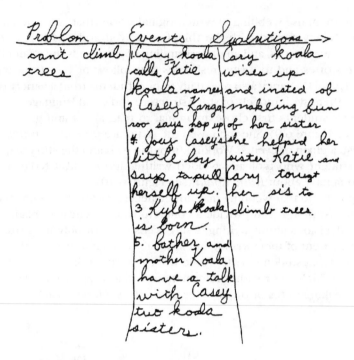

Figure 6.10   Shelly's story map outline.

with webs as a strategy for prewriting and use them consistently. Webbing does not need to become a ritual that everyone uses each time they write; rather, it should be a strategy that students use until they find what works best for them.

Literature Response Journals and Webs

In addition to helping children plan and organize their writing, webbing can be an important vehicle for responding to literature and recording the responses. Writing is a more personal and private means of expression than is participating in an open discussion, and so it can allow students a less risky forum for voicing a reaction or response than a class sharing session might.

Many teachers have their students begin a literature response journal in September so students have a record of their reading during the year (Bromley, 1994; Wolman-Bonilla, 1991). For each book her third-graders read, Nancy often asked her students to make a web on one page in their journal to represent the story in some way. On another page, they wrote a personal opinion or response to the book. Of course, there are many other ways to use webbing with journals. Figure 6.11 offers a variety of journal prompts in a web format to encourage students to think and write divergently. Prompts like these give direction to writing for reluctant writers or for those students who tend to respond minimally in their journals. Having each student in a small group begin a journal entry with a different prompt provides for varied responses and leads to interesting discussions of what was read when the journal entries are shared first before talking. In this way, Nancy's students have a record of the title, author, setting, characters, plot, theme, and point of view of each book they have read, as well as their response to each book.

A journal of this kind gives students a sense of their progress in reading and allows them to look back at what they have read. Students can swap journals, look at each other's webs, and read the written responses to see if they want to read a book someone else has read. Students can also be paired with a buddy and write responses to each other's entries (Bromley, Winters, & Schlimmer, 1994). Response journals give students opportunities to practice writing that is meaningful to them. Response journals also provide important information

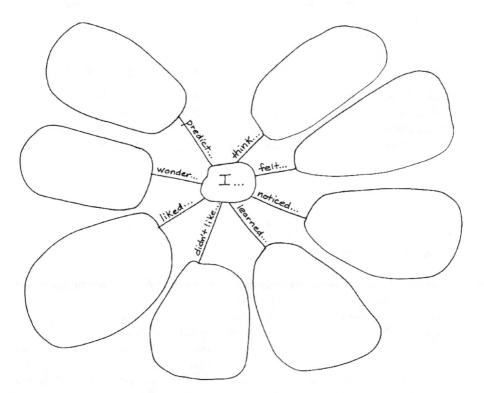

Figure 6.11 A web of journal starters to encourage divergent thinking and response to literature.

about what kinds of books and which authors children seem to like, so that you can make suggestions to broaden the range of literature your children read.

Literature response journals are a means to a deeper understanding and appreciation of literature. Calkins (1994) tells about a teacher who uses writing-reading response groups. In this classroom, small groups of children each read a different book, depending on the interests and abilities of the group. A group uses multiple copies of the same book, and each day they read for 30 minutes and then write responses in their journals. Following writing, they come together to share their responses and discuss questions the teacher provides. Calkins suggests that the most effective use of the responses is to have children voluntarily read them aloud to each other to begin the sharing time. In this way, children are encouraged to begin with and build on their own reactions to books. She says that as children hear how others respond and begin to interact and respond to each other, the ways in which they respond will change. They become more sensitive to a broader range of aspects that contribute to writing as well as reading, and their own opinions and feelings are confirmed. These response groups help children rethink books and stories from others' perspectives.

Learning Logs and Webs

Learning logs are another forum for responding to what is read or learned. A learning log is a journal in which students record and react to what they are learning in science, social studies, or math. The format can include webs, drawings, lists, maps, charts, sentences, or complete paragraphs. In learning logs, students can:

- Write information to remember
- Reflect on what was learned
- Discover gaps in knowledge
- Explore new concepts and ideas

Terry, a fourth-grade science teacher, realizes the power of learning logs for helping students summarize and review what they have learned. At the end of each class, Terry's students make sketches, drawings, or webs in their logs and label them with key words to show what they learned from their reading and/or from class activities. Sometimes Terry poses a question and has students write an answer in their logs. Then, for the first five minutes of each class, he has small groups of students share their entries with each other. Terry says this is not only a quick and easy way to review yesterday's class but also a way to check student learning so that he knows what needs to be reviewed or re-taught. In addition, because the logs include a variety of ways of representing information and ideas, Terry's students have learned to accept and appreciate these differences. Encourage students to keep learning logs and to use webs to show what they are learning in social studies and math as well.

Literature response journals and learning logs can be stepping stones to a deeper understanding and appreciation of literature and the diverse ways in which learning occurs. When students share their journals or logs in small groups by volunteering to read their entries aloud to each other and then talking about what they learned, they begin to construct new meanings together. They share personal thoughts and ideas, interact with each other, and learn from each other, not just from you as the teacher.

Webbing with Computer Software

For all students, but especially for those who have extreme difficulties with writing, the computer can be a real friend. For teachers as well, the computer is a wonderful tool for teaching as well as for planning curriculum and instruction. Figure 6.12 shows a web created on a MAC by Jennifer, a teacher who was involved in a unit on nutrition with her third-graders. Jennifer read her students the story *Apple Picking Time,* by Michele Slawson, and together they created the web to show characters in the story. Currently, there are many exciting software tools especially for creating webs on the computer. Appendix A includes further information and addresses for these tools.

- *Kid Pix* is compatible with both IBM and MAC computers and one of the easiest to use of the available programs that produce maps, even younger students can experience this motivating form of webbing. This program allows students to visualize a concept in a web format, label parts of the web, and outline information. With this software, students can move back and forth between the diagram and the written outline.

- *The Literary Mapper* is designed to be used with literature specifically. This program contains predeveloped maps that contain character, setting, and action so that students of any age can fill them in at the keyboard as they read a story. Brainstorming, listing, mapping, and editing to expand and change the webs students create are also possible with this software, which is MAC-compatible.

- *The Semantic Mapper,* while not designed for literature specifically, allows students of any age to create their own webs or maps and add labels. This software allows for brainstorming, listing, mapping, and editing to expand and modify maps. For students who are doing research, this software, which is MAC-compatible allows them to see visual representations of their research as it progresses.

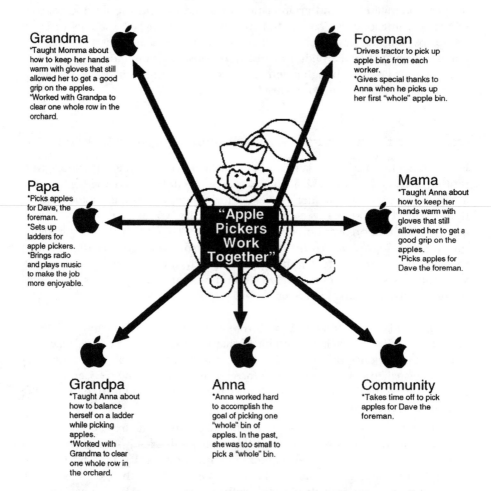

Character Web for:
Apple Picking Time
By Michele Benoit Slawson

Grandma
"Taught Momma about
how to keep her hands
warm with gloves that still
allowed her to get a good
grip on the apples.
"Worked with Grandpa to
clear one whole row in the
orchard.

Foreman
"Drives tractor to pick up
apple bins from each
worker.
"Gives special thanks to
Anna when he picks up
her first "whole" apple bin.

Papa
"Picks apples
for Dave, the
foreman.
"Sets up
ladders for
apple pickers.
"Brings radio
and plays music
to make the job
more enjoyable.

Mama
"Taught Anna about
how to keep her
hands warm with
gloves that still
allowed her to get a
good grip on the
apples.
"Picks apples for
Dave the foreman.

"Apple
Pickers
Work
Together"

Grandpa
"Taught Anna about
how to balance
herself on a ladder
while picking
apples.
"Worked with
Grandma to clear
one whole row in
the orchard.

Anna
"Anna worked hard
to accomplish the
goal of picking one
"whole" bin of
apples. In the past,
she was too small to
pick a "whole" bin.

Community
"Takes time off to pick
apples for Dave the
foreman.

Figure 6.12   A character web for a unit on nutrition created by Jennifer Nowacki using
a computer.

■ *Inspiration* is a tool that is a bit more complicated and probably is best
used by computer whizzes and adults. It models the thinking process by allowing the user to brainstorm ideas, create a web or diagram, and then write an
outline. It permits quick movement between web and outline, and changes

made in one appear automatically in the other. There are both IBM and MAC versions.

■ *Thinking Networks for Reading and Writing* uses semantic mapping or webbing to help the learner move from reading to restructuring what was read through rewriting and preorganizing and finally into drafting. It is MAC-compatible and probably best used by older students and adults.

Conclusion

This chapter dealt with webbing as a way to link reading and writing, support the writing process, and promote response to literature. It showed how webbing supports planning, organizing, notetaking, report writing, and sharing that students engage in as they read literature. Finally, it presented some software programs for creating webs on the computer.

REFERENCES

Bromley, K. (1993). *Journaling: Engagements in Reading, Writing and Thinking.* New York: Scholastic.

Bromley, K., Winters, D., & Schlimmer, K. (1994). Book buddies: Creating enthusiasm for literacy learning. *The Reading Teacher, 47*(5), pp. 392–403.

Calkins, L. M. (1994). *The Art of Teaching Writing.* Portsmouth, NH: Heinemann.

Graves, D. (1983). *Writing: Teachers and Children at Work.* Portsmouth, NH: Heinemann.

Smith, F. (1982). *Writing and the Writer.* New York: Holt Rinehart & Winston.

Wolf, S. A., & Gearhart, M. (1994). Writing what you read: Narrative assessment as a learning event. *Language Arts, 71*(6), 425–444.

Wolman-Bonilla, J. (1991). *Response Journals: Inviting Students to Think and Write about Literature.* New York: Scholastic.

Software

Inspiration 4.0: The Easiest Way to Brainstorm and Write. Portland, OR: Inspiration Software.

Kid Pix. San Rafael, CA: Borderbund Software.

The Literary Mapper. Gainesville, FL: Teacher Support Software.

The Semantic Mapper. Gainesville, FL: Teacher Support Software.

Thinking Networks For Reading and Writing. New York: Thinking Networks.

Children's Literature

Brandenberg, A. (1965). *A Weed Is a Flower: The Life of George Washington Carver.* Englewood Cliffs, NJ: Prentice-Hall.

Christelow, E. (1989). *Five Little Monkeys Jumping on the Bed.* New York: Clarion.

Fritz, J. (1976). *What's the Big Idea, Benjamin Franklin?* New York: Coward-McCann.

———. (1980). *Where Do You Think You're Going, Christopher Columbus?* New York: Putnam's.

Hutchins, P. (1982). *Good-Night Owl.* New York: Macmillan.

Jones, C. (1989). *This Old Man.* Boston: Houghton Mifflin.

Martin, B. (1983). *Brown Bear, Brown Bear, What Do You See?* New York: Holt.

Numeroff, L. (1986). *If You Give a Mouse a Cookie.* New York: Scholastic.

Ormondroyd, E. (1969). *Broderick.* Berkeley, CA: Parnassus.

Polacco, P. (1992). *Chicken Sunday.* New York: Philomel.

Robart, R. (1986). *The Cake That Mack Ate.* Boston: Little Brown.

Slawson, M. B. (1994). *Apple Picking Time.* New York:Crown.

VanLaan, N. (1987). *The Big Fat Worm.* New York: Knopf

Children's Literature Review Part I: Annotated Bibliography, Web Illustrations, and Teaching Ideas

This chapter contains annotations and webs for approximately 50 books, both picture books and books for older students that are primarily text. The bibliography includes Caldecott and Newbery Medal and Honor books, IRA Children's Choices books, books chosen by the Children's Book Council as outstanding science and trade books, and other examples of quality literature for K–8 children and youth. The selections reflect a diversity of subject matter and cultural heritages, including African, Asian, European, Hispanic, and native American. Multicultural literature is noted with an asterisk (*).

Each annotation includes: a *Summary* of the story; a *Setting* that includes time and place; a list of *Characters;* a *Theme,* or underlying idea; a list of potentially difficult *Vocabulary* in the book; a brief description of the *Illustrations; Grade Level/Content Area,* which identifies grades for which the book is appropriate and themes or units in science, social studies, math, health, art, or physical education with which the book can be used; and suggestions for using the web with students in the classroom.

The books are categorized by genre: folktale, fantasy, realistic fiction, historical fiction, biography, poetry, and information books. Within each genre, books are in alphabetical order according to the author's last name.

Folktales

*Aardema, Verna. **Bringing the Rain to Kapiti Plain.** (Illus., Beatriz Vidal). New York: Dial, 1981.

Summary: A cumulative folktale from the Nandi culture of Africa in which a cow herder helps to bring rain to a drought-plagued plain where his thirsty herd feeds.

Setting: Many years ago in Kenya, Africa.

Characters: Ki-pat and the cows and animals that live on Kapiti Plain.

Themes: Problems can be solved with ingenuity. Natural events can be explained in many ways.

Vocabulary: Ki-Pat, Kapiti Plain, acacia, migrate, drought, thong.

Illustrations: Full-color drawings show the Kenyan plain realistically in shades of brown during drought, changing to patchy green during the rain, and finally lush green after the rain. Pictures cover entire pages and many double pages with small amounts of print accompanying each picture.

Grade Level/Content Area: This book is appropriate for students in grades 3–5 who are studying life on the plains, Africa, or folktales. The story contains the traditional elements of a story and is an example of how people from every culture seek to explain natural phenomena that are otherwise puzzling to them and difficult to understand.

Literary Elements Web: Part of this literary elements web, the setting and characters, might be shown to children first to introduce difficult vocabulary. Then the story can be read to them; or they can read it, talk about it, and reread it before they complete the remainder of the web. This cumulative tale is told in verse and should be read through or the effect is lost. The story lends itself to choral reading because of its repetitive lines and predictably sequenced events.

Students can explore folktales of other cultures that explain the origin of rain or perhaps write their own *how and why* tale about how an extinct culture might have explained drought and rain to their children.

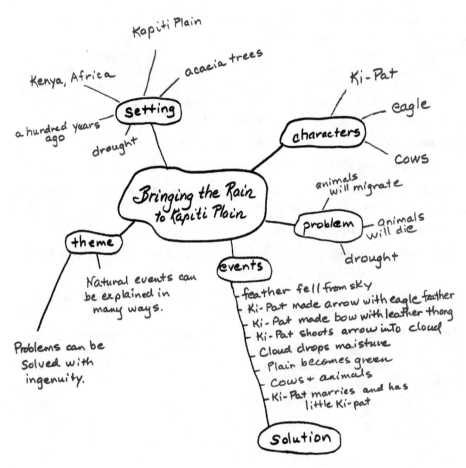

Figure 7.1 Literary elements web for *Bringing the Rain to Kapiti Plain* by Verna Aardema.

*Aruego, José, and Aruego, Ariana. *A Crocodile's Tale: A Philippine Folk Story.* New York: Scribner's, 1972.

Summary: Juan saves an ungrateful crocodile that then tries to eat him. Juan appeals to a basket and a hat to convince the crocodile that he is wrong, but they recount their own experiences with ingratitude and urge the crocodile to eat the boy. Juan appeals to a monkey who tricks the crocodile into freeing Juan. Juan shows his gratitude to the monkey.

Setting: The river near the banana farm of Juan and his father.

Characters: Crocodile, Juan, a basket, a hat, a monkey, and Juan's father.

Themes: Do unto others as you would have them do unto you. Gratitude is not always given when it is deserved.

Vocabulary: Gratitude, grateful, persuade, impatiently.

Illustrations: Simple outline drawings and the jungle colors of green, brown, and orange fit the setting of this humorous, entertaining story.

Grade Level/Content Area: K–6 students enjoy this story that can be used in a study of the Philippine Islands or of folktales.

Literary Elements Web: Give students the web with the literary elements on it and have them fill in supporting information. Students can use the completed web as a model for creating their own webs to guide them in writing their own folktales.

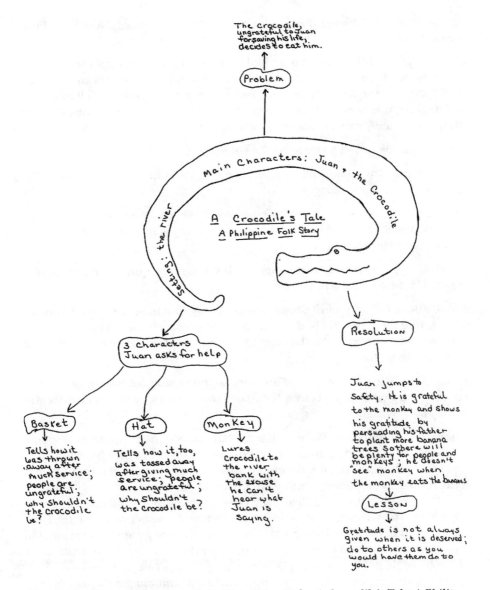

The crocodile,
ungrateful to Juan
for saving his life,
decides to eat him.

Problem

Main Characters: Juan + the Crocodile

Setting: the river

A Crocodile's Tale
A Philippine Folk Story

3 Characters
Juan asks for help

Basket

Tells how it
was thrown
away after
much service;
people are
ungrateful;
why shouldn't
the crocodile
be?

Hat

Tells how it, too,
was tossed away
after giving much
service; people
are ungrateful;
why shouldn't
the crocodile be?

Monkey

Lures
Crocodile to
the river
bank with
the excuse
he can't
hear what
Juan is
saying.

Resolution

Juan jumps to
safety. He is grateful
to the monkey and shows
his gratitude by
persuading his father
to plant more banana
trees so there will
be plenty for people and
monkeys; he doesn't
"see" monkey when
the monkey eats the bananas

Lesson

Gratitude is not always
given when it is deserved;
do to others as you
would have them do to
you.

Figure 7.2 Literary elements web by Diane Mannix for *A Crocodile's Tale: A Philippine Folk Story* by José Aruego.

*Martin, Rafe. **The Rough-Face Girl.** (Illus., David Shannon). New York: Putnam's, 1992.

Summary: This is an Algonquin Indian version of the Cinderella story in which Rough-Face Girl and her two beautiful but heartless sisters must prove they have seen the Invisible Being in order to win his affections. Full of magic and mystery, this powerful tale passes on the reality of the human heart where beauty is an energy that comes from within.

Setting: Long ago in a village by the shores of Lake Ontario.

Characters: Invisible Being, Rough-Face Girl, two older sisters, father, and sister of the Invisible Being.

Themes: Beauty is a matter of perspective. Believe in your own beauty and your spirit will not easily be shaken. Internal beauty is more enduring and life-giving than external beauty.

Vocabulary: Wigwam, scarred, moccasins, haughtily, quiver, runner, invisible, hard-hearted, charred, veil.

Illustrations: Color illustrations depict the Algonquin reverence for nature and capture the faces and body language of all those who scorn Rough-Face Girl, but deny the reader her face until the last page of the story where all disfigurement is transformed.

Grade Level/Content Area: This story supports study of Native American cultures, fairy tales, perspective, New York state history, or self-esteem for students in grades 3–6.

Character Perspective Web: This webbing activity helps students respond personally to the story, actively engage in discussion about the characters' perceptions of Rough-Face Girl, develop vocabulary, and visually represent their ideas related to the theme "Beauty is a matter of perspective."

After reading the story, divide the class into six groups and give each a copy of the story, a dictionary, a thesaurus, and the name of one character. First, ask each group to use or incorporate the shape of the wigwam into a symbol to represent the character they are assigned: father (log)—constant strength, sister of the Invisible Being (cornucopia)—goodness, sisters (megaphone)—needed attention, village people (clown's hat)—laughed at and mocked Rough-Face Girl, Invisible Being (ice cream cone)—desired by all, Rough-Face Girl (eye)— could see the Invisible Being. Then have each group write a description of their assigned character in words, using the story and the reference tools. Next each group can share with the whole class the meaning behind their symbol and the words they chose to describe a character's perspective. After discussing the story, students can create a personal response to the story and perhaps even a symbol and words to represent themselves as well.

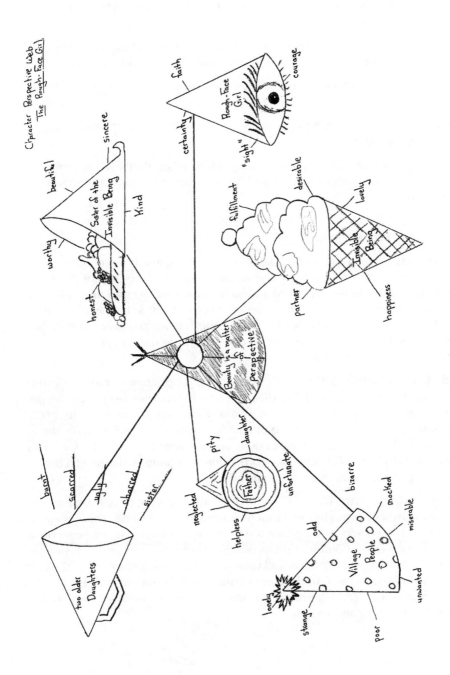

Figure 7.3 Character perspective web by Lisa Rieger for *The Rough-Face Girl* by Rafe Martin.

═══ *McDermott, Gerald. **Arrow to the Sun: A Pueblo Indian Tale.** New York: Puffin Books, 1986.

Summary: In this adaptation of a Pueblo Indian myth, a child searches for his father, and the story is told of how the sun comes to the world of man.

Setting: A Pueblo Indian village in southwestern United States and in the heavens.

Characters: Lord of the Sun, Young Maiden Boy, Pot Maker, Corn Planter, Arrow Maker, and other boys.

Theme: People can accomplish amazing things when they use their inner strength. With love, determination, and bravery, one can conquer the most powerful adversaries.

Vocabulary: Pueblo, ceremony, kiva, endure, transformed, rejoiced, emerged, mocked, serpents.

Illustrations: Earth tones of orange, yellow, brown, and black dominate illustrations of the earth prior to the presence of the spirit of the Lord of the Sun. After the spirit world is introduced, colors become brighter and more vibrant, and Young Maiden Boy brings these rainbow colors back to his people along with the spirit of the Lord of the Sun. Bright, rich colors and geometric shapes extend across full pages with text appearing as a minor part of each page in the open spaces of backgrounds.

Grade Level/Content Area: This folktale is appropriate for grades 1–3 and fits especially well with a social studies unit on communities around the world. Since it is about the Pueblo culture, it would also be appropriate in a study of the history of the Southwest. For upper-grade students, it provides an example of the culturally universal theme of a deity and son sent to earth. The story can be used in a study of folktales, since it contains the common theme of a hero who must prove himself by overcoming adversity.

Sequence Map: Maps like this, constructed after hearing or reading the story, make excellent models for student storytelling or writing. For younger children, a group story can be generated by having each child dictate or write a sentence to describe a different rebus picture. Older students enjoy retelling the story or writing descriptively and creatively about what happens to the boy as he passes through the four different Chambers of Ceremony: the Kivas of Lions, Serpents, Bees, and Lightning. This story can also be used as a springboard for creative thinking and writing.

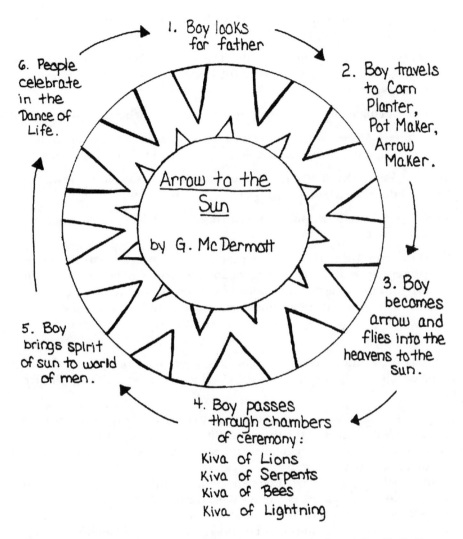

1. Boy looks for father

2. Boy travels to Corn Planter, Pot Maker, Arrow Maker.

3. Boy becomes arrow and flies into the heavens to the Sun.

4. Boy passes through chambers of ceremony:
   Kiva of Lions
   Kiva of Serpents
   Kiva of Bees
   Kiva of Lightning

5. Boy brings spirit of sun to world of men.

6. People celebrate in the Dance of Life.

Arrow to the Sun
by G. McDermott

Figure 7.4 Sequence map by Terri Judge for *Arrow to the Sun: A Pueblo Indian Tale* by Gerald McDermott.

*Steptoe, John. ***Mufaro's Beautiful Daughters: An African Tale.*** New York: Lothrop, Lee & Shepard, 1987.

Summary: This is an African tale about two beautiful girls who are called before the king, who is choosing a wife. The kindness of one of the girls results in her being chosen queen.

Setting: A long time ago in a small village and city in what is now Zimbabwe.

Characters: Mufaro, Manyara, Nyasha, Nyoka (character names are from the Shono language and reflect personality), small boy, old woman, and King.

Theme: Vanity, deceit, and greed lead to a downfall. Goodness is rewarded. "Pride goeth before a fall."

Vocabulary: Bountiful, stole, silhouetted, acknowledges, commotion, destination, transfixed, chamber.

Illustrations: The illustrations are paintings done in rich colors that reflect the lush vegetation of the African jungle and the beauty of the people. Pictures generally cover two pages, with dialogue and actions used to communicate character traits. Illustrations are authentic (Steptoe studied actual ruins located near the setting of the story) and reflect respect and love for the people of southern Africa.

Grade Level/Content Area: This book is appropriate for grades K–3 and would enrich a study of folktales or a social studies unit on Africa or foreign cultures.

Character Web: Before reading this story to children, show them the character web with the names of the daughters but with no descriptive words. Tell the children that the two daughters in this story are the same in some ways and very different in other ways.

After reading, talk with children to help them explore their responses to the story, and ask them to share what they think the moral or theme of the story is. Accepting all versions of theme that they come up with, as long as they can support their idea, helps the children understand that we all interpret things somewhat differently and that this diversity in ideas is good. Have children generate a list of words from the story that describes each daughter, adding their own descriptive adjectives. Discuss the ways that Steptoe develops his characters through action and dialogue.

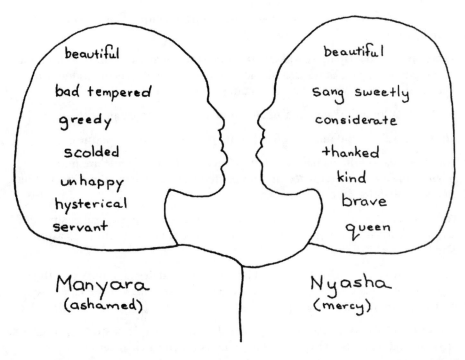

Figure 7.5 Character web by Regina Mardex for *Mufaro's Beautiful Daughters: An African Tale* by John Steptoe.

*Tompert, Ann. ***Bamboo Hats and a Rice Cake.*** (Illus., Demi). New York: Crown, 1993.

Summary: This Japanese folktale tells the story of an old man who trades a prized possession for other less precious items. His small acts of kindness are rewarded in the end when he receives unexpected good fortune.

Setting: A long time ago in a small mountain village in Japan.

Characters: An old man, his wife, some peddlers, and Jizo statues.

Themes: Good things happen to good people. Other people are important. Small favors are often returned in unexpected ways and many times over. What goes around comes around.

Vocabulary: Reluctantly, discouraged, offering, kimono, rice cake, shrine, sagging, scurrying, roly poly, trudged, enormous, flustered, tottering, astonished.

Illustrations: Colorful, traditional Japanese art and design coupled with Japanese characters accompany the text. The English meanings of the Japanese characters are found on each page.

Grade Level/Content Area: In grades 2–5, this story fits a study of folktales or Japan and could be used to introduce units on cultures, celebrations, or values.

Literary Elements Web: This web could be completed to introduce or reinforce story structure after reading the story and talking about its meaning. First define and discuss the elements of story, and then have a different group of students supply each element and the specific information about it to complete the web. This type of web is especially useful when comparing several folktales for similarities of theme and conflict.

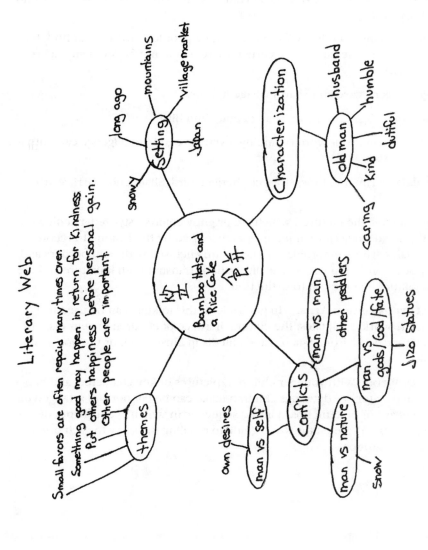

Figure 7.6 Literary elements web by Barbara Patten-Skellett for *Bamboo Hats and a Rice Cake* by Ann Tompert.

*Xiong, Blia. ***Nine-in-One, Grr! Grr!*** (Illus., Nancy Hom). San Francisco: Children's Press, 1989.

Summary: This is a folktale from the Hmong people of Laos about how Bird played a trick on Tiger and made certain there would not be too many tigers on the earth.

Setting: Tiger's cave and Shao's village in Laos.

Characters: Tiger, her mate, Shao (a god), and Bird.

Themes: Giving your word is binding, even for a god. Intelligence can outwit strength and size.

Vocabulary: Hmong, Laos, story cloth, tiger, bird, Shao, cubs, Grr!, 9 in 1, 1 in 9.

Illustrations: The pictures, which are brightly colored, stylized, needlework on cloth, called *story cloth,* imitate a practice used by the Hmong to record their folktales. These embroidered images are enclosed with bold borders and print appears on facing pages. The illustrations transmit both literature and the art of a culture that is close to extinction.

Grade Level/Content Area: In grades K–4, this folktale can be used in a study of the world's folktales, the cultural heritage of children in your class (if they have ancestors from Asia or Laos), media in illustration, or the *how and why* tale.

Sequence Web: With younger children, pictures of key characters and happenings in the story or drawings children make can be cut out and arranged on a flannel board or bulletin board in the sequence in which events happened. Children can use these pictures as a guide to retelling the story to each other in pairs or small groups.

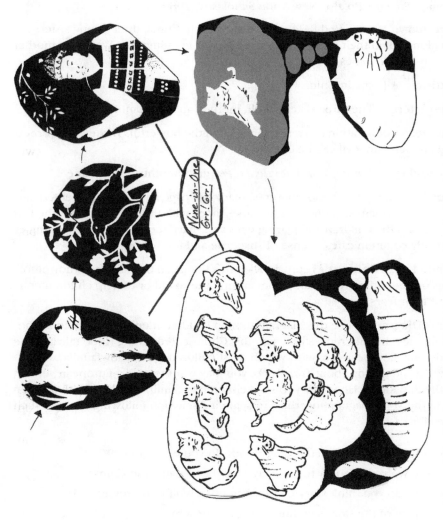

Figure 7.7 Sequence web by David K. Hall for *Nine-in-One, Grr! Grr!* by Blia Xiong.

*Young, Ed. **Lon Po Po.** New York: Scholastic, 1989.

Summary: In this Red Riding Hood story from China, three young sisters are left alone when their mother goes to visit their grandmother. While the mother is away a wolf comes to call.

Setting: A home in China.

Characters: The three sisters, wolf, mother, and grandmother.

Theme: Cooperation can result in defeat of the powerful. Through cleverness and cooperation, evil can be overcome.

Vocabulary: *Shang, Tau, Paotzie, Po Po* (grandmother), ginko tree.

Illustrations: Watercolor pictures, many full page and some segmented like flashes in a dream sequence, show dark shapes with little detail except the fearful faces of the children and glaring eyes and sharp teeth of the wolf. Young effectively communicates a sense of suspense and foreboding.

Grade Level/Content Area: In K–3, this book can be used in a study of folktales or Red Riding Hood tales from around the world or to help children confront their fears.

Venn Diagram: Use this diagram to help children identify and organize the similarities and differences between this Chinese Red Riding Hood tale and the traditional European tale with which most children are already familiar. After reading and talking about *Lon Po Po,* you may want to read a European version of the Red Riding Hood story to your children to familiarize them with it. Then fill in the Venn diagram together. To spark a discussion following this, ask such questions as:

- Which of the two Red Riding Hoods do you like better? Why?
- Are wolves a danger to us today? Are they a danger in China?
- Why do you think storytellers often use a wolf to represent evil?
- Which of the story's endings do you like? Why?

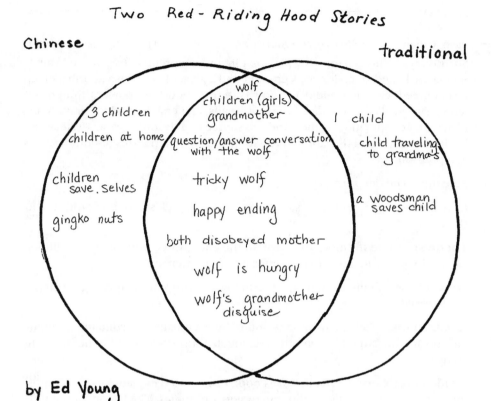

Two Red-Riding Hood Stories

Chinese

traditional

3 children

children at home

children save. selves

gingko nuts

wolf
children (girls)
grandmother

question/answer conversation
with the wolf

tricky wolf

happy ending

both disobeyed mother

wolf is hungry

wolf's grandmother
disguise

1 child

child traveling
to grandma's

a woodsman
saves child

by Ed Young

Figure 7.8   Venn diagram by Deb Pease for *Lon Po Po* by Ed Young.

Fantasy ═══

Base, Graeme. ***The Sign of the Seahorse.*** New York: Harry N. Abrams, 1992.

Summary: This is a morality play that includes a prelude, two acts of four scenes each, and an epilogue. A grouper and a gang of swordfish and sharks represent greed, violence, and deception as they demonstrate power through force. The smaller characters, the trout, snails, and crabs, stand for bravery, decency, and cooperation as they find the source of a deadly poison. Mystery and intrigue abound and the story ends with justice for all in terms of both rewards and punishments.

Setting: The deep sea.

Characters: Trout, groupers, crabs, a lobster, an eel, snails, a swordfish, and sharks.

Themes: Good triumphs over evil. In the end, justice prevails. The pollution caused by man can result in the suffering of other creatures.

Vocabulary: Finneus, soldier crab, moray eel, Gropmund, bootleg caviar, Molluc Mild.

Illustrations: Color illustrations, found on each page and containing rich detail and action, extend beyond the rectangular borders and invite the reader to study them.

Grade Level/Content Area: This book can be used in grades 4–8 to complement units on marine life, pollution, or aquatic studies. The beauty of the undersea world is depicted with realism as Base includes the names of many marine plants and fish.

Character Web: This web can be created to identify the cast of characters and to help students distinguish between protagonists and antagonists. After reading the story, solicit responses about which characters are on which side of the conflict. Then connect the characters to their group by bubbles. Another round of discussion can include identifying and listing the personality traits of each of the characters.

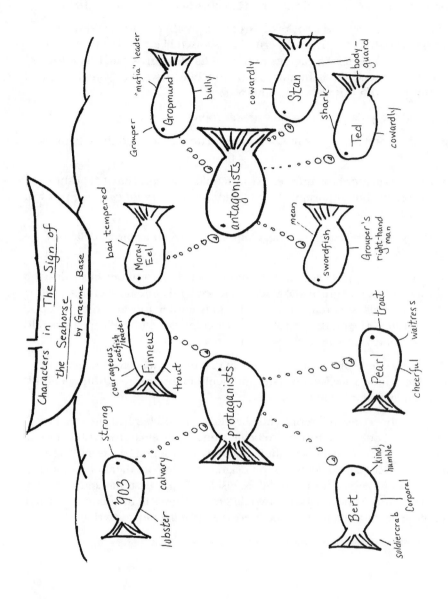

Figure 7.9 Character web by Deb Pease for *The Sign of the Seahorse* by Graeme Base.

Cannon, Janell. *Stellaluna.* New York: Harcourt Brace Jovanovich, 1993.

Summary: After an owl knocks her from her mother's clutch and she falls head first into a bird's nest, a baby fruit bat is raised like a bird until she is reunited with her mother. She adapts to the habits of her new family and learns the essence of friendship in humorous and touching ways. *Bat Notes* at the end of the story contain further facts about bats.

Setting: Present day in the tropics or subtropics.

Characters: Stellaluna, her mother, a surrogate mother, and three baby birds—Pip, Flitter, and Flap.

Themes: No matter how different two people or animals are, friendship is not only possible but important. Adaptability is necessary for survival. You will be accepted for who you are.

Vocabulary: Sultry, embarrassing, clumsy, anxious, murmured, delicious, mango, mystery.

Illustrations: Full-page acrylic and colored-pencil illustrations in shades of gray, brown, blue, and green show soft, detailed, and close-up pictures of adorable bats and birds. Text framed with a fine gray border appears on pages opposite the pictures. The mother bat's story, as it coincides with Stellaluna's, is told in tiny black and white drawings above the text.

Grade Level/Content Area: Students in grades 1–6 who are studying the tropics, bats, birds, survival, diversity, multiculturalism, or friendship will find much to enjoy and learn in this story.

Concept Web: This web represents the ideas one teacher had after reading this story. The book could be used to begin a unit on diversity, friendship, or multiculturalism. Pairs of students might first compare birds and bats using a Venn diagram. Then each pair could do a Venn diagram to compare themselves using such topics as physical appearance, likes, dislikes, family customs, and so on. Students could proceed to comparing two different cultures in the same way. Then any of these Venn diagrams could be used as a planning tool for writing.

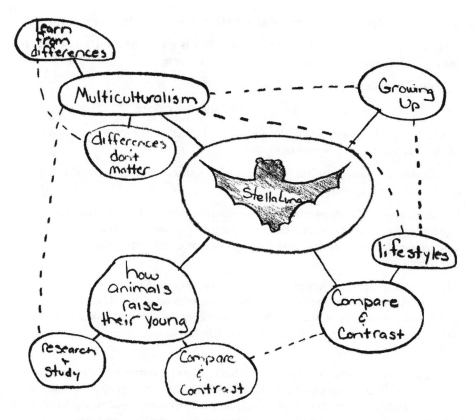

Figure 7.10 Concept web by Jennifer McManus for *Stellaluna* by Janell Cannon.

Gerstein, Mordecai. *The Mountains of Tibet.* New York: Harper & Row, 1987.

Summary: After dying, a Tibetan woodcutter is given the choice of going to heaven or living another life anywhere in the universe.

Setting: A valley high in the mountains of Tibet.

Characters: The woodcutter, his family, and the voice.

Theme: Most of us would make the same choices in our lives if we had them to make again. Life is a series of choices.

Vocabulary: Village, bright, universe, woodcutter, blazed, fireworks, frightened, pinwheel, sparkling.

Illustrations: The illustrations are of varied colors and intensities with a slightly stylized quality, suggestive of miniature paintings from the East. Shape and arrangement of pictures and location of text change in relation to choices the woodcutter has.

Grade Level/Content Area: This book is useful in grades 3–6 social studies units on communities around the world or on various cultural beliefs about death and dying since it deals with a mountain community in Asia and reincarnation of the soul. It also is useful as a vehicle for strengthening prediction skills.

Sequence Web: Students need some background information on this story to best ensure their comprehension. Begin by looking at a map of Asia, finding Tibet, and discussing the geography and life there. Children will profit from hearing about what *reincarnation* is and its importance to Eastern culture.

After hearing the story or reading it themselves, children can construct the story web shown, or one like it, that includes the important events and choices the woodcutter had. From this web, lead a discussion of theme, being sure to accept any theme a child can support reasonably well from the story. If the idea of reincarnation is new to your children, encourage them to do further reading in the library to find out more about Eastern culture.

This story lends itself well to creative writing. Ask the children to think about and write accounts of what they think will happen when they die or what their choices might be if they were given the option of reincarnation.

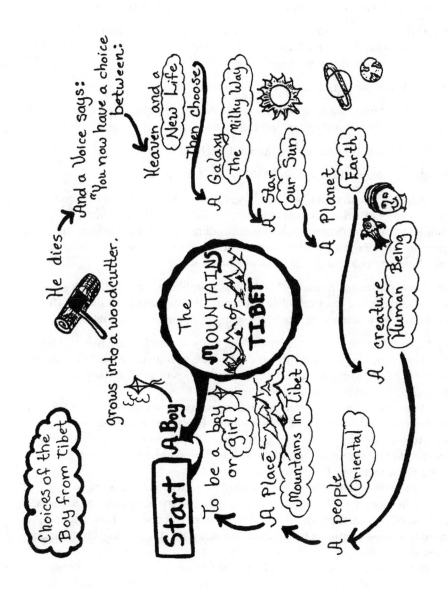

Figure 7.11 Sequence web by Charlotte De Almeida for *The Mountains of Tibet* by Mordecai Gerstein.

151

Shulevitz, Uri. ***One Monday Morning.*** New York: Macmillan, 1967.

Summary: This is a cumulative tale in which a king and queen and their growing entourage return each morning to a tenement house until the boy they have come to visit is at home to greet them.

Setting: A tenement apartment in a large city.

Characters: Little Boy, King, Queen, Little Prince, Knight, Royal Guard, Royal Cook, Royal Barber, Royal Jester, and Little Dog.

Theme: There is no limit to the human imagination.

Vocabulary: Names of the days of the week and characters.

Illustrations: Illustrations become larger and more colorful as the story progresses and Little Boy uses his imagination. Colors of the tenement buildings are dull and drab; in contrast, colors used to depict royalty are bright. Text and pictures are interwoven carefully so that the harder the Little Boy's imagination works, the more colorful the illustrations become.

Grade Level/Content Area: This book is suitable for grades K–2 as a purely enjoyable experience, as a vehicle for learning the names of the days of the week, or as a way of learning about the pattern of a cumulative tale.

Story Map: The cumulative nature of the story makes it good material for a directed listening-thinking activity since students can make predictions about who they think will visit next and which day comes next. The story also lends itself to choral reading or individual retellings.

As a way of helping children recall events, construct the story map shown here after reading the story. For young children who are nonreaders, it may be enough to include only the names of the days of the week. For children who can read, add the names of the characters as they appear in the story and have children retell the story from the map.

The illustrations in this book are excellent to use in developing young children's visual literacy skills. While children examine the shapes, colors, and arrangement of the illustrations, you can help them learn about how Shulevitz manipulates these elements to enhance the story. Be sure to have children compare the first picture, in which the Little Boy sits at a window on a dreary, rainy day, with the last picture, in which he sits at the same window and the sun is shining. Have children note the objects in both pictures that are clues about the origin of the boy's imaginary royal friends.

Weekly Appointment Book						
Monday	Tuesday	Wednesday	Thursday	Friday	Saturday	Sunday
King, Queen and Little Prince	King, Queen, Little Prince and Knight	King, Queen, Little Prince, Knight and Royal Guard	King, Queen, Little Prince, Knight, Royal Guard and Royal Cook	King, Queen, Little Prince, Knight, Royal Guard Royal Cook, and Royal Barber	King, Queen, Little Prince, Knight, Royal Guard, Royal Cook, Royal Barber and Royal Jester	King, Queen, Little Prince, Knight, Royal Guard, Royal Cook, Royal Barber, Royal Jester and a little dog

Figure 7.12   Story map by Lisa Milano for *One Monday Morning* by Uri Shulevitz.

153

*Sis, Peter. ***Komodo!*** New York: Greenwillow, 1993.

Summary: A young boy who loves dragons is taken to Komodo Island by his parents where he visits a Dragon Show and meets a Komodo dragon. Contains much factual information about Komodo Island and the dragons that live there.

Setting: Present day apartment in a metropolitan area, a plane, a boat, and Komodo Island.

Characters: Boy, mother, father, and a Komodo dragon.

Theme: To truly encounter nature, you must look for it in remote, private places. Sometimes things happen just as we imagine they will.

Vocabulary: Dragon, Komodo, carnivore, reptile.

Illustrations: Pen-and-ink drawings in green, brown, and gold watercolors are framed in black and cover both pages. Text appears at left of each fully detailed picture. Illustrations include lots of *hidden* dragons. End pages include superimposed images of a world map, a star chart, and a giant dragon.

Grade Level/Content Area: Students in grades K–9 can enjoy this story filled with facts about a little-known reptile. The book can be used in studies of animals, reptiles, geography, endangered species, and the environment. Counting and graphing the hidden dragons make this book appropriate for developing math skills.

Concept Web: To reinforce the factual information contained in this story and encourage further research, you and your students can create a web like this one after the story has been read, reread, and enjoyed. It might be interesting to provide categories, such as *physical characteristics,* and have students in pairs or groups supply supporting information or allow students to create their own representation of the information the book conveys. The *reproduction* spoke is blank since Sis did not include this aspect of his subject, and it is one area your students can explore on their own.

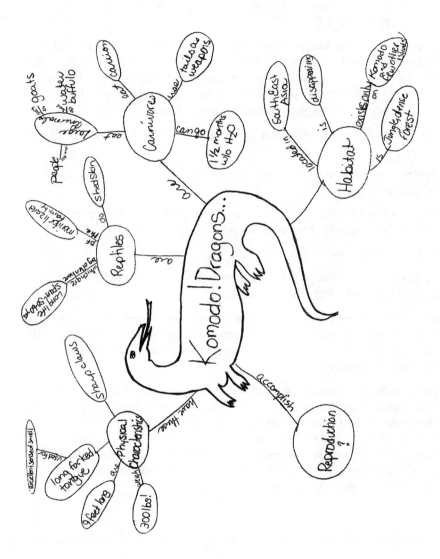

Figure 7.13 Concept web by Lisa Shrot for *Komodo!* by Peter Sis.

Swope, Sam. *The Araboolies of Liberty Street.* (Illus., Barry Root). New York: Charles N. Potter, 1989.

Summary: When the Araboolies moved to Liberty Street, everyone but the General and Mrs. Pinch were happy. The Araboolies are a family with many pets and children who come in many colors. Because of their strange looks and ways, General Pinch decided to get rid of them. But the children of Liberty Street banded together in a plan to save their new friends.

Setting: Liberty Street in any town where the houses and the people all look alike.

Characters: General and Mrs. Pinch, the children of Liberty Street, the Araboolies, and the army.

Themes: Being different depends on one's perspective. A good plan, hard work, and people working together can achieve a goal.

Vocabulary: Bullhorn, walkie-talkie, rumble.

Illustrations: These full-page illustrations in bold tempera enhance the descriptions of the fun-loving Araboolies.

Grade Level/Content Area: This book appeals to children in all primary grades and can be read just for fun or to teach the lesson of acceptance. With older students, it can be used to teach acceptance, cooperation, problem solving, and comparison/contrast.

Comparison Web: Another story about acceptance and tolerance is Joan Blos' *Old Henry,* which can also be read to children and discussed, comparing it to *The Araboolies of Liberty Street.* Both of these stories represent intolerance in both a fantasy and realistic setting with Swope's solution being very different from Blos' ending, which implies a compromise. After reading and discussing, students can complete the blank Venn diagram either individually or in groups and then share their work.

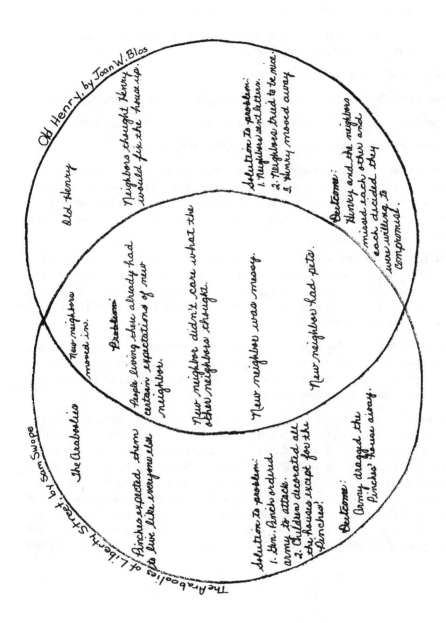

Figure 7.14 Comparison web by Jill H. Baker for *The Araboolies of Liberty Street* by Sam Swope.

157

Van Allsburg, Chris. ***The Polar Express.*** Boston: Houghton Mifflin, 1985.

Summary: A magical train ride on Christmas eve takes a boy to the North Pole to receive a special gift from Santa Claus.

Setting: The North Pole and a family's home.

Characters: Young boy, Santa Claus, Sarah, Mother, Father, and Conductor.

Theme: The magic of Christmas is real for those who believe in it.

Vocabulary: Christmas, Santa, nougat, North Pole, harness.

Illustrations: Full-color pastel drawings create a sense of mystery, wonder, and magic throughout this book. Subdued colors and shapes give the pictures a softness of texture that is enhanced by snow and the semidarkness of evening. Each picture covers both facing pages with text printed in a column on one side of a page.

Grade Level/Content Area: Use this story with K-6 children, who will enjoy it during the Christmas season. For children in grades 1 or 2, it enriches a study of the seasons; for students in grades 3-6, it is appropriate for the study of Christmas holiday celebrations around the world, variety in cultural beliefs, or fantasy as a literary genre.

Concept Web: Use the word *Christmas* as the organizing concept for a map of words to describe the concept. Using a concept map before reading the story helps assess and organize students' existing background knowledge and gives them a frame of reference for this story.

Sequence Web: Read the story to children and discuss the main actions of the plot. As children retell the story, transcribe what they dictate in the bubbles around the title, having them indicate where each action they relate fits in the sequence of events. To help children who might have trouble, write the first three or four words in each bubble and let the children supply the rest. Focus discussion on which actions in the story are based in fantasy and which in reality so that children learn to understand which elements of story are manipulated in this fantasy. You need to be sensitive both to children who hold beliefs in *the spirit* of Christmas and those who do not.

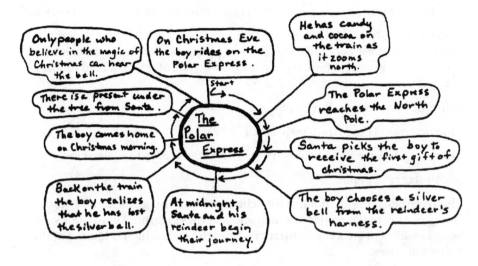

Figure 7.15 Sequence web by Lisa Milano for *The Polar Express* by Chris Van Allsburg.

Walsh, Ellen Stoll. ***Mouse Paint.*** San Diego: Harcourt Brace Jovanovich, 1989.

Summary: Three white mice who are safe from the cat as long as they stay on a piece of white paper find three jars of paint (the three primary colors) and in their ensuing antics show the reader how these colors are mixed to form new colors.

Setting: A piece of white paper.

Characters: Three white mice and a cat.

Themes: Learning can be fun. The color wheel is easy to understand.

Vocabulary: Simple.

Illustrations: Bright, bold, eye-catching collages using fabric and construction paper invite the reader to touch and feel these textured illustrations. A black border separates the illustrations from the text, which is located at the bottom of pages.

Grade Level/Content Area: Young children in grades PreK–2 enjoy this lighthearted story and as it is read to them easily learn the primary colors and how to mix them to form other colors. This book would be a good one to read as a stage-setter for painting or to keep close to an art center. The story also has the potential for developing mathematical concepts with older children. For example, three mice painted in three colors and then danced in each other's colors and produced three new colors. Are there other combinations they could have made? Why or why not? Can this story be represented with numbers?

Cyclical Organizer: After reading this story, children can participate in the construction of this organizer that centers on the actions of the mice. Picture clues and minimal words make it appropriate for fostering emergent reading behaviors. Colored markers could be used to reinforce colors and color words might also be added. Children can look on the labels of their crayons to find the proper spellings of color words and add them to the organizer or make their own picture version of how colors come to be.

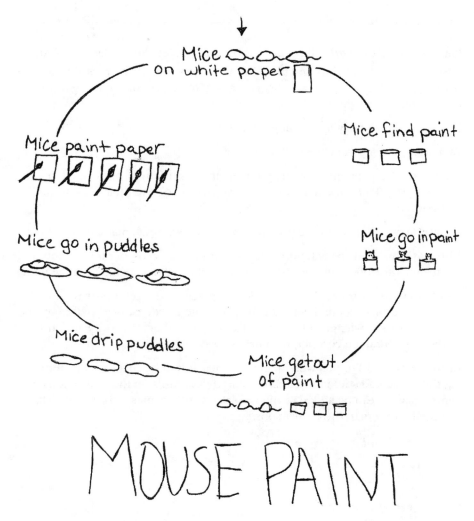

Figure 7.16 Cyclical organizer by Lisa Shrot for *Mouse Paint* by Ellen Stoll Walsh.

Realistic Fiction ═══════════════════════════════════

Bunting, Eve. ***The Wall.*** (Illus., Ronald Himmler). New York: Clarion, 1990.

Summary: A young boy and his father visit the Vietnam Veterans Memorial in Washington, D.C. They have come a long way to search for the name of the boy's grandfather who was killed in the conflict.

Setting: Present day in Washington, D.C.

Characters: A young boy and his father.

Themes: Many people still feel the pain and loss of loved ones killed in Vietnam. *The Wall* honors the men and women who gave their lives during that conflict.

Vocabulary: Vietnam, veteran, droopy, blurs, memorial, missing in action.

Illustrations: Full-page colored illustrations done in somber tones capture the feelings surrounding *The Wall* and support the detail included in the text.

Grade Level/Content Area: Students in grades 1–12, with proper support and explanations, can understand and appreciate the quest of a young boy and his father for knowledge of their grandfather and father. This story supports study of the Vietnam conflict, memorials, or death and loss.

Concept Web: Put this web on chart paper or butcher paper, and after reading the story, lead students in a discussion that focuses on these questions. Students' answers can be added to the web as can other questions they may have and their answers to these questions.

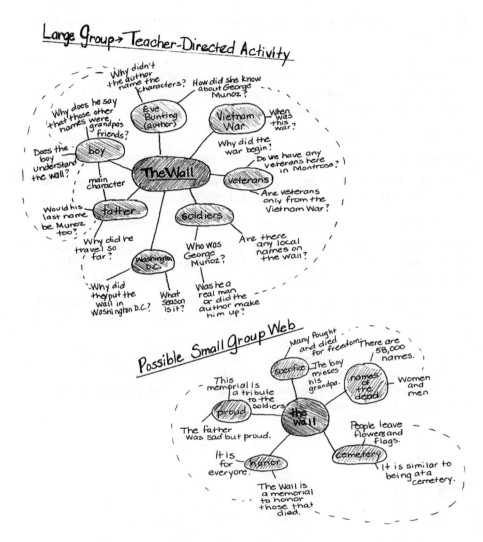

Figure 7.17   Concept web by Pam Pignatelli for *The Wall* by Eve Bunting.

Bunting, Eve. ***The Wednesday Surprise.*** (Illus., Donald Carrick) New York: Clarion, 1989.

Summary: Anna and her Grandma read together on Wednesday nights when Anna's mother and father are at work. Everyone thinks Grandma is teaching Anna to read. But it is the other way around, and Grandma reads to her son for the first time as his birthday gift.

Setting: Present day in Anna's home.

Characters: Anna, Grandma, Sam (Anna's brother), mother, and father.

Themes: It is never too late to learn something new. In close, caring families, family members give gifts of help, support, and love to each other.

Vocabulary: Business, surprise, astonished, imagining, wilting, speckled.

Illustrations: Realistic drawings in muted watercolors depict the people, furniture, and decorations in the softly lit rooms of Anna's cozy, comfortable home. Most pictures fill a page and a half with print to the left or right.

Grade Level/Content Area: In grades 1–4, this story can be used in a unit on the family or in a study of literacy. You might read it orally and then, in discussion, talk about illiteracy and its ramifications.

Character Web: A character web such as the one suggested here can be created following rereading and discussion to help students examine those attributes of each character that lead to the ability of family members to be helpful, caring, and loving.

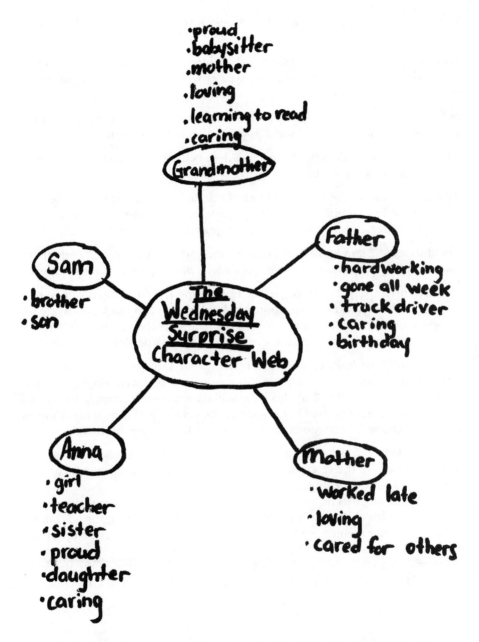

Figure 7.18 Character web by Kelly Hawley for *The Wednesday Surprise* by Eve Bunting.

George, Jean Craighead. *Julie.* (Illus., Wendell Minor). New York: Harper Collins, 1994.

Summary: In this sequel to *Julie of the Wolves,* Julie returns to her father's Eskimo village, where she struggles to save her wolves and her way of life in a changing Arctic world.

Setting: The Eskimo village of Kangik on the bank of the Avalik River in Alaska and the wilderness of the Alaskan tundra in the present.

Characters: Julie (Miyax), Kapugen, Ellen, Peter Sugluk, and four wolves (Kapu, Zing, Aaka, and Amy).

Themes: The actions of one individual can save an entire species. The value of education in a community can be progressive or regressive. Act on your beliefs. The struggle for survival can lead to growth as an individual.

Vocabulary: Bunting, cascade, tundra, and various Yupik words including *gussak, iglek, paipiuraq, qimmiq, qanitchaq, ptarmigan,* and *uminmaks.*

Illustrations: One full-color picture of Julie and her wolf pup covers the front of the book jacket. Throughout the book are several black and white sketches, usually occupying one to two full pages depicting Julie and Peter, Kapugen, the Alaskan tundra, a walrus, the wolves, a dog sled and so on.

Grade Level/Content Area: Students in grades 4–6 who are studying ecosystems, conservation, endangered species, wolves, or Alaskan geography are interested in and enriched by this poignant account of the struggle to save not only a population of wolves but also an entire culture and way of life. Units on conflict, survival, or Eskimo cultures are also enhanced by this novel.

Concept Web: This webbing activity allows for student exploration of personal responses to the story, develops the ability to analyze characters or themes, and builds vocabulary.

After reading this novel, groups of students might choose one concept or character for which they would like to create a web. Choosing various character traits or main themes, each group then cooperatively constructs a web to share with the class. As other books are read, add to the collection of webs. These webs can hang in the classroom throughout the period of the thematic unit and might be used for future comparisons of characters or concepts.

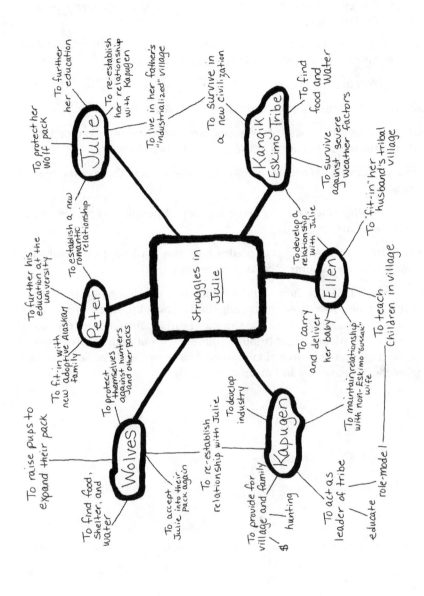

Figure 7.19 Concept web by Karen Wandell for *Julie* by Jean Craighead George.

MacLachlan, Patricia. ***All the Places to Love.*** (Illus., Mike Wimmer). New York: Harper Collins, 1994.

Summary: A young boy's recollection of the favorite places he shares with his family on his grandparents' farm in the country.

Setting: A farm in the country.

Characters: Eli, Grandmother, Grandfather, Mama, and Papa.

Themes: The simplicity and pleasures of farm life are many. Connections to the land are important. Beauty is in the eye of the beholder.

Vocabulary: Cattails, killdeers, marsh, meadow, barren, filed, rafter, bunchberry, trillium.

Illustrations: Realistic full-color paintings depict people and places on the farm and the surrounding land.

Grade Level/Content Area: For grades K–6, this book supports study of farms, family heritage, country life, or nature appreciation.

Concept Web: This web helps students examine the different aspects of the country that are best loved and the feelings and associations these places engender. It also presents a summary of the story and can be created after the story is read and reread. Students might bring in photographs of their favorite special places, glue them in the center of large pieces of paper, and create their own personal webs of memories and meaning for a place.

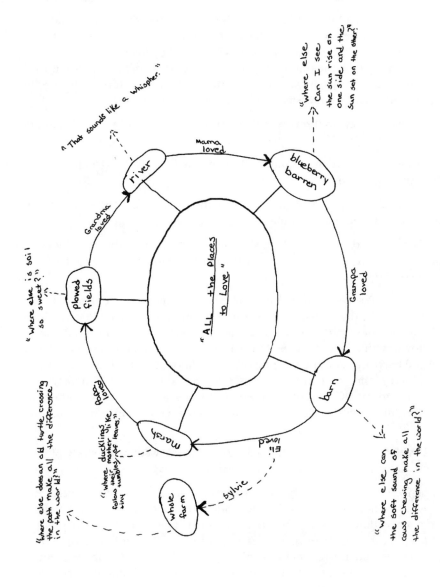

Figure 7.20 Concept web by Charlene Kempa for *All the Places to Love* by Patricia MacLachlan.

═══ *Martel, Cruz. ***Yagua Days.*** (Illus., Jerry Pinkney). New York: Penguin, 1976.

Summary: A young Puerto Rican boy is bored as he watches from his father's *bodega* (grocery store) as the rain falls on the streets of New York City. On a visit to his cousin in Puerto Rico, he discovers that they love rainy or *yagua* days because they take the outer part of a palm frond, a *yagua,* and use it to slide down a wet hill into the water. He comes back to New York with a brighter outlook and a better understanding of his culture and family.

Setting: Present day on the Lower East Side of New York City and also in Puerto Rico.

Characters: Adan, his father and mother, mailman Jorge, *Tio* (Uncle) Ulise, and *Tia* (Aunt) Carmen.

Themes: Our heritage is part of our family and of our lives. There are special things that tie us together as families and people.

Vocabulary: There are many Spanish words that can either be introduced first or explained in context. The Spanish-English dictionary in the back of the book is a good reference.

Illustrations: Black and white pencil sketches using crosshatching and shading bring to life the dreary day in New York City and the fun-filled Puerto Rican days. Drawings show in detail the blades of grass left standing tall and those slicked down with rain and crushed under the weight of children sliding down the hill and barreling into the river below. In addition, the illustrations reflect Adan's relatives who come in "all shapes, sizes, and colors" and demonstrate that there are many different types of Puerto Ricans, just as there are other citizens of the United States, whose skin tones and hair colors range from light to dark.

Grade Level/Content Area: In grades 2–4, this story supports study of immigration, diversity, Puerto Rico, or the Spanish language.

Concept Web: Show students the glossary of Spanish words at the end of the book and introduce these words before reading the story. This web might be created after reading the story, or it could be made as you read the story as a way of keeping track of information learned. After reading and discussing the story, help your students reflect on the themes they find in it. List these themes, and then help students look at each one to see if and how it might be relevant in their own lives, thus underscoring the similarities between Puerto Ricans and other citizens of the United States.

You can read this story on a rainy day and have students brainstorm and then write about what they each do that makes a rainy day a fun day. Then compile a book of fun things to do on a rainy day.

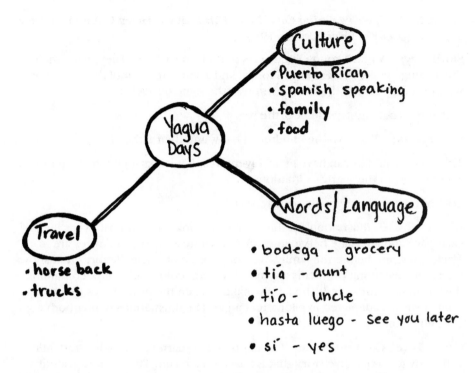

Figure 7.21 Concept web by Kelly Hawley for *Yagua Days* by Cruz Martel.

Rosen, Michael. ***We're Going On a Bear Hunt.*** (Illus., Helen Oxenbury). New York: Margaret K. Elderry Books, 1989.

Summary: A brave young family sets out on a bear hunt. They make their way through grass, a river, mud, a forest, and a snowstorm until they find a bear who promptly chases them back through the same obstacles.

Setting: The countryside near the sea.

Characters: Three young children, a baby, and their father.

Themes: Families can have great adventures. If it sticks together, a family can get out of even the scariest situations.

Vocabulary: Oozy, goggly, swishy, swashy.

Illustrations: Illustrations in this oversized book cover almost every inch of each page and alternate between black and white and color. Pictures are in black and white before the family overcomes each obstacle. Pictures that show the family mastering problems are in full, vibrant color with a box containing the vocabulary for sounds the family makes. When the bear chases the family, each obstacle is depicted in a long rectangle. The illustrations depict both comedy and drama.

Grade Level/Content Area: Preschool, kindergarten, and older students will enjoy this repetitive story that is based on a chant. The book repeatedly uses the directional words *under, over,* and *through.* The book could be used to introduce a study of bears or to motivate the writing of a story. Since there is no dialogue included in the story, older students might write it and then dramatize the story for younger children.

Concept Web: Together you and your students can list the obstacles the family encountered, which will help them review the plot of the story. Then students can refer to the text to find the descriptive words Rosen uses to tell about each obstacle, and these can be added to the web. Students can then add other adjectives to describe each obstacle. The web could be used as a prereading prediction activity in which the teacher lists the obstacles and students predict adjectives that might be used; list them on the web; then read to confirm predictions.

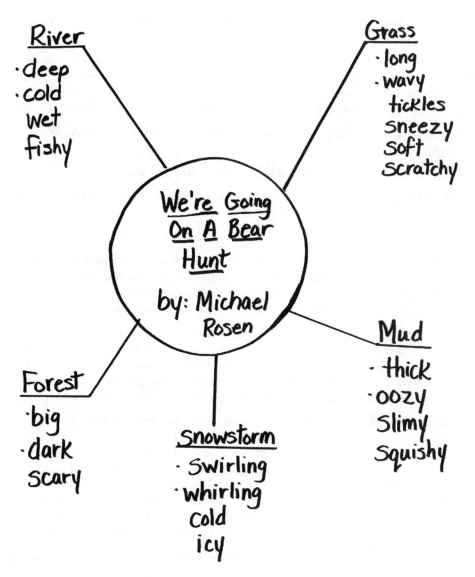

Figure 7.22 Concept web by Meredith Jewett for *We're Going on a Bear Hunt* by Michael Rosen.

Rylant, Cynthia. ***The Relatives Came.*** (Illus., Stephen Gammell). New York: Bradbury, 1985.

Summary: A big crowd of relatives arrive from Virginia to spend the summer. They travel a long distance in a little car to meet their smiling family. They hug, laugh, eat, sleep, tend the garden, and fix broken things together. Finally the relatives pack their ice chest and head back home, and the family misses them.

Setting: A small family farmhouse one and one-half day's drive north of Virginia.

Characters: Two families of relatives—both children and adults.

Themes: A family gathering is a happy time. Close-knit families enjoy visiting even when living conditions are not ideal.

Vocabulary: Relatives, Virginia, station wagon, bologna, particular.

Illustrations: Full-page, softly colored-pencil drawings in shades of primary colors show round friendly people doing all the things that usually happen when families get together to visit. Pages are filled with people or show the winding road on which the journeys north and back home occur.

Grade Level/Content Area: This book can be used in grades K–6 to support a unit on the family or to inspire writing. For students who feel they have nothing to write about because nothing extraordinary has ever happened to them, this simple, vivid, and touching story can motivate a similar type of tale about their experience visiting relatives or when someone came to visit them.

Time Line: This time line can be constructed after students have heard the story, reread it, and talked about it and the feelings it elicited. Record factual events along the top of the line in the order in which they occur, and record emotions or feelings the relatives might experience as a result of each activity along the bottom of the line. Then each student can create a similar time line about a visit of their own, which they remember. Students can use this time line as a planning tool for writing their own reflections on a visit. Volunteers can share these with the class, and/or drafts can be revised and published as gifts for family members.

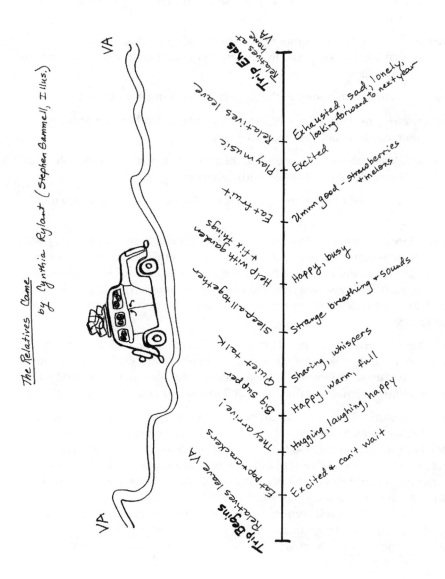

Figure 7.23 Time line for *The Relatives Came* by Cynthia Rylant.

Rylant, Cynthia. ***When I Was Young in the Mountains.*** (Illus., Diane Goode). New York: Dutton, 1982.

Summary: A woman remembers her childhood, reflecting on foods eaten, shopping, playing, working, and living with her grandparents in the mountains of rural Appalachia.

Setting: A rural community in the Appalachian mountains in the 1950s.

Characters: The author (as a young girl), her little brother, Grandmother, Grandfather, cousins, and various townspeople.

Themes: No matter where one lives, the place is special to the people who live there. Every childhood is filled with memories.

Vocabulary: Fried okra, pinto beans, johnny-house, pasture, congregation, baptisms.

Illustrations: Drawings done in soft earth tones and pastel watercolors with colored pencils match the warm and homey tone of this book. Print is separate from the drawings and is set in white space with an occasional small illustration appearing nearby almost as a remnant from the accompanying larger drawing. Both drawings and text are gentle and nostalgic and encourage reminiscences of times past.

Grade Level/Content Area: This book is suitable for grades 1–8 and for adults also. It can be used in a study of a rural culture in a coal-mining community or of the family. The prose is an excellent model and can inspire students to write in a similar vein about their own childhood and memories they hold dear.

Venn Diagram: This diagram can be used to develop skill in finding similarities and differences. Students will need to review the events in the story and to remember their own childhood experiences. Students can first list places and activities in Rylant's childhood that they would not find today in their own hometowns. Then they can list places and activities that they would find at home but not in the book. Finally they can list places and activities that are found in both. When each student creates their own Venn diagram, it can be used as a springboard to writing a similar type of prose. A bound book of childhood memories makes a valued gift to parents or family at holiday time.

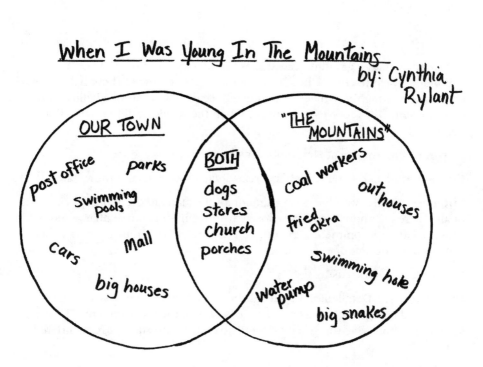

Figure 7.24 Venn diagram by Meredith Jewett for *When I Was Young in the Mountains* by Cynthia Rylant.

=== Sheldon, Dyan. ***The Whale's Song.*** (Illus., Gary Blythe). New York: Dial, 1990.

Summary: Lilly's grandmother shares her memories of the whales from her childhood. Despite Great-Uncle Frederick's different view of the whales, Lilly dreams of hearing the whales' song herself. Leaving her gift of a yellow flower on the water, Lilly receives her reward when the whales call her name that night.

Setting: Present day at Grandmother's house at the seashore.

Characters: Lilly, Grandmother, Great-Uncle Frederick, and the whales.

Themes: Stories one hears on a grandmother's lap are the most special ones of all. There are animal species whose existence has become endangered because of careless commercial practices. People have different views on issues. With enough desire, one can achieve a dream.

Vocabulary: Pier, rustle.

Illustrations: Detailed oil paintings show the tender love between grandmother and granddaughter as well as the beauty of the environment. The use of light and texture give the story a dreamlike quality and suggest remembered times.

Grade Level/Content Area: This story is suitable for use in all elementary classrooms. It can be used in units on environmental issues and intergenerational studies.

Story-Starter Web: After the book is read and the feelings that the story conveys and evokes are discussed, you and your students can create a web by writing the feeling above each whale's tail. Each student can then choose one or more of the feelings to write about.

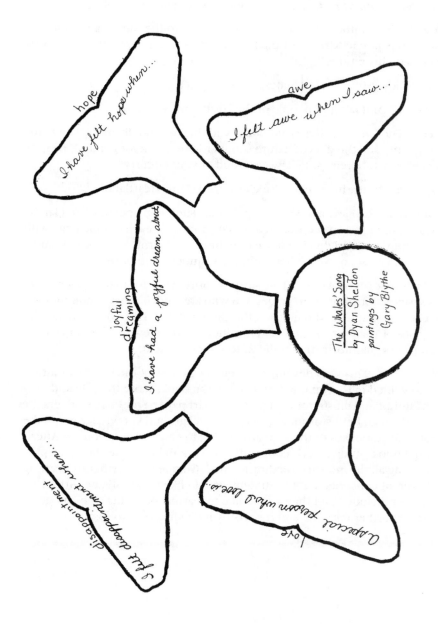

Figure 7.25 Story-starter web by Jill H. Baker for *The Whale's Song* by Dyan Sheldon.

The labels within the figure read:

- hope — I have felt hope when...
- awe — I felt awe when I saw...
- joyful dreaming — I have had a joyful dream about...
- disappointment — I felt disappointment when...
- love — I appreciate /learn who I love is...

The Whale's Song
by Dyan Sheldon
paintings by
Gary Blythe

Siebert, Diane. ***Heartland.*** (Illus., W. Minor). New York: Crowell, 1989.

Summary: The author dedicates this as "A hymn to the American farmer." It is a continuous poetic text about the land, animals, and people of the Midwest with detailed illustrations.

Setting: Midwestern United States.

Characters: Animals and people of the Heartland.

Themes: The United States is abundant with beauty and diversity. The hard work of people and the gifts of nature should not be taken for granted. Despite man's power, nature reigns. Be always proud of your country.

Vocabulary: Pride, hues, ebb, rise elevators, reigns, Heartland.

Illustrations: Realistic and vivid oil paintings stunningly portray rural landscapes and close-up farm scenes. Pictures cover most of each double page with text appearing on the right side of each picture. Neat farms, clean cows, and perfection can be seen everywhere in this romanticization of rural life.

Grade Level/Content Area: This story is appropriate for many ages but perhaps best suited for students in grades 3–6 who are studying rural communities, farm life, or geography and regions of the United States. This book can supplement studies of weather, climate, and nutrition. Current events that impact the Midwest can be an informative addition to the poetic text.

Concept Web: This web develops student awareness of the variety of information contained in this text. Before reading the book, write the title and names of author and illustrator on a piece of chart paper. Show the students the book; and through brainstorming, elicit their background knowledge about the Midwest. Add responses to the web attempting to categorize as you go. After reading the book, students can cooperatively work to complete the concept web including all the information they learned. Go one step further by creating another web of concepts that the students would like to investigate further or that were not included and they would like to learn about. This web can give direction for further research and reports by individuals or groups.

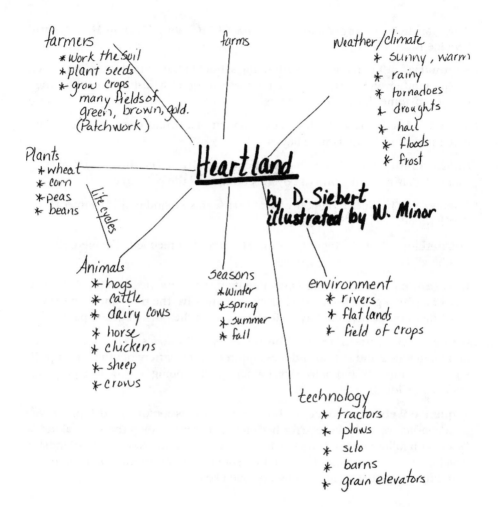

Figure 7.26 Concept web by Ann Maria Zevotek for *Heartland* by Diane Siebert.

*Surat, Michelle M. *Angel Child, Dragon Child.* (Illus., Vo-Dinh Mai). Milwaukee: Raintree, 1983.

Summary: A Vietnamese girl attending school in the United States and lonely for her mother who is still in Vietnam makes a friend whose idea enables the mother to come to the United States.

Setting: The home and school environment of a young Vietnamese girl who recently arrived in the United States.

Characters: Ut, her father, her mother, Little Quang (her brother), Chi Hai (her older sister), Raymond (a boy at school), and the principal.

Theme: Sometimes a person who at first seems unkind may turn into a wonderful friend.

Vocabulary: Tilted, jangled, rushing, twittered, screeched, gleamed, slung, pinched.

Illustrations: Pastel colored-pencil drawings portray the sensitive and shy nature of a young girl who misses her mother and give the trees and flowers in some pictures an Oriental flavor. Text appears at the bottom of the pages.

Grade Level/Content Area: This book fits well into a social studies curriculum for grades 2 and 3. It introduces children to the variety of ethnic groups living in a community and helps develop an understanding of how foreign policy effects individuals.

Sequence Web: Introduce the book with a discussion of friendship, the Vietnam conflict, or a child's love for her mother before reading the story aloud. Discussion following the story can focus on how Ut's and Raymond's friendship developed and its results. Help children summarize this discussion by constructing the sequence map shown or one like it.

Figure 7.27 Sequence web by Charlotte De Almeida for *Angel Child, Dragon Child* by Michelle Surat.

Thomas, Abigal. *Wake Up, Wilson Street.* (Illus., William Low). New York: Holt Rinehart & Winston, 1993.

Summary: A young boy and his grandmother awake early one morning and observe the peaceful beginning of a new day in a small town. They watch the paperboy, grocers, painters, and others proceed with their daily routines while sharing a quiet moment together.

Setting: Wilson Street as viewed from a window in the living room of a home in a neighborhood somewhere in the United States.

Characters: A young boy, his grandmother, and various other residents of and visitors on Wilson Street.

Themes: Daily rituals and routines are essential to our way of life. A great deal of activity that we are not aware of occurs in our world.

Vocabulary: Grocer, awake.

Illustrations: Oil paintings on rag paper become increasingly brighter as the sun rises. Some pictures take on a bird's-eye-view perspective, and others appear to be done from the ground looking upward, suggesting the nonhuman creatures that also wake up early to watch people.

Grade Level/Content Area: In grades K–2, this story fits well with a study of communities or families.

Sequence Organizer: The pictures on this organizer can be drawn and labeled to document children's discussion of the story and to help them visualize all that happens before they wake up in the morning. Children can think of adjectives to describe the events/people, and these words can be added. They can also decide if these things are in evidence in their own neighborhoods, and a *Y* (for *yes*) or *N* (for *no*) can be added. If the organizer is drawn on chart paper, it can be hung on a bulletin board or wall to be used later by children as an aid to story retellings.

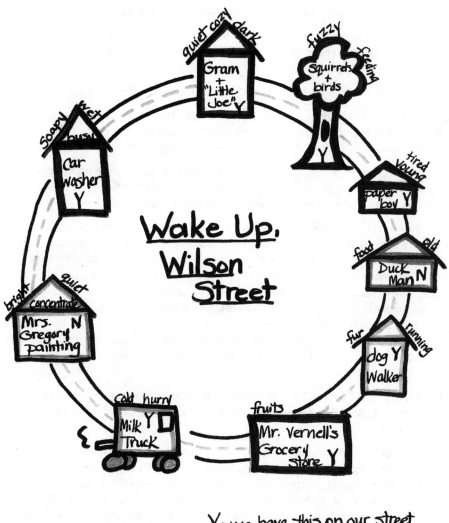

Figure 7.28 Sequence organizer by Meredith Jewett for *Wake Up, Wilson Street* by Abigal Thomas.

Wardlaw, Lee. *Seventh Grade Wierdo.* New York: Scholastic, 1992.

Summary: In this humorous story, a 13-year-old recalls his first weeks in seventh grade: encounters with the eighth-grade bully, "The Shark"; embarrassment over his family; and a crush on an eighth-grade girl.

Setting: Present day in Rob's home and at Jefferson Junior High.

Characters: Christopher "Rob" Robin, Logan Teplansky (his best friend), Winnie Robin (his 6-year-old genius sister), Nina Robin (his mother who loves Winnie-the-Pooh), John Robin (his father who is an ex-professional surfer).

Theme: Even the worst situations can be worked out. People are only as powerful as we allow them to be. Believe in yourself and your family. It is OK to be different. Communication and cooperation bring success.

Vocabulary (by chapter):   Chapter 1: jealous, grimace, keeled, prodigy; Chapter 2: quivered, harsh, genius, impersonation; Chapter 3: ominous, careened; Chapter 4: unconditional surrender, flanked, cronies, fumbling, piranha; Chapter 5: silhouette; Chapter 6: latchkey kid, winced; Chapter 7: bizarre, keen, script; Chapter 8: ferocious, bulging, pillar; Chapter 9: exasperated, pneumonia, realistic; Chapter 10: underestimate; Chapter 11: traitor, contagious; Chapter 12: ultimatum, concocting plans; Chapter 13: obstruction, blackmail, urgently; Chapter 14: frantic, supervision, ingenious; Chapter 15: lead zeppelin, threatened, suspended; Chapter 16: repercussions, grueling, extraordinary; Chapter 17: colliding.

Illustrations: There are no illustrations except for one on the cover showing Rob climbing the school steps with "The Heffalump" (his mother's van) in the background.

Grade Level/Content Area: Students in grades 6 or 7 who are struggling with family or peer relationship difficulties can benefit from this account that touches on areas such as problem solving, coping with stress, diversity in families, and growing up. Before entering junior high, this book can be helpful for initiating discussions about self-esteem, family values, coping, and problem solving.

Character Relations Web: After the book has been read and a full discussion of it has taken place, the concept "point of view" should be defined and examined. Role playing can be used to simulate parts of the story and demonstrate point of view. Then, provide students with a map that contains characters names and faces connected with two directional arrows. In pairs, small groups, or as a class, students can write in how the characters relate to or view one another. Students can then "step into" a character's shoes, take his or her point of view, and debate or interact with other students who have taken on different characters' roles.

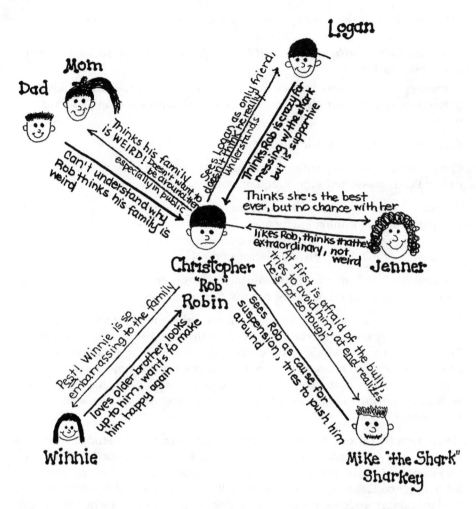

Figure 7.29 Relationship web by Shannon Smith for *Seventh Grade Wierdo* by Lee Wardlaw.

Historical Fiction

Cushman, Karen. *Catherine, Called Birdy.* (Jacket Illus., Trina Schart Hyman). New York: Clarion, 1994.

Summary: In this story written in diary format, a 14-year-old girl avoids an arranged marriage and searches for romance and adventure during medieval times.

Setting: An English manor in 1290.

Characters: Birdy, her father, her mother, her nurse, a peasant goatboy named Perkins, assorted suitors, and manor visitors.

Themes: Growing up is a difficult process of learning self-discipline and self-acceptance and of gaining independence. People's actions are influenced by the culture in which they live. Today we have much to be grateful for, especially in the areas of public health and disease control.

Vocabulary: Vellum, privy, dousing, abbot, baron, spindles, minstrels, guilds, manor, medieval, humility, abbey, pagans, herbal remedies, noble classes.

Illustrations: The book jacket shows Birdy writing in her diary, caged birds behind her that she feels have more freedom than she has, and an evil fairy. Through the manor's windows the countryside, homes of the common people, and the village church can be seen. Somber tones represent the darkness of the manor and pre-Renaissance ignorance. The first word in each chapter begins with a pen-and-ink calligraphic letter much like those seen in medieval manuscripts.

Grade Level/Content Area: For ages 12 and older who are studying the Middle Ages. The Afterword contains fascinating information on medieval society, for example, the cure for open sores was an application of raven droppings. A list of other children's books on medieval life is also provided. If this book is read to younger students, some scenes may be omitted, such as when Birdy sees two servants romantically involved in a hay mound and then comments that the girl will no longer be able to play the Virgin Mary in the Christmas pageant.

Comparison-Contrast Organizer: Have students list features of daily life in medieval times on the manor tower and corresponding features of contemporary life on the house. On the bridge between the two structures, ask students to list things that are the same so they can see that people in all times are alike in many ways. Use this organizer to stimulate critical thinking in a discussion format or as an assessment of students' understanding of the book.

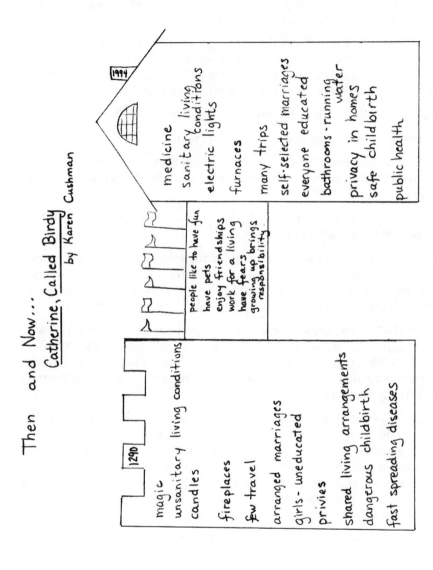

Figure 7.30 Comparison-contrast organizer by Deb Pease for *Catherine, Called Birdy* by Karen Cushman.

Harvey, Brett. *Cassie's Journey: Going West in the 1860's.* (Illus., Deborah Kogan Ray). New York: Holiday House, 1988.

Summary: A young girl relates the hardships, dangers, and excitement of traveling west with her family in a covered wagon during the 1860s. Her family decides it will be easier and more profitable in California, so they bid family and friends goodbye and join a caravan of wagons going westward.

Setting: The trail west from Illinois to California in the 1860s.

Characters: Cassie, Papa, Mama, Alice, and Plato.

Themes: Pioneers dreamed of new life in a new land, but realization of that dream brought many dangers and much loss. To achieve a dream one must have conviction and fortitude.

Vocabulary: Caravan, "seeing the elephant," alkali dust, canvas, buffalo chips, axle, *Oh Susanna!,* stampede.

Illustrations: Black and white drawings, many with a soft, shadowy appearance, emphasize the harshness of the journey. Pictures often include a distinguishable feature in the foreground and the horizon in the distance, thus giving the impression of the many miles to be covered on the long journey.

Grade Level/Content Area: This book is appropriate for students in grades 3–8 studying pioneer or frontier life, the westward expansion of the United States, or following a dream. It is based on actual diaries of pioneer women who kept written accounts of their experiences traveling west, and the text portrays a journallike memory of the past.

Geographical Organizer: Give students a web with Illinois in the East and California in the West, providing the strands *losses, bad weather,* and so on. Then have the students, either with you, in small groups, or individually, add the information to complete the web. Since the book ends before Cassie actually arrives in California, the web can be extended to include possible events of the rest of the trip. Then this web can be used to help students write different endings, either as journal entries or perhaps even as a play.

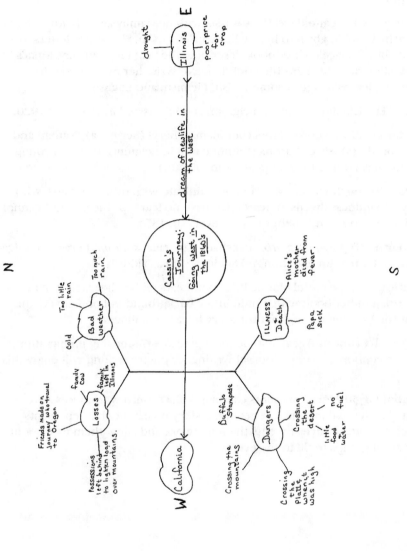

Figure 7.31 Geographical organizer by Diane Mannix for *Cassie's Journey: Going West in the 1860's* by Brett Harvey.

*Hesse, Karen. ***Letters from Rifka.*** (Cover Illus., Diana Zelvin). New York: Puffin, 1993.

Summary: A 12-year-old girl flees Russia with her family and a beloved book of poetry by Pushkin given to her by her cousin, Tovah. She writes letters to Tovah in the blank spaces of her book describing the year-long journey. Rifka's literacy develops and she gains the confidence to write her own poetry. In addition, she learns to speak some Polish, Flemish, and English.

Setting: The Ukraine in Russia, Belgium, and Ellis Island in 1919 and 1920.

Characters: Rifka Nebrot, Ethel (her mama), Beryl (her papa), Nathan and Saul (her brothers), Sister Catrina (Catholic nun in Belgium), Pieter (a young sailor), and Ilya (young Russian peasant immigrant).

Themes: Through writing we can communicate with others but also with ourselves. "Kindness dwells in hearts that have no fear" (p. 140). "A girl cannot depend on her looks. It is better to be clever" (p. 137).

Vocabulary: Typhus, *mitzvah,* ruckshack, steerage, *shalom,* herring, fumigation, HIAS (Hebrew Immigration Aid Society), *tallis,* Yiddish.

Illustrations: A beautiful blonde Rifka with tears on her face is shown on the cover writing in her book with a train in the background. A hood covers the hair that she is losing throughout the story because of illness.

Grade Level/Content Area: Students in grades 3–7 studying immigration, Jewish persecution, journeys, journal writing, or poetry writing will enjoy this book.

Sequential Organizer: Students can map Rifka's journey from Russia to the United States and rate the events in the story on a scale that represents *obstacles–triumphs.* Give students the framework and allow them to work in pairs or small groups to fill in the events.

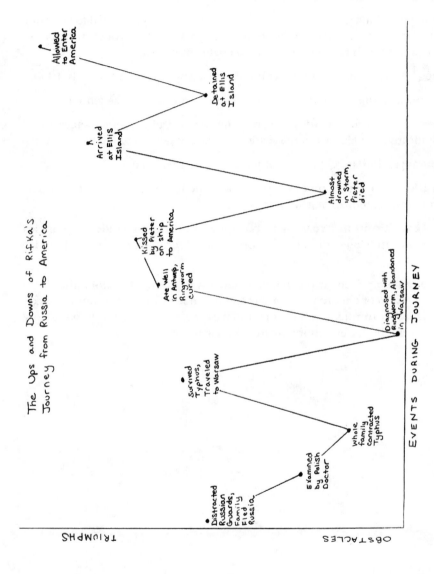

Figure 7.32 Sequential organizer by Kelly Haight for *Letters from Rifka* by Karen Hesse.

Mills, Lauren. *The Rag Coat.* Boston: Little Brown, 1991.

Summary: Minna goes to school for the first time and is ridiculed for wearing a "coat of rags" by the other children until she explains the wonderful memories and stories each patch in her quilted coat symbolizes.

Setting: A mountain or mining community of Appalachia in the early 1900s.

Characters: Minna, Quilting Mothers, Father, and students at school.

Themes: Names and words can sometimes be hurtful unless we share and communicate our ideas. Communication is a key to getting along with others.

Vocabulary: Burlap, Quilting Mothers, soot, Appalachian.

Illustrations: Pictures on every page show the important concept or situation from the accompanying written page.

Grade Level/Content Area: This book is appropriate for students in grades 2–5 who are studying early settlers, Appalachia, discrimination, or communication.

Character Web: This web can be created as you discuss the story after reading it to a group of children. The focus can be on how people communicated with each other throughout the story and parallels can be drawn showing how classmates might better communicate with each other.

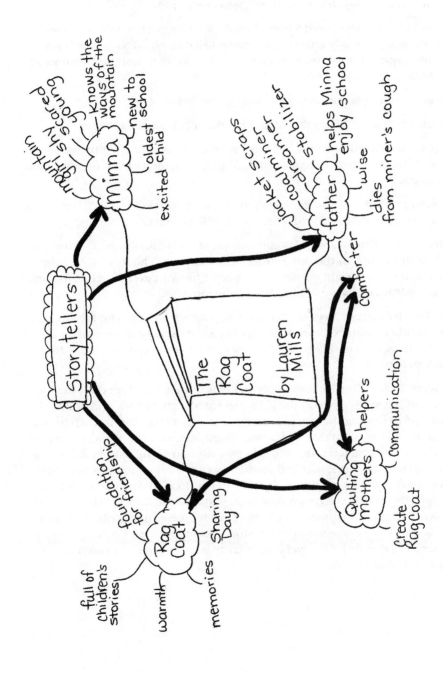

Figure 7.33 Character web by Michelle McDonald for *The Rag Coat* by Lauren Mills.

*Paulsen, Gary. **Nightjohn.** New York: Delacourte, 1993.

Summary: Twelve-year-old Sarny's brutal life as a slave becomes even more dangerous when a newly arrived slave named Nightjohn offers to teach her to read. This powerful story about literacy is "meticulously researched, historically accurate, and artistically crafted."

Setting: A slave plantation in the south in the 1850s.

Characters: Sarny, Nightjohn, Mammy (Old Delie), and Old Waller.

Themes: It is worth wanting to better your life no matter what the consequences. There are some things worth suffering for. Literacy leads to power and independence.

Vocabulary: Witchin', breeder, birthing Mammy, the sticks, spec'lators, sassafras tea, trough, calabash gourd, corn-shuck pallets, crackers, extremity.

Illustrations: One black and white illustration of Nightjohn with a torch in one hand and a book in the other introduces this story. The word *BAG* is imprinted on the lower right corner of the book's brown cover which is the first word Sarny learns to write with a stick in the dirt.

Grade Level/Content Areas: Students in grades 5 and up who are studying slavery, Southern history, literacy, or conflict are moved by this poignant account. Some aspects of this gripping story may be omitted when it is read to younger audiences.

Character Web: This webbing activity helps students explore their personal response to the story, develop the ability to analyze characters, and builds vocabulary. After reading the story to students, assign a character to each of the four corners of the room (Sarny, Mammy, Nightjohn, and Old Waller). Have students choose the character they thought was most powerful or complicated, go to that character's corner, and find another person with whom to share their opinion. Have pairs share with each other so that four students hear each others' responses, and then have groups share with the entire class. After a full discussion of the book, students can create character webs to describe a character with adjectives and evidence from the story to support their choices. Provide dictionaries or thesauri. This webbing activity is also useful as a planning tool for writing a character sketch.

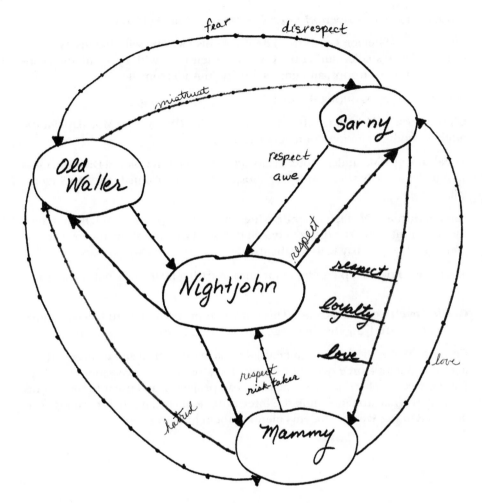

Figure 7.34 Feelings web for *Nightjohn* by Gary Paulsen.

*Polacco, Patricia. ***Pink and Say.*** New York: Philomel (1994).

Summary: Sheldon Curtis (Say) describes his meeting with Pinkus Aylee (Pink), a black soldier during the Civil War, their time with Pink's mother, capture by Southern troops, and imprisonment in Andersonville.

Setting: Georgia during the Civil War.

Characters: Sheldon Curtis (Say), Pinkus Aylee (Pink), Moe Moe Bay (Pink's mother), and marauding Confederate troops.

Vocabulary: Marauders, tote, mahogany, Forty-Eighth Colored Division, Ohio Twenty-Fourth Division, root-cellar, mustered, Union, Confederate, Andersonville, smote.

Illustrations: Detailed color drawings in this large picture book help draw the reader into the friendship between the two boys and show the love and concern Moe Moe Bay feels for them.

Themes: Friendship crosses color lines. A caring heart does not recognize skin tone.

Grade Level/Content Area: This book is appropriate for students in grades 4–6 who are studying the Civil War, slavery, friendship, or integration.

Concept Web: This web can be used to develop critical and divergent thinking. It. highlights three quotations from Moe Moe Bay's conversation with Say. Put the web on chart paper or the overhead projector, and use it to prompt discussion of what students think the three statements mean. Their meanings can be added to the web as students mention them in discussion.

Figure 7.35 Concept web for *Pink and Say* by Patricia Polacco.

=== *Say, Allen. **Grandfather's Journey.** Boston: Houghton Mifflin, 1993.

Summary: This story documents the journey of Say's grandfather across the Pacific Ocean from Japan and his exploration of North America. As his grandfather ages and gains a family, he moves back to his homeland but always yearns to see California "one more time."

Setting: North America and Japan from approximately 1920 to 1940.

Characters: *Grandfather* from boyhood to his death; the narrator; and the narrator's grandmother, mother, and father.

Theme: We are deeply connected both to our families and to the land we call home. Having more than one land to call home yields rich experiences to be shared with others.

Vocabulary: European, steamship, astonished, enormous, bewildered, marveled, warblers.

Illustrations: Gentle watercolor drawings of the same size appear on each page with print below them, reminding the reader of a photo album. Pictures appear posed as if they were actual photographs, and this format complements the family history nature of the text. Six illustrations predominantly feature landscapes of Japan and North America, communicating the importance of the two lands in the author's life as well as the significance of nature in Japanese culture.

Grade Level/Content Area: This book is suitable for use in grades 2–6 during a unit on Japan because two ideas important to Japanese culture are main themes of the book: respect for the elderly and for nature. It complements a unit on the family since it details three generations of family members and can be used to illustrate the concept of *family tree* graphically. It is not only a cross-generational story, but also shows cross-cultural relationships and can be used in units on multiculturalism, immigration, or aging.

Sequence Map: This web shows students visually how the story begins and ends with the same action; a young man leaving his homeland (Japan) to explore a new world (North America). It documents the events in Grandfather's life, but can also show that events such as birth, death, marriage, and travel occur in every family across cultures. This web highlights our similarities as people, not the differences between cultures.

   The class can create the web together after reading and discussing the story, and it may inspire students to interview their own grandparents or other elderly persons. The students can use this *time cycle* as a model, asking questions concerning monumental events in the relatives' lives and then creating a similar web based on their interviews.

Figure 7.36 Sequence map by Meredith Jewett for *Grandfather's Journey* by Allen Say.

Slawson, Michele Benoit. *Apple Picking Time.* New York: Crown, 1994.

Summary: A young girl, named Anna, and her family harvest apples in the orchards with the rest of the townspeople in this descriptive story based on the author's own experiences from childhood.

Setting: Autumn in the Yakima Valley, Washington state or any apple-growing region where apple trees grow in valleys and on hillsides.

Characters: Anna, Mama, Papa, Grandma, Grandpa, and Dave (the foreman).

Themes: Working together as a team is an efficient and special way to share and learn. Determination and hard work help achieve goals. Family traditions are an important and powerful part of life.

Vocabulary: Harvest, orchard, bins, breath, clouds, foreman, graceful, harness, half-moon, canvas, procession.

Illustrations: Impressionistic illustrations of scenery and people show autumn landscapes and apple pickers engaged in the harvest.

Grade Level/Content Area: This book supports study of harvesting, community, family, apples, autumn, teamwork, and cooperation for students in grades K–4.

Character Web: This webbing activity helps students understand how the characters worked together to accomplish a task. After reading the story and talking about it, assign a character to each group to discuss the character's role and contribution as an apple picker. Have one child in each group summarize their group's discussion for the class. Write these descriptions on the web as each group reports. The one shown here is just one way to make a web or graphic organizer for this story. The students' contributions will undoubtedly be somewhat different.

Character Web for:
Apple Picking Time
By Michele Benoit Slawson

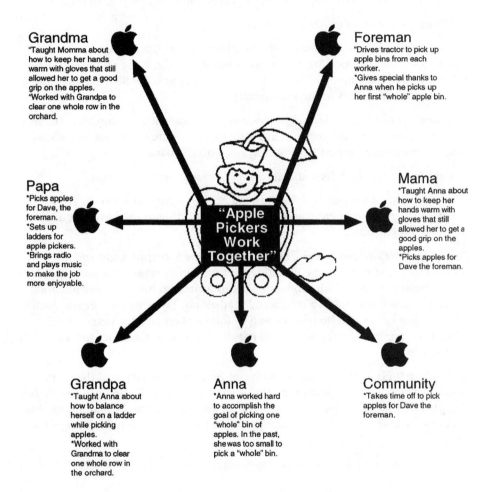

Grandma
"Taught Momma about how to keep her hands warm with gloves that still allowed her to get a good grip on the apples.
"Worked with Grandpa to clear one whole row in the orchard.

Foreman
"Drives tractor to pick up apple bins from each worker.
"Gives special thanks to Anna when he picks up her first "whole" apple bin.

Papa
"Picks apples for Dave, the foreman.
"Sets up ladders for apple pickers.
"Brings radio and plays music to make the job more enjoyable.

"Apple Pickers Work Together"

Mama
"Taught Anna about how to keep her hands warm with gloves that still allowed her to get a good grip on the apples.
"Picks apples for Dave the foreman.

Grandpa
"Taught Anna about how to balance herself on a ladder while picking apples.
"Worked with Grandma to clear one whole row in the orchard.

Anna
"Anna worked hard to accomplish the goal of picking one "whole" bin of apples. In the past, she was too small to pick a "whole" bin.

Community
"Takes time off to pick apples for Dave the foreman.

Figure 7.37 Character web by Jennifer Nowacki for *Apple Picking Time* by Michele Benoit Slawson.

—— *Taylor, Mildred D. **Roll of Thunder, Hear My Cry.** New York: Dial, 1976.

Summary: This is the story of a black family, the Logans, whose warm ties to each other and their land give them the strength to defy rural Southern racism during the Depression. Told from the perspective of Cassie, the 12-year-old daughter, this is a powerful, rich, and warm account of one year in their lives.

Setting: Mississippi in 1933.

Characters: The Logan family: Mama (Mary), Papa (David), Big Ma (Grandmother), Uncle Hammer, Mr. Morrison (a hired man), and the children (Cassie, Stacy, Christopher-John, and Little Man). The Avery and the Sims families and various other members of the community.

Themes: Courage, pride, and independence come with owning land. Indignities, discrimination, and personal anguish are overcome when one possesses family loyalty, love, honesty, pride, and strength of character.

Vocabulary: Night riders, sharecroppers, tenant families, revival.

Illustrations: One pen-and-ink drawing of the Logan family on the front porch of their home opens the book. Other than this and the cover picture, there are no illustrations.

Grade Level/Content Area: Students in grades 5–8 appreciate and are enthralled by the strength and commitment of this family who experience the cruelty of racism yet prevail. In units on African American history, discrimination, or racism, this book makes a wonderful read-aloud. Taylor's more recent stories of the Logan family can be read as well to follow them in later years. Three other titles are: *Let the Circle Be Unbroken, The Yellow Cadillac,* and *The Friendship.*

Character Web: This character web can be created as you read the story aloud to a class or as students read the story themselves. An organizer such as this provides a quick reference as to who a particular character is and how that character fits into the large community of people who move in and out of Cassie's life.

argaret. ***Let the Celebrations BEGIN!*** (Illus., Julie Vivas) New York:
d Books, 1991.

ary: As World War II draws to a conclusion, Miriam, a child of the Ger-
ncentration camps, helps the women of the camp make toys to be given
ounger children at the celebration they will have when the liberating
arrive.

: A German concentration camp for Jews in 1945 or 1946, probably
-Belsen.

ters: Miriam, Sarah and David (her young friends), Jacoba and the
women of the camp, and the soldiers.

es: Children have a desire for play, even under the most dire circum-
. People who have little to share will nonetheless share what they have.

ulary: Shawl, *dumnkopfs,* rheumatism, precious, patchwork, liberate,
s.

ations: Muted watercolors show scenes in the camp, while bright col-
w Miriam's memories of home. The soft drawings and colors of camp
shield the reader from the harsh reality of the deprivation and despair in
entration camp.

Level/Content Area: With older elementary students and middle-
students, this book will make an important contribution to units on sur-
nternment in concentration or refugee camps, or World War II.

cter Web: After reading the story and discussing the conditions in the
hat affect all of the people in the camp, it would be valuable to talk about
ese circumstances influence the way the characters act. Some character-
re explicitly and easily identified, while others may require insight and
sion. A web with just characters' names might be provided to students
rough class or small-group discussion, attributes can be added for each
ter. This web shows the character attributes the reader knows or can in-
be true within the barbed wire of the concentration camp.

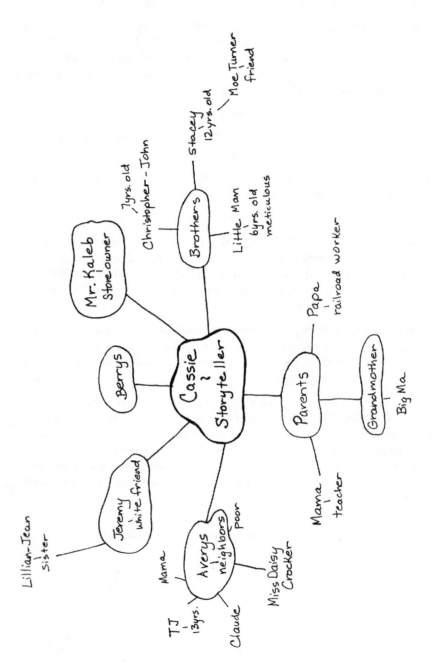

Figure 7.38 Character web for *Roll of Thunder, Hear My Cry* by Mildred D. Taylor.

Van Allsburg, Chris. ***The Widow's Broom.*** Boston: Houghton Mifflin, 1992.

Summary: A widow receives a clever broom from a witch. The hard-working broom helps around the house and entertains the widow but is seen as evil by the neighbors. One day some misbehaving neighborhood children receive a thrashing from the broom and the widow must give up her companion. In a surprise ending, the widow and the broom trick everyone.

Setting: A rural community and Widow Shaw's farm.

Characters: A magical broom, Minna Shaw (the widow), Mr. Spivey, the nasty Spivey children, and various townspeople.

Theme: It is wrong to condemn what you do not understand. There is often more to a situation than meets the eye.

Vocabulary: Cloaked, embers, hearth, pasture, horrified, bristles.

Illustrations: In a book that is longer and narrower than usual, its shape suggests a story unusual. Haunting images in charcoal or pencil create a spooky, hazy texture that enhances the story. Print always appears on the page opposite the illustration and is framed by two small, rectangular drawings of pumpkins. At three places, there are double-page illustrations that show action.

Grade Level/Content Area: This story is suitable in grades 4–6 to be read for enjoyment or to spark imagination. If you read it aloud, stop at various points to encourage predictions. The book lends itself to a study of fantasy, magic, or Van Allsburg's entire works.

Literary Elements Web: The web can be used as a way to document student discussion of the story. The categories and their content can be student-generated, or you can provide the story elements and have the students supply the specific information as they discuss and analyze the story. The story might be compared with others of Van Allsburg's by creating and comparing similar webs. Analyses such as these help students prepare for writing and illustrating their own ghost stories or Halloween tales.

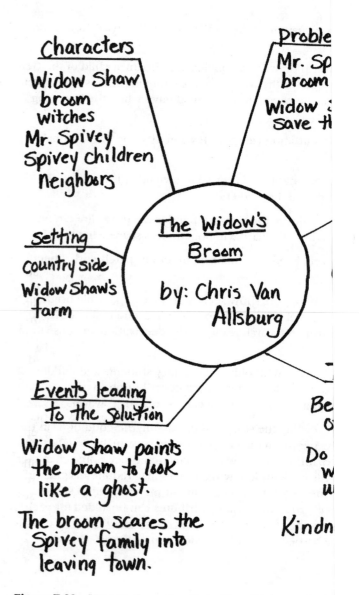

Figure 7.39   Literary elements web by Meredith Jewett for *Th...* Chris Van Allsburg.

Wild,
Orcha

Summ
man c
to the
soldie

Settin
Berga

Chara
other

Them
stance

Vocal
barrac

Illust
ors sh
scene
a con

Grad
grade
vival,

Char
camp
how
istics
discu
and t
chara
fer to

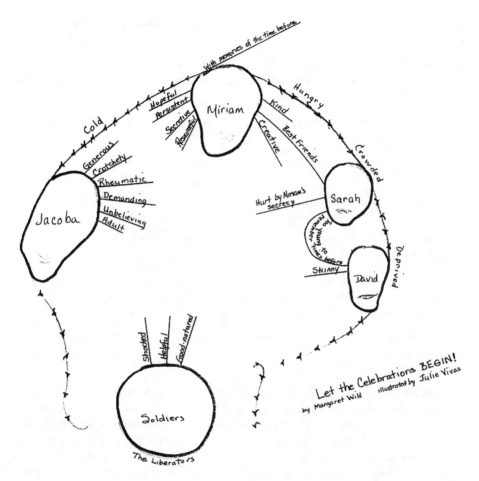

Figure 7.40 Character web by Jill H. Baker for *Let the Celebrations BEGIN!* by Margaret Wild.

Woodruff, Elvira. ***Dear Levi: Letters From the Overland Trail.*** (Illus., Beth Peck). New York: Knopf, 1994.

Summary: As he travels the Overland Trail to Oregon in 1851, twelve-year-old Austin Ives writes letters to his younger brother, Levi, back in Pennsylvania about the hardships, sorrows, and adventures of traveling by wagon train.

Setting: From Pennsylvania to Oregon on the Overland Trail from April to September of 1851.

Characters: Austin Ives, Tom Morrison, Frank Hickman, Hiram Buckner, and Reuben McAlister Rice.

Themes: People survive difficult times by setting their sights on dreams for the future. Follow your dreams for a better life.

Vocabulary: Covered wagon, oxen, yoke, buffalo, critter, concoction, kinship, harness.

Illustrations: The cover illustration in color shows a boy sitting in a covered wagon and writing. There are five black and white illustrations in the book showing covered wagons and the people in various activities.

Grade Level/Content Area: Students in grades 3–6 who are studying westward expansion, pioneers, frontier life, or the genre of historical fiction will enjoy this child's eye view of wagon train life.

Character Web: This webbing activity encourages personal response, builds understanding of characters, and develops vocabulary. After reading the story, have each student choose one of the five main characters and then form groups according to characters to discuss if or how the character changed or grew throughout the story or what admirable traits the character possessed. Have students make a web to depict their discussion and include supporting information from the story. Groups can share their webs with the class, and additions or modifications can be made to the webs during class discussion.

Main Idea Web: This webbing activity encourages personal response, builds understanding of main ideas and supporting details, and builds vocabulary. After reading the story, arrange students in small groups, and have them brainstorm the main ideas, issues, or concepts in the story. They can put these ideas on a web and add supporting information. Webs can then be shared with the entire class and main ideas compared.

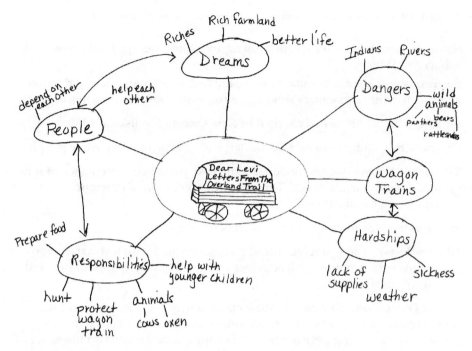

Figure 7.41 Character web by Diane Doherty for *Dear Levi: Letters from the Overland Trail* by Elvira Woodruff.

Biography ═══

═══ *Coles, Robert. **The Story of Ruby Bridges.** (Illus., George Ford). New York: Scholastic, 1995.

Summary: Six-year-old Ruby Bridges, the first African American girl to integrate an all-white elementary school, confronts the hostility of segregationists.

Setting: Frantz Elementary School In New Orleans, Louisiana, 1960.

Characters: Ruby Bridges, Miss Hurley, and crowds of angry white people.

Themes: Knowledge and understanding ease prejudice. Acceptance of others leads to acceptance of self. Through the exploration of differences comes the realization of similarities.

Vocabulary: Segregation, persuade, federal marshals.

Illustrations: Large, double-spread pictures created with soft watercolor hues convey the emotions and activities of Ruby, her family, Miss Hurley, and crowds of angry citizens.

Grade Level/Content Areas: Students in grades 1–6 who are studying school integration, racism, or African American culture are moved by this poignant story of a young girl's heroism. It is appropriate for units on the genre of biography, African American women, and educational reform.

Character Web: This web is a tool for a character study. It can also be used for the comparison/contrast of various characters. Students can choose a character from the story that they identify with or are most interested in and create a character web to share with the class. On completion, webs can be displayed as students present their character sketches and compare characters.

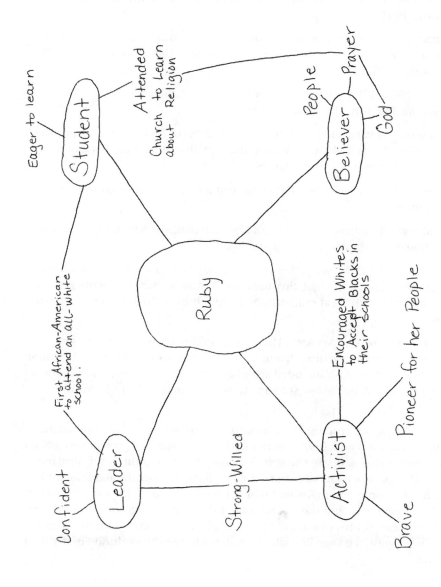

Figure 7.42 Character web by Karen Wandell for *The Story of Ruby Bridges* by Robert Coles.

*Haskins, Jim. ***Black Eagles: African Americans in Aviation.*** New York: Scholastic, 1995.

Summary: This nonfiction text features the biographies of several African American pilots, both men and women, and their flights, with a look into the future of *Black Eagles.*

Setting: 1903–1992, various locations including California, Texas, New York, Chicago, Washington, D.C., and Europe.

Characters: Several pilots, including Gene Bullard, Jesse Brown, James Herbert Banning, Bessie Coleman, Hubert Julian, William J. Powell, Benjamin O. Davis, Jr., and Daniel (Chappie) James.

Themes: The actions of one individual can inspire an entire group. Strive to attain your goals.

Vocabulary: Bombardment, inaugurated, aviation, aircraft, Air Corps, combat, technology, turbulent, correspondents.

Illustrations: A full-color jacket featuring eleven pilots, a black and white photograph of one of the first airplanes, and several pictures of pilots and their planes throughout the text enhance the biographies and make them *real* to the reader.

Grade Level/Content Areas: These biographies are well suited to grades 4–8 units focusing on aviation, famous African Americans, World War II, nonfiction, or biographies. Also included are a bibliography, an index, and a chronological time line, which allow students to see the progression of African American pilots.

Time Line: Before reading these biographies, draw a time line for students with the dates 1903 and 1992 at either end. Ask students to predict dates of important events that occur in the text, including the invention of the airplane, the first African American woman to earn a pilot's license, the founding of the U.S. Army Air Force, the first solo flight across the Atlantic, the creation of the first black flying unit, and the assignment of the first black naval aviator. After reading the text, return to the time line and place the events with the correct dates. This completed time line allows students to see the evolution of the field of aviation.

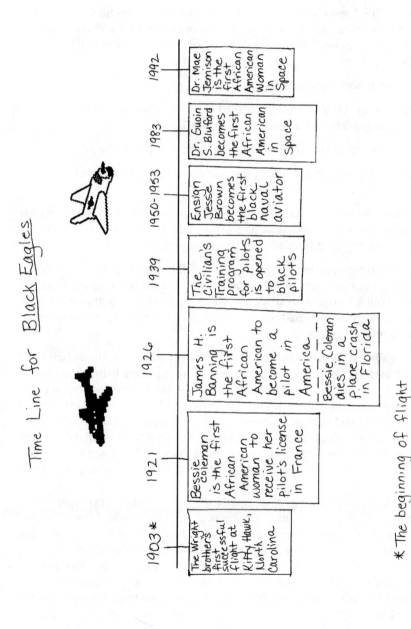

Time Line for Black Eagles

| 1903 * | 1921 | 1926 | 1939 | 1950-1953 | 1983 | 1992 |

1903 * — The Wright brothers first successful flight at Kitty Hawk, North Carolina

1921 — Bessie Coleman is the first African American woman to receive her pilot's license in France

1926 — James H. Banning is the first African American to become a pilot in America

Bessie Coleman dies in a plane crash in Florida

1939 — The Civilian's Training program for pilots is opened to black pilots

1950-1953 — Ensign Jesse Brown becomes the first black naval aviator

1983 — Dr. Guoin S. Bluford becomes the first African American in space

1992 — Dr. Mae Jemison is the first African American Woman in Space

* The beginning of flight

Figure 7.43 Time line by Karen Wandell for *Black Eagles: African Americans in Aviation* by Jim Haskins.

*Haskins, Jim, and Kathleen Benson. **Space Challenger: The Story of Guion Bluford.** Minneapolis: Carolrhoda Books, 1984.

Summary: This 1984 Outstanding Science Tradebook is about Guion (Guy) Bluford, the first black American in space, who was part of the crew of the space shuttle "Challenger." The story depicts his struggle through school and his family's support in helping him achieve his goals.

Setting: Guy at home and at school.

Characters: Guy, his mother and father, brothers—Eugene and Kenneth, wife—Linda, and children—Guion III and James T.

Theme: Determination and work can make a dream come true.

Vocabulary: Aerospace, technical, simulator, satellite, pharmaceutical, McDonnell Douglas.

Illustrations: Both color and black and white photographs are interspersed with text and show Guy at different stages in his life. Direct quotes from conversations among family members add realism to the pictures.

Grade Level/Content Area: This book fits well in grades 3–6 social studies units on careers or explorers or in science units on rocketry or space travel. It is also a good book to use with students who have learning disabilities or reading difficulties because Guy had trouble in school with reading but overcame his problems with family help.

Character Web: You can introduce this character web to students before they read or listen to the story so that they have a purpose for their reading. As you discuss the vocabulary in the rocket, tell students that each arrow stands for potential problems or obstacles for which Guy had to find solutions in order to overcome them and become successful. After reading the book, have students discuss the problems and solutions the text identifies as well as any they can think of that he may have had but were not discussed and ways that he might have solved them. Write these under "problems" and "solutions" on the web.

Use the completed web as a springboard for discussion of possible problems your students might have in achieving their own dreams and some plans of action they might employ to overcome these problems. This story of a real person's life is an excellent one for helping students begin to identify and explore their own aspirations. Students might write their own biographies based on the structure of the character web, using vocabulary that describes their own projected growth and predicting possible problems and solutions that their own futures might hold.

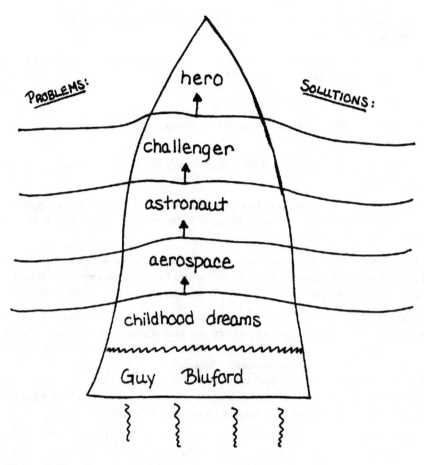

Figure 7.44 Character web by Lisa Milano for *Space Challenger: The Story of Guion Bluford* by Jim Haskins and Kathleen Benson.

Lepsky, Ibi. ***Albert Einstein.*** (Illus., Paolo Cardoni). Woodbury, NY: Barron's Educational Series, 1982.

Summary: A young boy fails in school but triumphs over this adversity to become one of the greatest scientists of our time.

Setting: Germany almost a century ago.

Characters: Albert, Mama, Papa, Maja (Albert's sister), Albert's teacher, and his classmates.

Theme: A person should not be judged solely on the basis of his or her outward appearance.

Vocabulary: Absentminded, ignored, company, colony, history, geography, memorize, incapable, gymnastics, granite, improvise, compass, curtly, anguish, genius, theories, distracted, precise.

Illustrations: Pastel colors and cartoonlike illustrations accompany text. The style of characters' clothing appears authentic for the time period in which Albert lived, and the simple, yet distinctive illustrations support the text well.

Grade Level/Content Area: This book supports grades 2–4 units of study in the physical sciences on energy, matter, the atmosphere, and the universe. It also provides a personal introduction to the life of a scientist for students in grades 3–7 who are studying careers. Since Albert experienced difficulties in school yet overcame them, this story also is excellent to share with children who have problems with learning. Albert's life can inspire a student who has a negative self-concept and thus serve as a positive model.

Character Web: As students listen to this story or read it themselves, have them fill in either the words that describe Einstein (on the strands of the web) or sentences from the story that describe his habits or actions (in the bubbles at the ends of the strands). After the story is read, have students fill in unfinished parts of the web.

If students can benefit from a vocabulary extension activity, ask them to supply synonyms for the descriptors on the strands. Have them use a dictionary or thesaurus to identify new words that mean the same thing as the words they have on the web.

With an individual student or small group that experiences learning difficulties, lead a discussion of how students feel they may or may not be similar to Einstein. Be sure to focus on Einstein's triumph over adversity and his tremendous contribution to science and technology today.

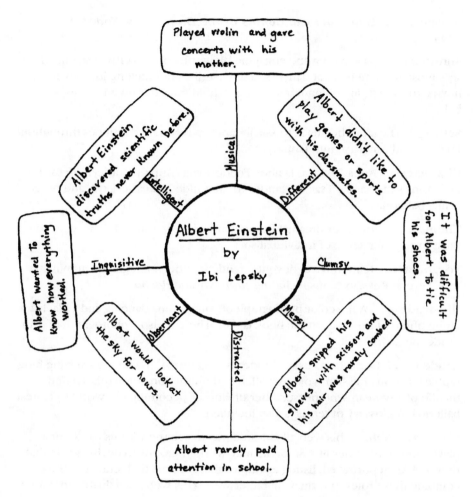

Figure 7.45 Character web by Lisa Milano for *Albert Einstein* by Ibi Lepsky.

═══ *Levine, Ellen. **Anna Pavlova: Genius of the Dance.** New York: Scholastic, 1995.

Summary: A fascinating and engaging biography of Anna Pavlova, one of Russia's most acclaimed ballet dancers, that describes her lifelong journey from novice to expert, including her struggle to hold onto her own traditions and beliefs.

Setting: The story begins in Russia in January 1881 and continues throughout England and America until January 23, 1931.

Characters: Anna Pavlova, Lyubov Feodorovna (Anna's mother), Victor Dandre (Anna's husband), Tsar Alexander III, Mathilde Kchessinskaya, and other prima ballerinas.

Themes: Follow your dreams! Perseverance is rewarding. To succeed, you must foster your sense of individualism.

Vocabulary: Icon, novice, devout, grandeur, ethereal, regimen, administrators. Several Russian terms including *samovar* and *dacha*.

Illustrations: A full-color photograph of young Anna dancing and a black and white photo of Anna adorn the book jacket. There is also a photograph of Anna inside the novel.

Grade Level/Content Areas: Students in grades 4–8 who are studying biographies, famous Russian women, ballet, and nonfiction enjoy this account of the life of a woman who pursued her dreams of becoming the world's greatest ballerina. A glossary of terms is also included.

Character Web: This web allows students to see the various roles Anna played throughout her life. Students may work in groups to devise a role that they feel Anna portrayed, listing examples that support their choices. As a class, combine these roles to form a character web. This web is a valuable tool for a character sketch or for comparisons among various characters.

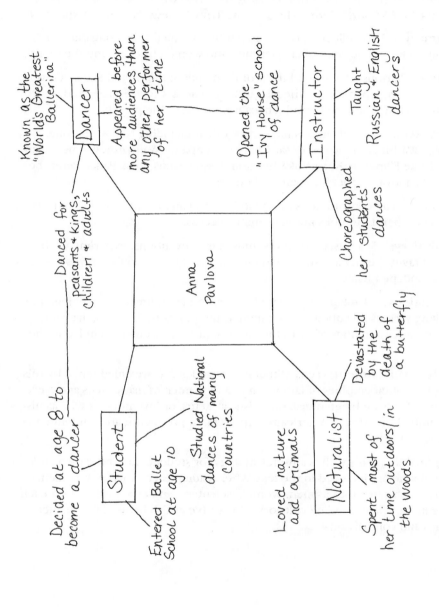

Figure 7.46 Character web by Karen Wandell for *Anna Pavlova: Genius of the Dance* by Ellen Levine.

*Marzollo, Jean. ***My First Book of Biographies: Great Men and Women Every Child Should Know.*** (Illus., Irene Trivas). New York: Scholastic, 1994.

Summary: This collection of 45 biographies highlight the contributions in various fields of endeavor of famous men and women from around the world.

Setting: Various sites around the world, including the United States, Europe, Mexico, India, Japan, Egypt, the East Indies, Austria, Chile, Switzerland, space, and the moon. The time period ranges from 69 BC to the present.

Characters: Several famous men and women including Neil Armstrong, George Washington Carver, Cesar Chavez, Cleopatra, Walt Disney, Amelia Earhart, Duke Ellington, Katsushika Hokusai, Jesse Owens, Rosa Parks, Peter the Great, Sequoya, Harriet Tubman, and others.

Themes: The contributions of one individual can benefit an entire population. Financial status does not determine success.

Vocabulary: Scientists, explorers, musicians, inventions, experiments, biography, gravity, pesticides, strike, radium, electricity, abolitionist, boycott, segregation, independence.

Illustrations: A full-page animated illustration compliments each biography, detailing various inventions, experiments, and portraits. The book jacket features pictures and titles of 11 of the famous men and women included in the text.

Grade Level/Content Area: Students in grades 2–8 are enlightened by this anthology of biographies of famous men and women of many races and backgrounds. Units on biographies, scientists, athletes, or inventors, as well as history units about African Americans, explorers, or presidents, are complimented by this text.

People Web: This web is a useful strategy for students to list the men and women who are included in the text. After reading each biography, students choose such categories as men, women, scientists, and explorers and list each name in the corresponding category. This web can also be used for character studies and comparisons.

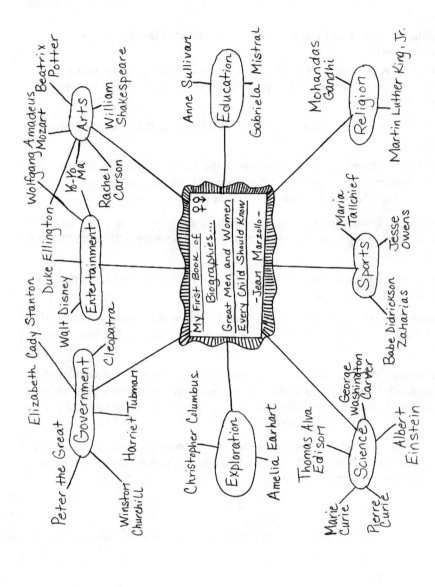

Figure 7.47 People web by Karen Wandell for *My First Book of Biographies: Great Men and Women Every Child Should Know* by Jean Marzollo.

Poetry

Begay, Shonto. *Navajo: Visions and Voices Across the Mesa.* New York: Scholastic, 1995.

Summary: A collection of 20 poems, chants, and short stories that provide an intimate look at Navajo life and its struggle for balance with the contemporary world.

Setting: Navajo Indian Reservation, Kiethia Valley, at the foot of the Shonto Plateau.

Characters: Shonto, various members of the Navajo tribe, First Man and First Woman, Mother Earth, Father Sun, Medicine Man, Changing Woman, and other characters from the Navajo spiritual world and Navajo rituals.

Themes: All living things depend on each other for survival. The balance between cultures is fragile and must be maintained. Harmony with nature leads to harmony with self.

Vocabulary: Mammal, plateau, gorges, mesa, hogan, diaspora, junipers, rituals, sacred, canyon, organic.

Illustrations: One full-color, well-detailed painted illustration is displayed for each of the 20 writings. Painted in earth tones, these pictures feature hues of the desert.

Grade Level/Content Areas: Students in grades 3–8 who are studying Navajo culture or tribes, the geography of the Southwestern United States (especially Arizona), the comparison of cultures, or poetry are enlightened by these tales and paintings of the Navajo lifestyle.

Literary Web: This web reinforces the characteristics of poetry. Posted on chart paper, students may categorize the poems while rereading them or may choose to categorize the class favorites.

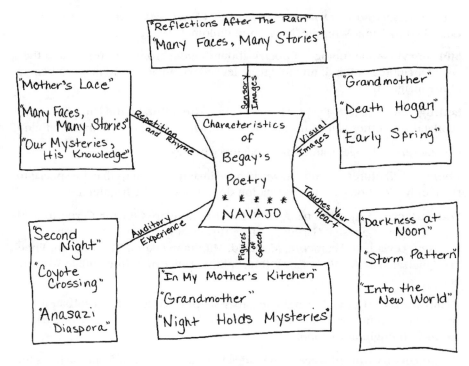

Figure 7.48 Literary web by Karen Wandell for *Navajo: Visions and Voices Across the Mesa* by Shonto Begay.

Carle, Eric. ***Dragons, Dragons and Other Creatures That Never Were.***
Compiled by Laura Whipple. New York: Philomel, 1991.

Summary: An anthology of poetry about dragons from cultures around the
world including cultural, mythological, legendary, ancient, and modern beings
of the imagination.

Setting: Asia, Africa, Egypt, Mexico, Japan, Great Britain, the United States,
Scotland, and other places around the world where imaginary beings are found.

Characters: Dragons and other imaginary beings.

Themes: Cultures around the world have imaginary beings that are special to
them only. Creations of the imagination do not have to be frightening.

Vocabulary: Amphisbaena, Anansi, Basilisk, Bunyop, Centaur, Cerberus, Chi-
mera, Dragon, Ganesha, Garuda, Griffin, Hippocamp, Hippograff, Kappa,
Kracken, Leviathan, Manticore, Mermaid, Minotaur, Okolo, Pan, Pegasus, Phoenix, Quetzalcoatl, Rainbow Crow, Roc, Sphinx, Unicorn, White Buffalo Woman,
Yeti.

Illustrations: Cut and torn tissue paper shapes that have been splashed,
splattered, and fingerpainted with bright acrylic colors appear on white backgrounds throughout the book.

Grade Level/Content Area: In grades K–6, this book can form the basis for
a unit on dragons or imaginary creatures from around the world. The school art
teacher can help students experiment with Carle's distinctive collage approach.
This work might then be the impetus for writing about whatever imaginary beings they create. Revision and rewriting for publication can produce finished
pieces for a bulletin board or class anthology similar to Carle's.

Sequential Organizer: When this type of organizer is created using pictures
from the story as well as key vocabulary, it can be used as a tool for retellings to
strengthen the oral language of English-as-a-second-language (ESL) students. It
might also serve as a visual from which story summaries can be written.

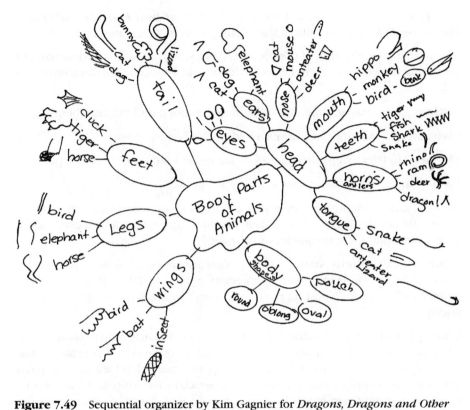

Figure 7.49 Sequential organizer by Kim Gagnier for *Dragons, Dragons and Other Creatures That Never Were* by Eric Carle.

━━ de Regniers, Beatrice Schenk. *A Week in the Life of Best Friends and Other Poems on Friendship.* (Illus., Nancy Doyle). New York: Atheneum, 1986.

Summary: A collection of poems describing some of the joys and sorrows of friendship between children, between parent and child, and between child and pet.

Setting: Everyday settings, including home, school, and neighborhood.

Characters: All kinds of parents, children, and a few pets.

Theme: In friendships there are both happy and sad times between people.

Vocabulary: No difficult words.

Illustrations: Pictures are delicately colored line drawings that complement the simple poetry selections. Half-page drawings appear on almost every page with poems filling the remainder of the page.

Grade Level/Content Area: These poems are appropriate for students in grades 2–5 for lessons in listening appreciation, for a health unit on self-understanding, or for a unit on poetry as a genre of literature or on writing poetry.

Concept Web: After reading the poems to students, lead a discussion about what makes friendships special relationships. Ask students to define the similarities and differences between friend and acquaintance, friend and enemy. Then have students supply words that describe a special friendship they have with someone and put these words in the arrows of a web similar to the one shown here. Students can then use these words to write their own poems.

   Encourage students to illustrate their original poems. The simple nature of the pictures in this book should promote the feeling that students can draw their own accompanying pictures. Some students in your class might want to write and illustrate their own book of poems.

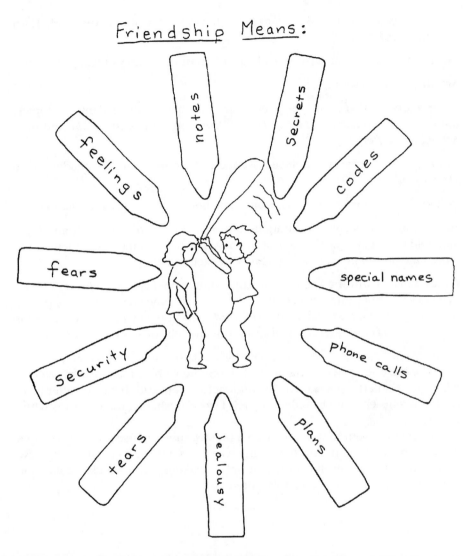

Figure 7.50 Concept web for *A Week in the Life of Best Friends and Other Poems on Friendship* by Beatrice Schenk de Regniers.

Hopkins, Lee Bennett. ***More Surprises.*** (Illus., Megan Lloyd). New York: Harper & Row, 1987.

Summary: This is an easy-to-read collection of the poetry of many authors.

Setting: Varied settings.

Characters: Subjects for the poems vary, but they are divided into six topics: *Some People, Body Parts, Living Things, How Funny, Hot and Cold,* and *In School and After.*

Theme: Themes vary, but the innocence and carefree nature of childhood are clearly evident.

Vocabulary: Inventing, somersault, stalk, lingers, wren, luscious, dapples.

Illustrations: Detailed illustrations appear in a range of colors—from bright and bold to soft and pastel—to suit the mood or topic of the poem they accompany. One or two illustrations appear with each poem.

Grade Level/Content Area: This collection of poems is suitable for children in grades K–3 and can be read to them for pure listening enjoyment. The poetry on *Living Things, Body Parts,* and *Hot and Cold* fit well with science units for these grades. These poems can also serve as models for student-created poetry.

Topic Web: Introduce the poems in this book to children with a simple topic web like the one shown in Figure 7.51. From the web, children can predict what they think the poems will be about before you read them, and after hearing the poems children can identify their favorites, sharing their reasons with the class.

If children want to write their own poems, they can use the topics shown in the web and write poems that fit in these areas. Or children can create new topics and write poems for these new areas, making their own class collection of poetry using Hopkins' topics as a model.

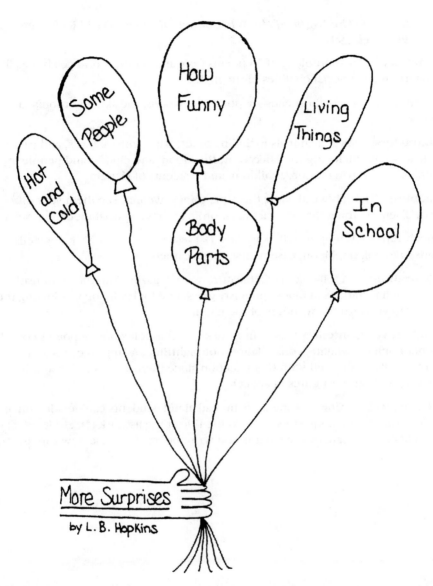

Figure 7.51 Topic web by Jill Zavelick for *More Surprises* by Lee Bennett Hopkins.

Larrick, Nancy. *The Night of the Whippoorwill.* (Illus., David Ray). New York: Philomel, 1992.

Summary: This anthology of 34 poems from all over the world celebrates the mysterious and special qualities of the night.

Setting: Various night scenes—a pond, the woods, the sky, and rooms indoors.

Characters: Several animals including foxes, bats, wolves, birds, and cats; spacial scenes including the Milky Way, the moon, and clouds; and people including poet David McCord, children, and residents of Harlem.

Themes: Though we all view the same things, we may see them very differently. Even the thing that appears most ordinary has a special hidden mystery.

Vocabulary: Whippoorwill, katydids, Harvest Moon, Milky Way, constellations, tranquil, doubloon, casements, barge, cathedrals.

Illustrations: A full-color jacket featuring a boy gazing into the night leads to full-color illustrations in blues and misty grays, one for each poem, allowing the reader to visualize the wonders of the night.

Grade Level/Content Areas: In grades 3–6, this collection of poems compliments a unit on wildlife, constellations, or nighttime. A language arts unit on poetry is also enhanced with this selection since there are several examples of imagery and various figures of speech.

Literary Web: After hearing a poem read aloud, students can decide which characteristic it demonstrates and add the title at the asterisk (*). Students may also choose to create new elements and write poems for these new topics.

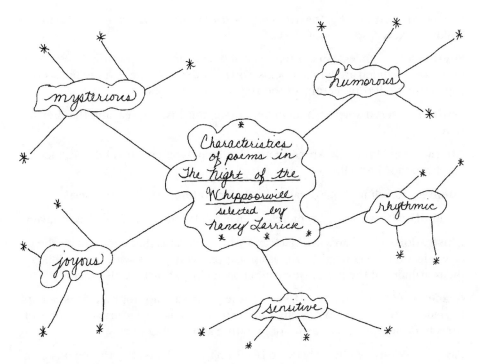

Figure 7.52   Literary web by Karen Wandell for *The Night of the Whippoorwill* by Nancy Larrick.

*Hughes, Langston. ***The Dream Keeper and Other Poems.*** (Illus., Brian Pinkney). New York: Knopf, 1994.

Summary: A collection of 66 powerful poems, many exploring the Black experience. Included are lyrical poems, songs, and blues. The text includes a two-page introduction/biography of the author and his works.

Setting: Everyday settings including home, the city, the sea, and the dream state.

Characters: Primarily African American men, women, and children, including the author himself.

Theme: Reach for your dreams! Settle for nothing less than the best!

Vocabulary: Barren, vast, merchant man, melancholy, strife, ebony, oblivion.

Illustrations: Pictures are black and white drawings that compliment the poetry selections. Half-page drawings appear on many pages with poems filling the remainder of the pages. Several full-page illustrations are also included.

Grade Level/Content Area Use: These poems are appropriate for students in grades 3–8 for units in African American history, language arts on figures of speech, or on poetry as a genre of literature and writing poetry.

Favorite Poems Web: This web is a listing of students' favorite poems compiled in the form of a Native American *dream catcher* which is a reference to Hughes' poem "Dream Keeper." After listening to each of the poems, students complete their own dream catchers with the titles or first lines of each of their favorite poems. This web could be used for future comparisons/contrasts between this and other poets and poems.

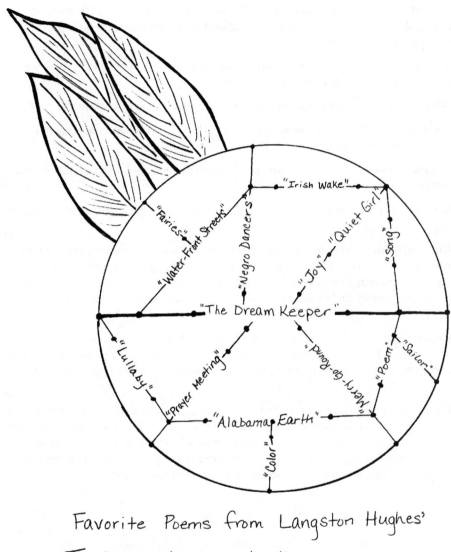

Favorite Poems from Langston Hughes'
The Dream Keeper and other poems.

Figure 7.53 Favorite poem web by Karen Wandell for *The Dream Keeper and Other Poems* by Langston Hughes.

Willard, Nancy. ***The Voyage of the Ludgate Hall: Travels with Robert Louis Stevenson.*** (Illus., Alice and Martin Provenson). San Diego: Harcourt Brace Jovanovich, 1987.

Summary: This is a poem based on the letters Robert Louis Stevenson wrote describing an adventurous ocean voyage.

Setting: On board a cargo steamer from London to New York in the 1800s.

Characters: Robert Louis Stevenson, his family, various animals (such as apes, baboons, monkeys, and eels), and a few passengers.

Theme: Even a difficult ocean crossing can be a delight and pleasure to the senses.

Vocabulary: Voyage, journey, squall, mutton, buttermilk, gabardine, confirming, hearty embrace, retractable.

Illustrations: Done in a primitive style, these flat, one-dimensional acrylic paintings effectively portray the people and buildings of a hundred years ago. These award-winning illustrations, the inclusion of part of an actual letter written by Stevenson on his voyage, and Willard's introduction confirm the authenticity of this lovely book.

Grade Level/Content Area: Suitable for students in grades 3–6 to promote appreciative listening or to learn about the characteristics of poetry. It also can enrich social studies units on types of transportation or the England and America of the 1800s.

Element Web: Use this web to reinforce the characteristics of poetry only after students have heard the story read orally at least twice. Then give students the web with the characteristics printed on each strand and have them supply examples of each characteristic from the text of the poem itself. This poem provides many fine examples of the characteristics of good poetry.

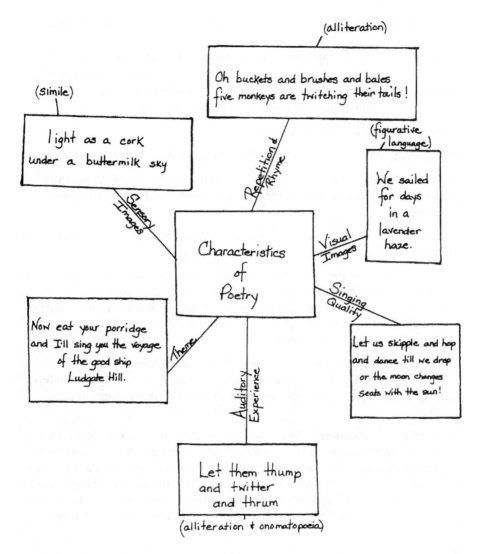

(alliteration)

Oh buckets and brushes and bales
five monkeys are twitching their tails!

(simile)

light as a cork
under a buttermilk sky

(figurative
language)

We sailed
for days
in a
lavender
haze.

Repetition &
Rhyme

Sensory
Images

Characteristics
of
Poetry

Visual
Images

Now eat your porridge
and I'll sing you the voyage
of the good ship
Ludgate Hill.

Theme

Singing
Quality

Let us skipple and hop
and dance till we drop
or the moon changes
seats with the sun!

Auditory
Experience

Let them thump
and twitter
and thrum

(alliteration & onomatopoeia)

Figure 7.54 Element web by Mary Johnson for *The Voyage of the Ludgate Hall: Travels with Robert Louis Stevenson* by Nancy Willard.

Information Books

Cherry, Lynne. ***The Great Kapok Tree.*** New York: Harcourt, 1990.

Summary: The animals and other creatures that live in a Brazilian rain forest whisper in a sleeping man's ear all the reasons he should not cut down a tree and finally convince him to drop his ax and leave the forest.

Setting: Present day rain forest in Brazil.

Characters: Man, snake, bee, monkeys, birds, and a native child.

Themes: Trees are necessary for the survival of all creatures. Destruction of the world's ecology can be avoided. The rainforest is a resource that needs protection.

Vocabulary: Emergents, canopy, shrub layer, understory, toucan, iguana, jaguar, three-toed sloth, macaw.

Illustrations: Vibrant, full-color, detailed, realistic pictures show life in each layer of the rainforest from the understory to the canopy. Around the border of each picture are some of the exotic animals of the forest and picture charts of the vertical layers of forest life. Maps inside the front and back covers show locations of the world's rain forests.

Grade Level/Content Area: In grades K–6, this book can be used to develop environmental awareness, geographical knowledge of the rain forest, understanding of endangered species, and awareness of the destruction of rain forests.

Hierarchical Organizer: Before or after reading this book, explain the various levels of life in a rainforest to your students as they are described in the preface. After this and following reading, create a web that includes the names of the layers of the forest. Then have your students reread the story and place each of the creatures as they appear in the story in the proper layer of the forest. This web can be used to initiate a discussion of the food chain and life cycles.

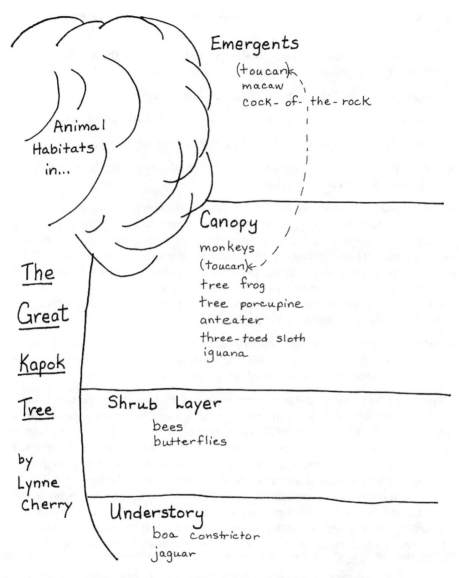

Figure 7.55 Hierarchical organizer by Deb Pease for *The Great Kapok Tree* by Lynne Cherry.

de Paola, Tomie. ***Charlie Needs a Cloak.*** Englewood Cliffs, NJ: Prentice-Hall, 1973.

Summary: A shepherd shears his sheep, cards and spins the wool, weaves and dyes the cloth, and sews a beautiful new red cloak.

Setting: The story takes place on Charlie's sheep ranch.

Characters: Charlie the shepherd, Charlie's sheep, and a small mouse.

Theme: Men and animals enjoy an interdependent relationship.

Vocabulary: Shear, card, spin, weave, sew, cloak (these words are listed in a mini-glossary at the end of the book).

Illustrations: Pictures are pencil drawings with muted colors, except the bright red of Charlie's cloak, which is the most important element in the story. A small mouse appears in every picture. Text is printed at the top of each page, and it documents the process Charlie uses to make a new cloak for himself. Pictures occupy the remainder of the page, and they depict a series of hilarious errors that take place in the process. One sheep in particular is not pleased with the way Charlie uses the wool and uses trickery that has comical results to try to keep Charlie from finishing his project.

Grade Level/Content Area: Appropriate for K–2 children, this book enriches a social studies unit on the interdependence of man and animals, a unit on textile manufacturing, or a lesson on sequence of events.

Sequence Map: Have children listen to this story, look at the pictures, and discuss and enjoy the process of making a cloak and Charlie's humorous problems. Then help children establish the sequence of factual events that resulted in a finished cloak, and transcribe the steps they identify. Discussion will result in a sequence map like the one in Figure 7.56. Or jumble the five steps in the process and help children rearrange them until they are in order.

Do not overlook the possibilities of exploring the humor in this book. Since the pictures tell a different story than the text does and since children enjoy finding these humorous differences, help them find the hilarious errors Charlie makes and transcribe them onto the map at the appropriate point in the cloak-making process.

The illustrations can also serve as the basis for composing a story from a different point of view. Children can orally tell or rewrite the story from the perspective of the sheep that used trickery on Charlie. This story lends itself to roleplaying as well as storytelling since children can invent their own dialogue between Charlie and his sheep.

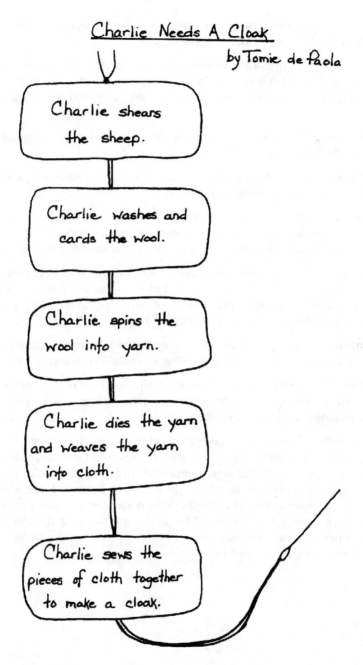

Figure 7.56 Sequence map by Lisa Milano for *Charlie Needs a Cloak* by Tomie de Paola.

George, Jean Craighead. *One Day in the Tropical Rainforest.* (Illus., Gary Allen). New York: Harper Collins, 1990.

Summary: The future of the Rainforest of the Macaw depends on a young Indian boy, Tepui, and a scientist as they search for a nameless butterfly. Written in log form, the story tells of their journey in the forest and their race against time.

Setting: The Rainforest of the Macaw in the state of Monagas, South America, on January 21 from 6:29 AM to 6:15 PM in present day.

Characters: Twpui, Dr. Juan Rivero, various unnamed scientists, and 20 "Chainsawyers" hired to destroy the forest.

Themes: Extinction is forever. The actions of one individual can save an entire species. The destruction of one culture affects the world. Conservation is the key to the future. Consider the consequences before you act on your ideas.

Vocabulary: Various scientists—ornithologist, mammalogist, botanist, herpetologist, lepidopterist; various animals and plants—macaw, potoo, kiskadee, margay, katydids, peccaries, sloth; canopy; emergents; understory; bracts; species; buttresses; bivouac; ominous; lanky; corollas.

Illustrations: Twelve full-page black and white illustrations accompany the text, and the book cover is a full-color illustration of Tepui and several animals.

Grade Level/Content Area: This book supports study of the rainforest, ecological destruction, ecological conservation, living things, water cycle, human ecology, or jungle ecology for students in grades 3–6.

Concept Web: This webbing activity develops personal response to the literature, the ability to analyze characters and themes, and new vocabulary. Begin with the three pie charts that depict important percentages graphically for students and put *Rainforest of the Macaw* at the core of a web. Discuss the pie charts and ask students to add a different component of the rainforest with supporting information for each strand. The web can be hung in the classroom and, as further reading and study occurs, more information can be added. Character webs can also be created by the class in a similar way.

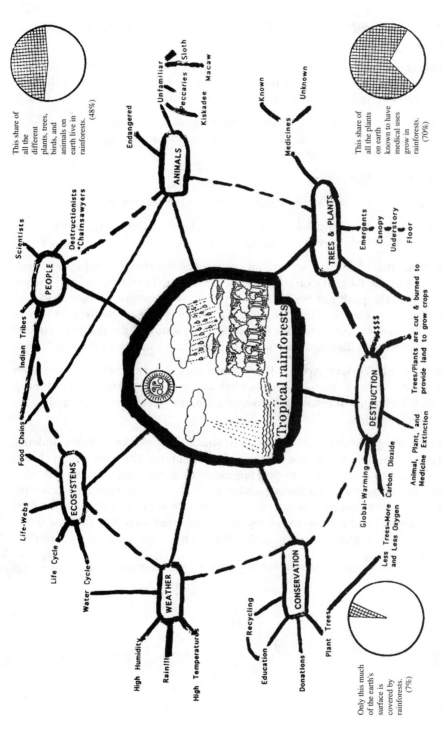

Figure 7.57 Concept web by Karen Wandell for *One Day in the Tropical Rainforest* by Jean Craighead George.

Lewis, Naomi. ***Puffin.*** (Illus., Deborah King). New York: Lothrop, Lee & Shepard, 1984.

Summary: This story traces the life of a young sea bird born on an island off the northern coast of Scotland. It discusses the bird's birth, care by mother and father, growth, independence, migration, and return to begin its own family.

Setting: The setting ranges from a north coastal Scottish island, across the Atlantic Ocean, to Newfoundland and Nova Scotia in Canada, and back again to where the puffin was born in Scotland.

Characters: The puffin.

Theme: The cycle of life for a sea bird ends where it begins.

Vocabulary: Fledgling, shallows, tide, prey, breakers, breeding, murk, skuas, secluded, boulders, burrows, nestling, oil slick.

Illustrations: Full-page watercolor pictures on the right side of every page supplement the narrative on the left side of the page to tell the story of the puffin's life. As the puffin grows and develops, so do his colors. Vibrant shades of blue and green capture the ocean, while pictures at sunset and the first light of morning show varying intensities of color. The picture of the puffin encountering the oil slick is dark and communicates the deadly nature of these accidents.

Grade Level/Content Area: This book is appropriate for children in grades 2 and 3 in a study of the life cycles of birds and animals or ecology in general. It fits well with units in grades 4–6 on migration, the oceans, ecology, and environmental hazards.

Factual Web: Before reading the story, solicit any prior knowledge students have about puffins by making a list of what they know. Then help them classify their facts into categories (physical appearances, food, home, and so on), and start a factual web that includes each category and the facts the students supplied. After students read or hear the story you (or they) can add information (both categories and facts) to the partially completed web. The finished web gives students a guide for retelling the story or for writing a report about the puffin.

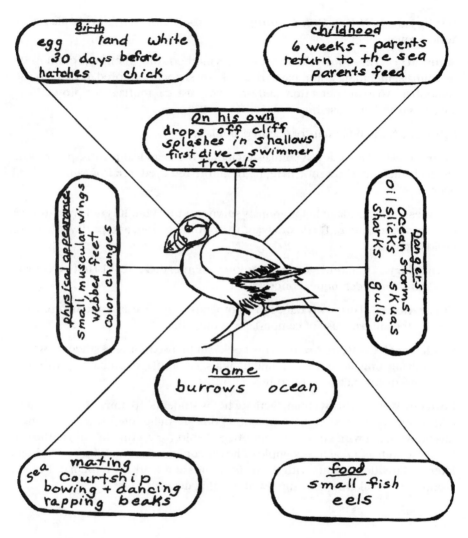

Figure 7.58 Factual web by Suzanne S. French for *Puffin* by Naomi Lewis.

Martin, James. *Hiding Out: Camouflage in the Wild.* (Illus., Art Wolfe). New York: Crown, 1993.

Summary: This book tells about various methods of camouflage employed by animals, including color, pattern, and body shape. Both predators, who use camouflage to avoid detection, and prey, who use camouflage for protection, are shown and discussed.

Setting: Natural habitats of featured animals.

Characters: Thirty-seven animals including the dead leaf mantis, polar bear, jewel chameleon, showshoe hare, night heron, red-eyed tree frog, and blacktail deer.

Themes: Camouflage helps animals survive in the wild. It is not wise to stick out like a sore thumb. Predators want to avoid detection, and prey want to avoid detection.

Vocabulary: Camouflage, predator, prey, mimic, disguise, disruptive coloration, carnivore, technique, concealment, habitat.

Illustrations: Forty-two full-color photographs of creatures and nature emphasize the animals' use of camouflage in the wild.

Grade Level/Content Area: This book can be used for K–3 students who are studying animals in their natural habitats, camouflage, predator/prey relationships, or the balance of nature.

Concept Web: This webbing activity helps students organize the ideas and information contained in this nonfiction book. To build interest after reading this book, begin with an actual camouflage T-shirt (or picture of one) at the center of the web as a real-life example of how people use camouflage and to build interest. Provide students with the main strands and work with them either as a group or in small groups to supply supporting details.

Figure 7.59 Concept web by Maria Moy for *Hiding Out: Camouflage in the Wild* by James Martin.

Nixon, Joan Lowery. *If You Were a Writer.* (Illus., Bruce Degen). New York: Macmillan, 1988.

Summary: In this story of a 9-year-old girl who wants to become a professional writer like her mother, the girl follows her mother's suggestions as she practices the craft. She thinks of words that make pictures and ways to describe actions. She tells silly stories about everyday situations, makes up suspenseful ones, and finally her mother gives her a pad and pencil to begin writing.

Setting: Present day home of a writer's family.

Characters: Melia, her mother, and Nikki and Veronica (younger sisters).

Themes: Creative writing comes from creative words and ideas. Children can be writers. Literacy is an important family value.

Vocabulary: Slithery, bristly, murmur, stagger, quiver, huddle, prowl, book jacket.

Illustrations: Illustrations support the creativity theme. There is no pattern to the size or arrangement of the pen, ink, and watercolor drawings or their borders that range from plain brown to leaves and berries or nothing. Some pictures cover either right or left pages and some cover only top or bottom halves of pages with print in blank spaces.

Two aspects of text stand out. When the setting changes in the story, the first letter of the text is large and green. When Melia thinks of words to use when writing, the words are italicized.

Grade Level/Content Area: In grades 2-5, this book can be used to support writing and vocabulary development or in units on careers, publishing, or creativity.

Concept Web: After reading the story, give the children a partially completed web that includes only the labeled circles. As you read the book a second time, pause at appropriate places to allow children to fill in Melia's ideas. Then they can use different colored pencils or pens to add their own ideas of what they could write about. In this way, their ideas are shown as distinctly different than Melia's. Then children can use this finished web to give direction to their own writing.

You might also talk about other, more positive titles for the story and have children rename it. They may come up with such titles as *You Are a Writer* or *A Family of Writers.*

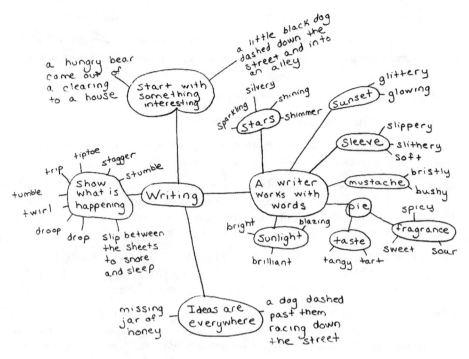

Figure 7.60 Concept web by Kelly Haight for *If You Were a Writer* by Joan Lowery Nixon.

Powzyk, Joyce. ***Wallaby Creek.*** New York: Lothrop, Lee & Shepard, 1985.

Summary: This is an informative and beautiful book about the animal wildlife that lives near a creek in Australia with in-depth information about many species.

Setting: Wallaby Creek in Australia in 1983.

Characters: The author and assorted wildlife.

Themes: When humans learn about wildlife, they will respect it. The animals that live near a creek form their own special community.

Illustrations: Watercolor paintings in realistic colors and text on each double page present a different animal native to Australia. Backgrounds are more impressionistic, thus calling attention to the animals that are the focus, and sometimes extend beyond page borders, making them seem three-dimensional.

Grade Level/Content Area: Students in grades K–6 who are studying ecosystems, animals, food chains, or Australia will enjoy this informative book. It could also be used in an art class that is studying watercolors.

Concept Web: Put a map of Australia on chart paper, and make it a class project to fill in the details using yarn for the lines and index cards for the information. Students can work in groups on animals of their choice, adding information to the web and reporting to the class on what they found.

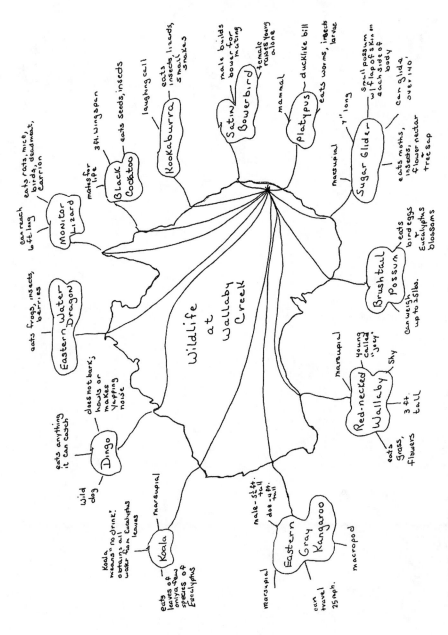

Figure 7.61 Concept web by Dianne Mannix for *Wallaby Creek* by Joyce Powzyk.

chapter 8

Children's Literature Review Part II: Annotated Bibliography and Teaching Ideas

These 148 annotations include both picture books and books for older students that are primarily text. Webbing can be used with these books as you integrate them with the content areas of science, social studies, mathematics, language arts, health, music, or art. They include Caldecott and Newbery Medal and Honor books, IRA Children's Choices books, titles chosen by the Children's Book Council as outstanding science and trade books, and other examples of quality literature for grades K-8. These annotations include examples of books about children with handicaps and various heritages, including African, Asian, European, Hispanic, and native American. Multicultural literature is noted with an asterisk (*).

Each annotation includes a bibliographic reference with a section called *Summary* and a section called *Grade Level/Content Area*. With the information provided, you can decide whether and how to use webs with these books to promote children's enjoyment and appreciation of a certain topic and/or teach, reinforce, or enrich certain ideas or information included in your curriculum.

The books are categorized by genre: folktale, fantasy, realistic fiction, historical fiction, biography, poetry, and information books. Within each genre, books are in alphabetical order according to the author's last name.

Folktales ═══

═══ *Bruchac, Joseph. **The First Strawberries; A Cherokee Story.** (Illus., Anna Vojtech). New York: Dial, 1993.

Summary: In this Cherokee folktale with luminous watercolor illustrations, the author retells the story of the creation of strawberries.

Grade Level/Content Area: Students in grades 3–6 studying Native Americans, folktales, *how and why* tales, or foods will enjoy this simply told story. It may provide impetus for students to write their own stories about how a fruit, a vegetable, or an everyday object came to be.

═══ *Clement, Claude. **The Painter and the Wild Swans.** (Illus., Frederick Clement). New York: Dale Books, 1986.

Summary: A famous painter in rural Japan of the past sees wild swans and must capture their beauty. His quest causes him to forfeit everything else, and in doing so, he learns the nature of true beauty and becomes a swan.

Grade Level/Content Area: In a K–5 art class, this book can be used to introduce a discussion of beauty. In social studies, it supports a unit on other cultures or a discussion of how death is viewed in other cultures.

═══ *Climo, Shirley. **The Korean Cinderella.** (Illus., Ruth Heller). New York: Harper Collins, 1993.

Summary: This retelling of the story of Pear Blossom, the stepdaughter chosen by the magistrate to be his wife, is the Korean version of the Cinderella tale. Illustrations inspired by patterns on Korean temples make this story come to life.

Grade Level/Content Area: Students in grades K–6 enjoy this story and can find similarities and differences with the traditional Cinderella story. It can accompany study of Korea or a comparative unit on folktales.

═══ *Goble, Paul. **The Lost Children.** New York: Bradbury, 1993.

Summary: A Native American Blackfoot myth that explains the origin of the Pleiades constellation and warns of the dangers of neglecting children. Goble documents his work with notes and endnotes that tell of the history of the myth, the Blackfoot nation, and their tepees. A bibliography of further reading about Native American traditions, myths, and legends is also included.

Grade Level/Content Area: This story can be used in grades K–9 in studies of Native American cultures or astronomy. In a cross-cultural study, the Blackfoot's explanation for the origin of the Pleiades can be compared with that of the ancient Greeks who also had an explanation.

Greene, Carol. *The Old Ladies Who Liked Cats.* (Illus., Loretta Krupinski). New York: Harper Collins, 1991.

Summary: When a group of old ladies is no longer allowed to let their cats out at night, the delicate balance of their island ecology is disturbed with disastrous results. Soft, full-color painted illustrations cover each page with print at the top and bottom of pages.

Grade Level/Content Area: Students in grades K–3 enjoy this folktale, which focuses on ecology, food chains, and animals' dependence on each other for survival. A social studies unit on community jobs or cooperation would also be enhanced by this tale that originated with Charles Darwin.

*Greene, Ellin. *The Legend of the Cranberry: A Paleo-Indian Tale.* (Illus., Brad Sneed). New York: Simon & Schuster, 1993.

Summary: This legend from the Delaware Indians is a story of mastodons, Stone Age hunters, and cranberries. It is a powerful tale about conflict and peace.

Grade Level/Content Area: Students in grades K–6 who are studying the history of the Northeast, Native Americans, conflict, or foods will enjoy this story with its strong accompanying illustrations.

Hamilton, Virginia. *Jaguarundi.* (Illus., Floyd Cooper). New York: Scholastic, 1995.

Summary: In this environmental tale, two animals of the rainforest, Rundi Jaguarundi and Coati Coatimundi, leave their friends (16 additional animals rarely seen by humans) in search of a new home because their rainforest is being destroyed by encroaching civilization.

Grade Level/Content Area: Students in grades 1–7 who are studying the environment, destruction of the rainforest, or animal migration will enjoy this environmental story that is also an information book. It includes a visual glossary with a picture of each animal in the book and numerous facts about them.

*Hamilton, Virginia. *The People Could Fly: American Black Folktales.* (Illus., Leo and Diane Dillon). New York: Knopf, 1987.

Summary: This collection of 24 stories and 40 illustrations represents the main body of black folklore. There are trickster tales, in which Bruh Rabbit outwits stronger animals, frightening devil tales, tales full of riddles and humor, and moving tales of freedom. It is written so that both readers and storytellers can capture the rhythms of the language.

Grade Level/Content Area: In grades 1–6, this book fits social studies units on folklore or African American heritage. It provides a variety of tales that might be read and discussed during Black History Month or to complement a study of the Civil War, slavery, or storytelling.

*Krensky, Stephen. ***Children of the Earth and Sky; Five Stories About Native American Children.*** (Illus., James Watling). New York: Scholastic, 1991.

Summary: This book includes five stories about Native American children who began helping their families at early ages. Stories from the Hopi, Comanche, Mohican, Navajo, and Mandan tribes relate these experiences. A glossary defines the tribes and names of their respective homes, and a map shows where the tribes lived on the North American continent.

Grade Level/Content Area: Students in grades 2–4 who are studying Native Americans of the past and their families and communities or Indian cultures will enjoy hearing these five informative and interesting stories about the children of these tribes.

*Martin, Rafe. ***The Boy Who Lived with the Seals.*** (Illus., David Shannon). New York: Putnam's, 1993.

Summary: A boy disappears one day while playing by the Great River. His parents do not give up hope although his people think he is lost forever. One day many years later he is seen swimming with seals. He returns to his tribe but finds it strangely changed and so leaves for good. This Chinook Indian legend is accompanied by luminous acrylic paintings in rich earth hues.

Grade Level/Content Area: Used in grades 3–6, the story fits well in units on North American Indian legends, the Chinook tribe, or ecology. This classic story from the Columbia River area of the Pacific Northwest is about the sacredness of life and carries the message that we cannot take endlessly from nature but that we must return its gifts to maintain harmony.

*Morgan, William (Ed.). ***Navajo Coyote Tales.*** Santa Fe: Ancient City Press, 1988.

Summary: This collection of six tales follows the adventures of Coyote as he encounters various animals including Rabbit, Fawn, Crow, Snake, Skunk, and Horned Toad. These myths and legends, collected directly from the Navajo, are accompanied by several black and white sketches of the featured animals.

Grade Level/Content Area: Young students in grades K–3 enjoy these tales for entertainment or instruction. Written in storytelling format, these legends enhance social studies units on the Navajo culture, interrelationships, or morals. Language arts units on storytelling, dialogue, or word selection are also enriched by this book.

═══ *Polacco, Patricia. ***Rechenka's Eggs.*** New York: Philomel, 1988.

Summary: Babushka is making colored eggs for the Easter Festival in Moskva. She finds an injured goose and nurses it back to health only to have it break all her eggs. The next day Rechenka, the goose, lays a decorated egg and continues to do so until there are 13 eggs for Babushka. When the goose leaves for the wild, it lays one exquisitely decorated egg, which hatches into a gosling that stays with Babushka forever.

Grade Level/Content Area: This book, set in Eastern Europe or Russia of the past, can be used in grades K–3 where traditions in other cultures are being studied in social studies.

═══ *Romanova, Natalia. ***Once There Was a Tree.*** (Illus., Gennady Spirin). New York: Dial, 1985.

Summary: A tale, originally published in the Soviet Union, about the life of a tree and the food chain it supports. Delicate, detailed, and earth-toned, these distinctive illustrations show lovely landscapes, large animals, tiny insects, and the trees that shelter them. The story contains a message about man's responsibility to trees and the earth.

Grade Level/Content Area: For students in grades 2–6, this story carries the message that we must respect and protect trees because, like the earth, they are home to many insects and animals as well as being very important to man. In study of ecology, the environment, trees, animals, insects, or Russian tales, this story provides an example of literature that has won wide acclaim for both its lovely artwork and its powerful message.

═══ Schwartz, Alvin. ***Scary Stories to Tell in the Dark.*** (Illus., Stephen Gammell). New York: Harper & Row, 1986.

Summary: This is a collection of U.S. folklore first told by the pioneers and now retold by the author. It includes tales of horror about ghosts, skeletons, witches, "jump" stories, scary songs, and modern-day tales of fright that bring "shivers of pleasure." Schwartz provides notes and sources to validate and explain the origin of his tales.

Grade Level/Content Area: This collection enriches a social studies unit in grades 3-9 on western settlement or a unit on American folklore and storytelling.

Scieszka, Jon. ***The Frog Prince Continued.*** (Illus., Steve Johnson). New York: Viking, 1991.

Summary: This story, written from the perspective of the Prince, is an extension of "The Frog Prince" which finds the Prince and Princess living *not so happily ever after.* The Prince becomes bored with castle life, leaves, and has misadventures with three witches and a fairy godmother that lead him to realize his love for the Princess.

Grade Level/Content Area: This book is most appropriate for students in grades 3–9 since younger students often miss the humor, perhaps because they are not familiar with the original story or are conditioned to accept the *happily ever after* we have learned to expect in such tales. It can be used as a model for students' own writing. They can be encouraged to read fairy tales and continue past the author's *the end* with their own versions of how life might occur. Scieszka's disregard of boundaries between tales is a good model of creativity in thinking and writing and encourages interesting student-authored stories.

Scieszka, Jon and Lane Smith. ***The Stinky Cheese Man and other Fairly Stupid Tales.*** New York: Scholastic, 1992.

Summary: This is a collection of eight satirical remakes of such original fairy tales as Chicken Licken, Jack and the Beanstalk, The Ugly Duckling, Cinderella, and others. Every other page features a full-color humorous illustration.

Grade Level/Content Area: Students in grades 3–6 are amused by these outrageous versions of well-known tales. Language arts units on parts of a book, descriptive word choices, parts of a story, point of view, and figures of speech (including satire) are enriched by this book, which supports a process approach to writing.

Wilsdorf, Anne. ***Princess.*** New York: Greenwillow, 1993.

Summary: A modern version of "The Princess and the Pea," this is the story of Prince Leopold's quest to find a genuine princess. Set in medieval times, this story ends with a faulty assumption made by Leopold's mother and his marriage to a shepherd's daughter named Princess.

Grade Level/Content Area: In grades preK–6, this fairy tale with a contemporary twist teaches students that gender and social class do not always determine a person's worth. It might be used in comparison with the original or in a unit on fairy tales. Older students can use it as a model for rewriting other traditional fairy tales in more equitable ways. It is a good book for teaching structural analysis as a way of determining meaning from words by using the names of the evil monsters in the story.

*Siberell, Anne. ***Whale in the Sky.*** New York: Dutton, 1982.

Summary: This Northwest Indian tale, the retelling of an authentic legend, is illustrated with woodcuts and tells the story of totem-pole carvings. Thunderbird (a golden eagle), Whale, Frog, Raven, and Salmon are the characters in this tale about why whales live in the ocean and not in rivers.

Grade Level/Content Area: Children in grades 1–3 studying animals, the Northwest Indians, legends, or folktales enjoy this simple tale of the weak and strong.

*Winter, Jeanette. ***Follow the Drinking Gourd.*** New York: Knopf, 1988.

Summary: Based on a folk song of the same name, the story tells about an old sailor who traveled to the plantations teaching the slaves the song that contained a secret message about how to escape to freedom in Canada by following the Big Dipper, which points north. It describes the journey of a brave group of runaway slaves who listened to the song and made their escape.

Grade Level/Content Area: Students in grades 4–7 studying slavery and the Underground Railroad in social studies enjoy this story, which can be enriched with the actual song and music.

*Wolkstein, Diane. ***The Banza: A Haitian Story.*** (Illus., Marc Brown). New York: Dial, 1981.

Summary: Tiger and Goat become friends, and Tiger gives timid Goat a *banza*—or banjo—for her protection. When Goat finds herself up against 10 hungry tigers, she plays a ferocious song that frightens the tigers away. Textured drawings are done in bright, Caribbean colors.

Grade Level/Content Area: This book can be used with children in grades 2–3 who are learning about other cultures. The flora, fauna, and symbols of Haiti and the Caribbean are found in this book.

Fantasy ═══

Capucilli, Alyssa. ***Inside A Barn in the Country.*** (Illus., Ted Arnold). New York: Scholastic, 1995.

Summary: In this rhyming tale that begins with a quiet night in the country, first a mouse squeaks, then one by one, all the other barn animals speak, and finally the farmer wakes up and makes a racket. The story follows the format of "The House That Jack Built" and contains rebus picture words that encourage reading.

Grade Level/Content Area: Students in grades PreK–2 will enjoy this rebus read-along story that supports study of the farm, animals, or sounds animals make.

Carle, Eric. ***The Very Quiet Cricket.*** New York: Philomel, 1990.

Summary: In this multisensory book, a young male cricket who wants to rub his wings together and make a sound, as many other insects do, finally achieves his wish. Bold, colorful pictures show the creatures the quiet cricket meets before he meets a female cricket and learns to chirp; locust, praying mantis, worm, spittlebug, cicada, bumblebee, dragonfly, mosquitoes, and luna moth.

Grade Level/Content Area: The repetitive text and cricket's chirp heard as the last page of the book is turned make this an excellent interactive story for emergent readers. This book would fit well in units on insects or sounds or in a study of Carle's works in their entirety.

Conly, Jane Leslie. ***R-T, Margaret, and the Rats of NIMH.*** (Illus., Leonard Lubin). New York: Harper & Row, 1990.

Summary: This is a continuation of the adventures of the superintelligent rats who escaped from the National Institute of Mental Health (NIMH) and established their own community of Thorn Valley. Two children who are lost in the woods; R-T who cannot speak but builds a friendship anyway, and Margaret who learns about hard work for the first time in her life, become companions of Racso, Christopher, Isabella, and other members of the rat community until they must return home.

Grade Level/Content Area: This book is a good read-aloud for students in grades 3–6 because of its fast-paced action. Its themes of survival, self-sufficiency, cooperation, and environmental awareness make it appropriate for units on any of these topics as well. It is the third in the series of *Mrs. Frisby and the Rats of NIMH,* written by Robert O'Brien, and *Racso and the Rats of NIMH,* written by Jane Conly, O'Brien's daughter.

Duke, Kate. *Aunt Isabel Tells a Good One.* New York: Dutton, 1992.

Summary: In this fairytale, a mouse named Penelope and her Aunt Isabel make up an exciting bedtime story about the adventures of Prince Augustus and Lady Nell.

Grade Level/Content Area: In grades K-3, this fantasy is enjoyed for its adventurous storyline as well as for its graphically detailed illustrations. The pictures, which cover most of each page, are done in soft watercolors and, in addition, feature a small pertinent item in the corner of each page next to the large illustration. This story enhances any language arts/reading unit on storytelling, writing styles, parts of a story, sequence of events, or figures of speech.

Fleischman, Sid. *The Whipping Boy.* (Illus., Peter Sis). New York: Greenwillow, 1987.

Summary: In a kingdom of the past where it is forbidden to spank the heir to the throne, an orphan named Jemmy is made to serve as the whipping boy of "Prince Brat." Jemmy and the Prince run away together and the Prince learns about friendship and caring.

Grade Level/Content Area: For students in grades 3-6, this book is enjoyable as a coming-of-age story and for the adventures it describes. It would be appropriate in a unit on friendship, responsibility, or fantasy.

Lobel, Arnold. *Frog and Toad Are Friends.* New York: Scholastic, 1970.

Summary: Five funny stories titled: "Spring," "The Story," "A Lost Button," "A Swim," and "The Letter," are included in this book about a special friendship between two gentle creatures. This is one of a series of books by Lobel about these two friends.

Grade Level/Content Area: In grades K-2, these stories support thematic units on friendship, animals, or wetlands. Lobel's delightful stories can be used as models for students' own writing as well.

Lowry, Lois. *The Giver.* Boston, Houghton Mifflin, 1993.

Summary: In this "haunting novel," Jonas is given his lifetime assignment at the Ceremony of Twelve, which is to become the receiver of memories shared by only one other in his community. In this role he discovers the terrible truth about the society in which he lives and makes a decision that will change his life.

Grade Level/Content Area: This book is a frightening description of a futuristic society that could possibly exist one day if people are denied personal freedoms. It is a provocative story that might be read as an adjunct to a study of democracy or fantasy.

Sandford, John. *The Gravity Company.* Nashville: Abingdon Press, 1988.

Summary: This is a story about how the automatic switch at the Gravity Company is accidentally turned off and everything in town becomes weightless until Mortimer realizes what is happening and turns the gravity back on slowly.

Grade Level/Content Area: Students in grades 1–3 studying the force of gravity or weightlessness in space enjoy this story. It generates creative discussion and can be a model for storytelling or story writing.

Van Allsburg, Chris. *Ben's Dream.* Boston: Houghton Mifflin, 1982.

Summary: On a rainy day, Ben falls asleep while studying for a geography test and has a dream. He and his house are adrift on a round-the-world course in which he gets a unique view of the great monuments of the world that were in his geography textbook.

Grade Level/Content Area: Students in grades 3–8 will be challenged to identify the 10 world landmarks drawn in black and white by Van Allsburg that show these monuments from different perspectives. The book supports units on world geography, architecture, landmarks, dreams, or floods. List the names of the ten monuments after the book is read, and have students match names with pictures.

Realistic Fiction

*Ackerman, Karen. *Song and Dance Man.* (Illus., Stephen Gammell). New York: Knopf, 1988.

Summary: Three children go to visit their grandpa who takes them on a nostalgic visit to the attic where he finds his old banjo and puts on a song and dance show from his vaudeville days. Bright colored illustrations communicate the gaudy glamor of the vaudeville stage.

Grade Level/Content Area: In K–3 social studies, this book fits a unit on the family. Respect for what our elders have experienced and have to offer is also portrayed, as well as some of the history of drama in the United States.

Blume, Judy. *Tiger Eyes.* Scarsdale, NY: Bradbury, 1985.

Summary: When her father is killed, a fifteen-year-old girl named Davey, her mother, and younger brother move from Atlantic City to New Mexico to stay with relatives. This is the story of how each of them progresses through the grieving process, and how Davey matures as well.

Grade Level/Content Area: For students in grades 8–12, this book provides background for a social studies unit on nuclear war and disarmament since Davey gets herself involved in this issue.

— Cleary, Beverly. ***Dear Mr. Henshaw.*** (Illus., Paul O. Zelinsky). New York: Dell, 1983.

Summary: In this Newbery Medal book, sixth-grader Leigh Botts moves to a new school and experiences the separation and divorce of his parents. The text is a series of letters he writes to his favorite author and journal entries in which his life is humorously described.

Grade Level/Content Area: This book reinforces journal and letter writing in language arts and shows how a young boy deals with problems and makes friends in a new community.

— *Clifton, Lucille. ***Everett Anderson's Goodbye.*** (Illus., Ann Grifalconi). New York: Holt, Rinehart & Winston, 1983.

Summary: A young black boy has a difficult time coming to terms with his grief after his father dies. The story takes him through the grieving process, from denial, anger, bargaining, and depression to acceptance. It is written as rhymed poetry that expresses the boy's emotions and his mother's quiet support.

Grade Level/Content Area: In grades K–3, this story supports a unit on the family or death and dying.

— Drescher, Joan. ***My Mother's Getting Married.*** New York: Dial, 1986.

Summary: This is the story of Katy's reservations and uncertainty about her mother's remarriage and her acceptance of her new stepfather, who indeed does not take all her mother's love.

Grade Level/Content Area: Children in grades K–1 learning about different types of families in social studies enjoy this story of a successful blended family.

— *Filipovic, Zlata. ***Zlata's Diary: A Child's Life in Sarajevo.*** New York: Viking, 1994.

Summary: This is the personal account of an eleven-year-old girl who keeps a diary for two years in Sarajevo before coming to the United States. She calls her diary "Mimmy," writes letters detailing the horrors of life in this war-torn city, and includes actual colored photographs of her life.

Grade Level/Content Area: Students in grades 6–12 who are studying recent changes in Eastern Europe or immigration will learn about war and courage in this personal account of two troubled years in a young girl's life.

Girard, Linda. *At Daddy's on Saturdays.* (Illus., Judith Friedman). Niles, IL: Albert Whitman, 1987.

Summary: A young girl named Katie learns to deal with the anger, concern, and sadness surrounding her parents' divorce. She discovers that she still has a close relationship with her father.

Grade Level/Content Area: This book fits a social studies unit in grades PreK–3 on the family.

*Greenfield, Eloise. *William and the Good Old Days.* (Illus., Jan Spivey Gilchrist). New York: Harper Collins, 1993.

Summary: This is the story of how his grandmother's stroke changes a little boy named William, his family, and the neighborhood. At first, confused and uncertain, William continues to show his love for his grandmother, who is blind and in a wheelchair, by visiting and caring for her every day.

Grade Level/Content Area: Children in grades K–3 will learn about illness, old age, and the love of family in this book about a black boy and his grandmother's illness. In a unit on grandparents or the family this book presents a sensitive portrayal of a strong woman who has a new place in her community after a stroke.

*Hamilton, Virginia. *Plain City.* New York: Scholastic, 1992.

Summary: A twelve-year-old girl searches for the truth about her own past and her missing father in this story of unconditional love, family loyalty, and compassion.

Grade Level/Content Area: Students in grades 5–8 who are studying family history or genealogy will be touched by this story of one girl's inquiry into her own family's past.

*Hesse, Karen. *Lester's Dog.* (Illus., Nancy Carpenter). Boston: Little Brown, 1993.

Summary: A boy with a hearing impairment and his friend conquer their fear of an intimidating dog. At the same time they save a kitten and give it to a lonely neighbor.

Grade level/Content Area: Students in grades 3–6 who are studying diversity, social responsibility, or friendship will enjoy this sensitive story that elicits feelings related to people caring about one another.

*Hoffman, Mary. *Amazing Grace.* (Caroline Binch, Illus.). New York: Scholastic, 1991.

Summary: Realistic full-color drawings show Grace, a young Black girl, taking parts of main characters and acting out stories she has heard. When a classmate tells her she cannot be Peter Pan in her class play, her Trinidadian grandmother takes her to see "Romeo and Juliet." Grace learns how to do ballet, wins the part, and finds she can do anything she puts her mind to.

Grade Level/Content Area: In grades 1–2, this story supports a study of careers, gender identity, or creative dramatics. Grace's grandmother is from Trinidad and lives with her daughter and granddaughter in a city, so the story has other possibilities for connecting to stories with similar settings or families that are nontraditional as well.

Klass, David. *California Blue.* New York: Scholastic, 1994.

Summary: After discovering a previously unknown species of butterfly, seventeen-year-old John struggles with his beliefs about the environment and his feelings for his dying father who is supported by a lumber company that endangers the fragile balance of forest life.

Grade Level/Content Area: Students in grades 6–9 who are studying California's environment, endangered species, or lumbering will find this story interesting and will be able to identify with the main character's journey toward self-realization as well.

*Lord, Bette Bao. *In the Year of the Boar and Jackie Robinson.* (Illus., Marc Simont). New York: Trumpet, 1987.

Summary: Set in Brooklyn in the 1950s, this episodic story tells about a Chinese immigrant, Bandit, and her family's immersion in a culture that is foreign to them. Baseball finally becomes Bandit's passion and helps her make the link between dragons and New York City.

Grade Level/Content Area: This book fits grades 3–4 social studies units on the nature of cities, immigration, Asiatic cultures, and the problems of being new and different.

*Mazer, Anne (Ed.). *America Street: A Multicultural Anthology of Stories.* New York: Persea Book, 1993.

Summary: This book is an anthology of short, high-interest stories written by U.S. authors from diverse racial and cultural backgrounds. Included are stories about childhood from Duane Big Eagle, Robert Cormier, Nicholasa Mohr, Lensey Namioka, and others.

Grade Level/Content Area: Children ages 10–14 enjoy and relate to these tales of childhood that enrich social studies units on multicultural beliefs and traditions and geographical information of featured countries. This anthology is an excellent resource for teaching about such moral issues as friendship, loyalty, honesty, respect, right versus wrong, and nondiscrimination.

=== McFarlane, Sheryl. *Waiting For the Whales.* (Illus., Ron Lightburn). New York: Philomel, 1993.

Summary: This story is about an old man's love for whales and his relationship with his granddaughter who learns his appreciation and continues the family traditions after his death.

Grade Level/Content Area: Students in grades K–3 who are studying whales, nature and life cycles, ocean life, or the elderly will enjoy this beautiful tale.

=== *Paulsen, Gary. *The Monument.* New York: Dell, 1991.

Summary: Thirteen-year-old Rocky, adopted daughter of Fred and Emma, learns about art, love, and life from Mick, an artist and Vietnam veteran. Mick is commissioned to help the people of Bolton, Kansas decide what kind of monument they will construct to commemorate the sons and husbands of their community who were killed in Vietnam.

Grade Level/Content Area: This book can be enjoyed by students in grades 7-12, either as good reading or for supporting material in a study of the Vietnam conflict or what makes art. Although Rocky's racial heritage is mixed and she has a physical handicap (her left leg is stiff from surgery to correct a congenital problem that resulted in a fused kneecap), both factors are minor to the story.

=== *Pearson, Susan. *Happy Birthday, Grampie.* (Illus., Ronald Himler). New York: Dial, 1987.

Summary: Martha gives her 89-year-old Swedish grandfather, who is blind and in a home for the aged, a special birthday gift. She makes him a card that he can read with his fingers—with raised letters, a doily, and a felt heart—to which he responds warmly.

Grade Level/Content Area: In grades 2–3 social studies, this book supports the study of cultural diversity and promotes understanding of the aged and blindness.

Peterson, Jeanne Whitehouse. *I Have a Sister, My Sister Is Deaf.* (Illus., Deborah Ray). New York: Harper & Row, 1977.

Summary: A sister shares positive experiences about her deaf sister and explains how deafness itself does not hurt but how her sister's feelings are hurt when people do not understand her disability.

Grade Level/Content Area Use: In PreK–2, this book increases understanding of the hearing impaired. It builds knowledge of finger spelling and lip reading and promotes an appreciation of how people with disabilities have many similarities to others.

*Pinkney, Gloria. *Back Home.* (Illus., Jerry Pinkney). New York: Dial, 1992.

Summary: Ernestine, an eight-year-old Black girl, returns to visit relatives on the North Carolina farm where she was born and her mama grew up. Ernestine is reunited with aunts, uncles, cousins, and grandparents in this gentle story of homecoming.

Grade Level/Content Area: In grades 1–3, this story supports study of farm life, the South, or families. Full-color pencil and watercolor drawings in hues of red, blue, yellow, and black show the farmlands around Lumberton, North Carolina.

*Rosenberg, Liz. *Monster Mama.* (Illus., Stephen Gammell). New York: Philomel, 1993.

Summary: In this story about the "unique and universal" mother–son relationship, Patrick Edward's mother terrorizes the neighborhood, is hairy and disfigured, and lives in a cave in the back of his house. But she is a fine mother who teaches him to use his powers of good, drives him to school on rainy days, and bakes cookies when his friends come over. In a confrontation with bullies, Patrick Henry is nonviolent until they malign his mother, and then he becomes a monster until his mother intervenes.

Grade Level/Content Area: Students in grades 1–5 can be urged to speculate about the underlying message in this story with its brilliant and almost abstract illustrations. The story fits well in a unit on the family or on differences among people. The mother is portrayed with a physical difference, yet it does not impact on her capacity for love, tenderness, or fierce motherly protection. Patrick Edward is a classic result of a child who has benefited as a result of his parent's difference, because it makes him independent, capable of taking care of himself, and strong in conviction and loyalty.

*Shreve, Susan. ***The Gift of the Girl Who Couldn't Hear.*** New York: Beech Tree (Morrow Junior Books), 1993.

Summary: The friendship of a talented young singer and a deaf girl is strengthened during the auditions for a junior high musical production.

Grade Level/Content Area: This book is appropriate for students in grades 6-9 involved in studying diversity, handicaps, or interpersonal relationships.

Vigna, Judith. ***Nobody Wants a Nuclear War.*** Niles, IL: Albert Whitman, 1986.

Summary: Two siblings who are worried about nuclear war set up their own shelter. When their mother discovers this, she discusses with them the things that people have done and are doing to make the world safe from nuclear weapons.

Grade Level/Content Area: For children in grades 1-3, this book supports a study of current issues and world peace in social studies.

Viorst, Judith. ***The Tenth Good Thing about Barney.*** (Illus., Eric Blegvad). New York: Macmillan, 1988.

Summary: When his cat Barney dies, a boy tries to think of the ten best things about his pet in an attempt to overcome his grief. His parents help him in gentle ways to accept the death.

Grade Level/Content Area: In grades 1-3, this book complements a social studies unit on the family or on death and dying.

*Whelen, Gloria. ***Goodbye, Vietnam.*** New York: Random House, 1993.

Summary: Mai and her family escape Vietnam hoping to find a better life in the United States. The story of their journey and arrival captures the pain and difficulty of immigration.

Grade Level/Content Area: Students in grades 4-6 who are studying immigration, journeys, or the Vietnam conflict will be touched by this vivid portrayal of an escape to freedom.

*Williams, Karen Lynn, ***Galimoto.*** (Illus., Catherine Stock). New York: Mulberry Books, 1990.

Summary: As he walks through his African village, Kondi, a young Malawei boy, from scrap heaps, shops, and friends finds all the materials he needs to make himself a *galimoto,* or car. In this contemporary tale, Kondi makes a special push toy that he creates from wires and shares with the other children at night in the moonlight.

Grade Level/Content Area: In grades 1–3, this story can be used to develop the theme that persistence and creativity can make dreams come true or that accomplishments often grow from small and inconspicuous beginnings. It is also appropriate in a study of contemporary Africa or, specifically, children or toys of other cultures. Use the story to motivate your students to unleash their own creativity to make similar cars or other types of toys once they see what Kondi has done.

═══ *Williams, Vera B. ***Cherries and Cherry Pits.*** New York: Greenwillow, 1986.

Summary: This is a story about Bidemmi, a young black girl, who tells and colorfully illustrates four stories, each of which contains a main character who leaves the subway carrying cherries home to eat and share with his or her loved ones. In the last story, she tells about herself and what she does with the pits left from her cherries. She plants and tends them until they grow and become trees loaded with fruit that she shares with her neighbors.

Grade Level/Content Area: Children in K–2 enjoy this story as an enrichment to a social studies unit on the family or urban communities or as a science unit on plants.

═══ Yolen, Jane. ***Owl Moon.*** (Illus., John Schoenherr). New York: Scholastic, 1987.

Summary: This Caldecott Medal book tells the story, in text and picture, of a father who takes his young child out into the woods on a still, cold night to look for owls. The special relationship between a father and a child, who is finally old enough for this long-awaited adventure, and a message of hope are found in this quiet story.

Grade Level/Content Area: This book supports grades 2–4 science units on the natural world, nature appreciation, or birds and social studies units on the family, self-identity, or rural life in winter time.

═══ Zolotow, Charlotte. ***William's Doll.*** (Illus., William Pene DuBois). New York: Harper & Row, 1972.

Summary: This is the story of a boy named William who wants a doll but is discouraged by his brother, the boy next door, and his father. His grandmother's realistic handling of the problem helps break old stereotypes and provides a sensible and caring solution.

Grade Level/Content Area: Children in grades 1–2 enjoy this book that complements social studies units on the family, becoming an individual, or changing roles of family members.

Historical Fiction ═══

═══ Conrad, Pam. *Pedro's Journal.* New York: Scholastic, 1991.

Summary: This is the story of Christopher Columbus told from the perspective of young Pedro, a cabin boy aboard the Santa Maria, as he keeps a journal of the trip. Sketches of ship life and sea animals and journal entries chronicle the danger and excitement of Columbus' first voyage to the New World.

Grade Level/Content Area: Students in grades 3–6 who are studying explorers or the discovery and colonization of America will enjoy this personal diary that Conrad bases on historical accounts of Columbus' life. In addition to learning much about the sea voyage itself and about the islands and inhabitants of the south seas, readers may be inspired to keep their own journals of actual or imaginary trips.

═══ Cooney, Barbara. *Only Opal.* New York: Philomel, 1994.

Summary: A lyrical adaptation of the writings of Opal Whitley, in which she describes her love of nature and life in an Oregon lumber camp at the turn of the century. Adopted by an Oregon family, this young girl found herself uprooted nineteen times as her family moved from one lumber camp to another.

Grade Level/Content Area: Children in grades 2–6 studying Oregon, frontier or pioneer life in a lumber camp, poetry, or journal writing will enjoy this adaptation of *Only Opal: The Diary of a Young Girl* by Jane Boulton which was first published in 1920.

═══ Herman, Charlotte. *Millie Cooper, 3B.* (Illus., Helen Cogancherry). New York: Puffin Books, 1986.

Summary: Set in 1946, Millie, a third-grader, wishes for a new Reynolds Rocket ballpoint pen so she can do well on spelling tests and write her own autobiography. In this humorous story, Millie seeks and discovers how different and special she really is from other third-graders.

Grade Level/Content Area: In units on writing or self-esteem, or just for the fun of it, this story is enjoyable for eight- and nine-year-olds. Millie and the setting have contemporary appeal, and her trials and ordeals are those experienced by most other third-graders.

═══ *Hesse, Karen. *Letters From Rifka.* New York: Holt, 1992.

Summary: In letters to her cousin, a young Jewish girl chronicles her family's flight from Russia in 1919 and her own experiences when she must be left in Belgium for a while when the others emigrate to America.

Grade Level/Content Area: Students in grades 6–12 studying World War I, the history of the Jewish people, or immigration will enjoy this vivid picture of immigrant courage, ingenuity, and perseverance.

Jackson, Louise A. *Grandpa Had a Windmill, Grandma Had a Churn.* (Illus., George Ancona). New York: Parents' Magazine Press, 1977.

Summary: The reader is taken back to the author's childhood home in the 1940s in rural Texas and memories of grandpa and grandma are recounted. Photographs accompany the text.

Grade Level/Content Area: In grades 2–4, this book can be used with children who are studying farm life or rural life in the South 50 years ago, or animals in science.

MacLachlan, Patricia. *Sarah, Plain and Tall.* New York: Harper & Row, 1985.

Summary: Anna and Caleb's father places a newspaper ad for a wife and mother and receives a letter from Sarah in Maine. Sarah brings her cat and comes for a month's visit to their prairie home, which is very much different from her home by the sea. This is a gentle story about love and the changes it brings to the lives of two lonely children and their father.

Grade Level/Content Area: This book is appropriate for children grades 3–6 and complements a study of family life in the colonies and pioneer settlement or a unit on death.

Marrin, Albert. *Cowboys, Indians, and Gunfighters: The Story of the Cattle Kingdom* New York: Atheneum, 1993.

Summary: This is a history of the Great Plains and of United States' cultural and ethnic diversity done in text, photographs, paintings, prints, and a map.

Grade Level/Content Area: Students in grades 4–12 studying the history of the midwestern plains states, grasslands, or U.S. diversity will enjoy this well-documented story.

*Nixon, Joan Lowery. *Land of Dreams.* New York: Bantam, 1994.

Summary: In this last of the Ellis Island trilogy, Kristin, a seventeen-year-old Swedish immigrant to the United States who endured the Atlantic crossing with Rebeka (Land of Hope) and Rose (Land of Promise), makes a new home on a farm in Big Lake, Minnesota. Kristin's struggles for gender equity and a *modern* life in a somewhat backward community make her an intriguing character.

Grade Level/Content Area: Students in grades 5–8 who are studying immigration or the Midwest in the early 1900s will enjoy this story built around a strong and appealing heroine.

═══ Paterson, Katherine. *Jacob Have I Loved.* New York: Crowell, 1984.

Summary: This is the story of twin 13-year-old girls growing up on a tiny Chesapeake island in the early 1940s. The story centers around the life of Louise, who befriends a mysterious sea captain, experiences a hurricane, becomes a waterman as she works with her father, and wishes for an education. She finally sets herself apart from her pampered sister, Caroline, and discovers what her values are.

Grade Level/Content Area: For students in grades 6–9, this book enriches a social studies unit on various cultures within the United States or on the eastern shore specifically.

═══ *Staples, Suzanne Fisher. *Haveli.* New York: Knopf, 1993.

Summary: In this story, Shabanu is nineteen, a member of a large household in Lahore, Pakistan, and the fourth of four wives married to Rahim, a Muslim feudal lord who is forty-two years older than she. The senior wives are jealous and make Shabanu's and her four-year-old daughter's lives so miserable that she must plan for their future after Rahim's death.

Grade Level/Content Area: Students in grades 6–8 who are studying Pakistan, the Muslim culture, or the changing role of women will enjoy this story, which is a sequel to *Shabanu: Daughter of the Wind,* the story of the coming of age of a young girl born into a poor nomadic tribe that tends a herd of camels, and lives in the desert of Punjab. In *Haveli,* a grown-up Shabanu has been married for six years to a Muslim and experiences life in a large and well-to-do family. Both books provide descriptions of disparate segments of Pakistani culture and show Shabanu as both loyal and rebellious in her search for safety and happiness for herself and her daughter.

═══ *Taylor, Theodore. *The Cay.* New York: Avon, 1969.

Summary: Just before World War II, eleven-year-old Phillip is on a ship bound from Curaçao, a Dutch island in the Caribbean, back to Virginia when the ship goes down. He finds himself blind from a head injury and shipwrecked on a barren island with a West Indian named Timothy. Taught by his mother not to befriend or trust blacks, Phillip struggles for survival, adjusts to his blindness, and comes to rely on and love the old man.

Grade Level/Content Area: This book fits a grade 5–9 social studies or science unit on the Caribbean and life in a temperate climate or a unit on racial and ethnic diversity or black history since it helps children appreciate human goodness and wisdom independent of race.

⸻ *Uchida, Yoshiko. **The Bracelet.** (Illus., Joanna Yardley). New York: Philomel, 1994.

Summary: During World War II, Emi, a U.S.-born Japanese girl, and her family are ordered to a relocation camp with other Japanese families. A friend gives Emi a gold bracelet, which is lost, and Emi learns that no one can take away what is in her heart even as her family prepares to move to another camp in the Utah desert.

Grade Level/Content Area: This picture book is appropriate for children in K–3 and can be used in a study of war, friendship, courageousness or hope. Yardley's illustrations open with shades of pinks, blues, and greens, but these colors darken to grays, browns, navy blue, and yellows to show the journey and the camp. At the end, bright colors evoke cheerfulness showing the reader that the empty gift box does not symbolize despair for Emi, rather it means hope and courage to her. Emi is also a character in Uchida's *Journey Home,* which could be read by or to older students. Some interesting cross-class discussion or study of this author are possible or both books can be used together in a study of our treatment of Japanese–Americans during World War II.

⸻ *Uchida, Yoshiko. **Journey Home.** (Illus., Charles Robinson). New York: Macmillan, 1978.

Summary: Yuki, a young Japanese girl, her mother, and father are released from a World War II concentration camp in the Utah desert and return to Berkeley, where they lived before the war. Discrimination fed by mistrust and misunderstandings, the critical support of family and loved ones in times of tragedy, and the importance of forgiveness are all themes in this story about the difficulties of life for the Japanese–Americans during and following the war.

Grace Level/Content Area: In grades 3–6, this book fits units on awareness and sensitivity about diversity and discrimination, the conflicts surrounding war or the history of the western region of the United States.

⸻ *Yep, Lawrence. **Hiroshima.** New York: Scholastic, 1995.

Summary: This story of Sachi, a young girl who survives, but is disfigured by an atomic bomb, is based on true-life accounts of survivors of the bombing of Hiroshima. It is a poignant tale of Sachi and Hiroshima, both trying to recover from the devastation of war, but healed by the courage to survive and rebuild.

Grade Level/Content Area: This book is appropriate for students in grade 4–8 who are studying World War II, Japan, or moral choices.

Ziefert, Harriet. *A New Coat for Anna.* New York: Knopf, 1986.

Summary: In this World War II story, probably set in England, Anna's mother decides she will trade the few valuables she has left for a winter coat for her growing daughter. She trades a gold watch, a lamp, a garnet necklace, and a teapot to a farmer, spinner, weaver, and tailor, who all help make Anna's coat. Based on a true story, this tale holds a simple lesson about love and patience, how clothing is made, and how hardship can give life to hope.

Grade Level/Content Area: In K–2 social studies, this book fits a study of how clothing is made, a European community of the past, the problems of wartime, or a mother's love for her daughter.

Biography

*Conner, Edwina. *Marie Curie.* (Illus., Richard Hook). New York: Bookwright, 1987.

Summary: This is the story of a famous woman scientist—her childhood in Poland; her determination to finish college in France; her marriage to another famous scientist, Pierre Curie; her discovery of radium; her appointment as the first woman professor of physics; her receipt of the Nobel Prize twice; her determination to be a good mother; her efforts to get X-ray equipment to soldiers in World War I; the slow deterioration of her health due to exposure to radium; and finally her death in 1934.

Grade Level/Content Area: Students in grades 4–6 studying the scientific method, radiation, or influential women in history in social studies enjoy this book about the power of knowledge, determination, and dedication.

Freedman, Russell. *Eleanor Roosevelt: A Life of Discovery.* New York: Clarion, 1993.

Summary: This biography shows Eleanor Roosevelt as an active, intelligent, warm, loyal person. Photographs document her life as a family person, the wife of the President, a working First Lady, and a world-famous leader.

Grade Level/Content Area: Students in grades 4–12 will enjoy this personal glimpse into the life of a woman who was perhaps ahead of her time. The book supports studies of women, the Presidency, or U.S. history at the time she was active.

*Greene, Carol. *Elie Wiesel: Messenger from the Holocaust.* Chicago: Children's Press, 1987.

Summary: This book is about Elie Wiesel, who survived the Holocaust and dedicated his life to speaking and writing about it. He was the winner of the 1986 Nobel Peace Prize.

Grade Level/Content Area: For students in grades 4–8, this book supports a social studies unit on Europe during World War II or on the creation of the state of Israel.

═══ *Greene, Carol. **Mother Teresa: Friend of the Friendless.** Chicago: Children's Press, 1983.

Summary: This is the story of Mother Teresa, the Catholic nun whose work with the poor in India, in response to her understanding of God's will, made her famous.

Grade Level/Content Area: This book fits grades 3–5 social studies units on careers, important women in history, world hunger, Nobel Prize winners, and racial acceptance.

═══ *Hopkinson, Deborah. **Sweet Clara and the Freedom Quilt.** (Illus., James Ransome) New York: Knopf, 1993.

Summary: This book is based on a true story of a young slave who created a map of the route to the north by stitching it as a pattern in a quilt. It is illustrated in vibrant colors by a slave who is a descendent of the slaves from the plantation on which the story is based.

Grade Level/Content Area: Students in grades K-6 who are studying slavery, southern history, or quilting will enjoy this picture book.

═══ Lasker, David. **The Boy Who Loved Music.** (Illus., Joe Lasker). New York: Viking, 1979.

Summary: This is the story of Joseph Haydn's time as music director at the summer palace of Prince Esterhazy in eighteenth-century Austria, and of a young boy named Karl who was a horn player in the Prince's orchestra. When the Prince stayed at his summer palace far into the fall and did not seem interested in returning to Vienna where his musicians longed to be, Haydn composed the *Farewell* symphony with a surprise ending that persuaded the Prince to return with his court.

Grade Level/Content Area: In grades 2–4, this book enriches a music appreciation unit, a study of men in the arts, or provides social studies background for a study of the history of Europe.

═══ Lauber, Patricia. **Lost Star: The Story of Amelia Earhart.** New York: Scholastic, 1988.

Summary: This is the story of one of America's first female fliers, who had a singular vision about herself and the airplane. Black and white photographs accompany this story of Amelia Earhart's life from the time she was 7 years old and jumping fences in Kansas until her death at age 40.

Grade Level/Content Area: In grades 3–7, this book supports a social studies unit on transportation or aviation, World War I, careers, or women as explorers and leaders.

Meltzer, Milton. ***Betty Friedan: A Voice for Women's Rights.*** (Illus., Stephen Marchesi). New York: Viking Penguin, 1985.

Summary: This is the story of Betty Friedan's life, from her birth in 1921 to the present. It documents her desire to do something with her life and the thinking that resulted in her most famous book *The Feminine Mystique* and the establishment of the National Organization for Women.

Grade Level/Content Area: In grades 3–7 social studies, this book fits a unit on the history of women and the women's rights movement. The book provides young girls with a strong role model, and without glossing over her faults, Friedan is presented as a free thinker with an inner fire.

Murphy, Jim. ***Across America on an Emigrant Train.*** New York: Clarion, 1993.

Summary: This adventure follows young writer Robert Louis Stevenson from his home in Scotland on a journey to join the woman he loves in California. Stevenson's words and the history of the building of the transcontinental railroad are intertwined with photographs, engravings, and lithographs. A bibliography is provided.

Grade Level/Content Area: This book supports studies of the development of the railroad, the history of the West, or the lives of famous writers, and students in grades 3–8 will enjoy it.

*Powers, Mary Ellen. ***Our Teacher's in a Wheelchair.*** Niles, IL: Albert Whitman, 1986.

Summary: Brian Hanson, a daycare teacher who is partially paralyzed and uses a wheelchair, is the subject of this biography. His life story includes the injury that caused the paralysis and his many accomplishments.

Grade Level/Content Area: In grades K–3, this book fits a social studies unit on careers and can help children accept and understand people with handicaps.

Ransom, Candice F. ***Listening to Crickets: A Story About Rachel Carson.*** (Illus., Shelly O. Haas). Minneapolis: Carolrhoda Books, 1993.

Summary: This is the story of Rachel Carson who combined her gift of writing with her love of nature to change how the world viewed DDT. She provides an excellent role model for children to follow to broaden their views of future careers.

Grade Level/Content Area: Students in grades 3–6 who are studying biography, women, or female writers will enjoy this story of commitment and persistence that allowed a woman to enter a world where few people had previously tread.

— *San Souci, Robert. **Cut from the Same Cloth: American Women of Myth, Legend, and Tall Tale.** (Illus., Brian Pinckney). New York: Philomel, 1993.

Summary: Fifteen stories about overlooked legendary U.S. women with a map showing where they grew up and black and white illustrations to accompany the text.

Grade Level/Content Area: Students in grades 2–12 studying U.S. women, myths, legends, or tall tales will enjoy these carefully researched stories about women who have been overlooked by the history books.

— *Schroeder, Alan. **Ragtime Tumpie.** (Illus., Bernie Fuchs). Boston: Little Brown, 1989.

Summary: This is a fictional account of entertainer Josephine Baker's childhood in New Orleans as she grew up in poverty and with a verbally abusive stepparent, yet held onto her love of music and dream of becoming a famous honkytonk dancer.

Grade Level/Content Area: Students in grades 1–8 studying famous women or African-American women, responsible citizenship, or the field of entertainment enjoy this story of an African-American female who overcame a difficult childhood to become a famous entertainer, war hero, and advocate for children and peace.

— *Stevens, Bryna. **Deborah Sampson Goes to War.** (Illus., Florence Hill). Minneapolis: Carolrhoda Books, 1984.

Summary: This book is about the early life of Deborah Sampson, who disguised herself as a man and went to fight as a soldier in the American Revolution. Despite her illnesses and injuries, no one learned of her true identity until near the end of the war.

Grade Level/Content Area: In grades 2–6, this book supports a study of the revolutionary war or women in U.S. history.

— Sufrin, Mark. **George Bush: The Story of the Forty-first President of the United States.** New York: Dell, 1989.

Summary: This book documents George Bush's life from his birth to his election as President, including the many different jobs he has held, from navy pilot to businessman, ambassador, head of the CIA, and Vice President. His roles as husband and father are also discussed.

Grade Level/Content Area: In grades 3–6 social studies, this book fits units on government, political leaders, or current events.

Wallner, Alexandra. *Betsy Ross.* New York: Holiday House, 1994.

Summary: This is the story of Betsy Ross, the woman history tells us sewed the first U.S. flag and whose home was taken over by British troops. The text and its old-fashioned paintings give a fascinating glimpse of colonial life.

Grade Level/Content Area: Students in grades 2–5 who are studying conflict, the American Revolution, or important women in U.S. history will enjoy this biography. In an Afterward, Wallner explains that there are conflicting stories about Ross's life.

*Weidhorn, Manfred. *Jackie Robinson.* New York: Atheneum, 1993.

Summary: This biography creates a portrait of the individual Jackie Robinson and vividly describes the context within which he struggled against the boundaries of social caste. It is illustrated with photographs.

Grade Level/Content Area: Students in grades 4–12 studying African-American history, the history of baseball, or biographies of role models will enjoy this biography, which is much more than a sports story.

Poetry

Blishen, Edward. *The Oxford Book of Poetry for Children.* (Illus., Brian Wildsmith). New York: Peter Bedrick Books, 1984.

Summary: Various poems, some well known and some less well known, on a variety of topics and characters, from a baby in a cradle to apples in an orchard; randomly illustrated.

Grade Level/Content Area: This collection of poems enriches a range of science and social studies topics in grades 2–6.

*Clement, Claude. *The Painter and the Wild Swans.* (Illus., Frederic Clement). New York: Dial, 1986.

Summary: A Japanese painter named Teiji wonders how he can ever hope to capture the beauty of a flock of wild swans that live on an island in the middle of a lake. He learns that real beauty is rare and impossible to capture.

Grade Level/Content Area: For students in grades 4–8, this story that also includes a poem makes a good accompaniment to a unit on art, artists, or Japan. The lyrical text, delicate Japanese calligraphy, and lovely acrylic paintings convey a feeling of uncluttered oriental simplicity in a story with an unusual ending.

Cole, Joanna. *A New Treasury of Children's Poetry.* Garden City, NY: Doubleday, 1984.

Summary: An anthology of more than 200 old and new poems, light verse, riddle rhymes, and limericks that will delight children's senses.

Grade Level/Content Area: These poems foster an appreciation for poetry and language, a knowledge of concepts, and identification with characters and situations for children in PreK–6. These poems serve as good models to imitate as children write their own poetry.

de Regniers, Beatrice Schenk, Moore, Eva, White, Mary Michaels, & Jan Carr. *Sing A Song of Popcorn.* (Illus., Marcia Brown, Leo and Diane Dillon, Richard Egielski, Trina Schart Hyman, Arnold Lobel, Maurice Sendak, Marc Simont, and Margot Zemach). New York: Scholastic, 1988.

Summary: This collection contains 128 poems, ranging from traditional to contemporary, with full-color illustrations by nine Caldecott Medal-winning artists. The poems, which are humorous, touching, profound, and nonsensical, are divided into nine themed sections: *Fun with Rhymes; Mostly Weather; Spooky Poems; Story Poems; Mostly Animals; Mostly People; Mostly Nonsense; Seeing, Feeling, Thinking;* and *In a Few Words.*

Grade Level/Content Area: Children in PreK–3 enjoy these short poems that complement the study of poetry and rhyme in language arts, or the study of animals, weather, other cultures, and self-awareness in science and social studies.

Fleischman, Paul. *I Am Phoenix: Poems for Two Voices.* (Illus., Ken Nutt). New York: Harper & Row, 1985.

Summary: This collection of fifteen poems about various birds including pigeons, egrets, doves, owls, warblers, and cormorants was written to be read aloud simultaneously by two students. *Joyful Noise,* also by Fleischman, is a similar collection about insects.

Grade Level/Content Area: Enjoyed by children in grades 3–6, this book fits a science unit on birds, extinction of the passenger pigeons, life cycle of the Phoenix, and appreciation for animals. A social studies unit on Greek mythology and legends would also be enhanced by this anthology, which contains several full-page, black and white drawings of various birds, statues, and people.

— Fleischman, Paul. *Joyful Noise: Poems for Two Voices.* (Illus., Eric Bed-
dows). New York: Harper & Row, 1988.

Summary: A collection of poems about insects for reading by two voices that
is a companion to *I Am Phoenix,* a collection about birds for two voices. It is
told from the point of view of the insects and includes the rhythm and sounds
of the insect world.

Grade Level/Content Area: In grades 1-6, this book can be used for choral
speaking in language arts or in science as an enrichment for a unit on the insect
world.

— *Hughes, Langston. *The Dream Keeper and Other Poems.* (Illus., Brian
Pinkney). New York: Knopf, 1994.

Summary: A reissue of an old classic with some new poetry, this collection
speaks to the hopes, dreams, and humanity of all. Black and white scratchboard
illustrations capture the essence of each poem.

Grade Level/Content Area: Students in grades 3-12 who are studying and
writing poetry or exploring the African-American experience or African-American writers will enjoy this poetry.

— Hughes, Shirley. *Stories by Firelight.* New York: Lothrop, Lee & Shepard, 1993.

Summary: This is a collection of winter stories and poems that includes a
child's learning about a. mythical sea creature, a wordless journey through a
dream, and a boy and his grandfather who build a bonfire kindled with a pine
tree and memorabilia.

Grade Level/Content Area: Students in grades K-6 studying storytelling
will be encouraged to tell stories from their own lives after hearing these
stories.

— *Lewis, Richard. *Out of the Earth I Sing: Poetry & Songs of Primitive Peo-
ples of the World.* New York: Norton, 1968.

Summary: This is a collection of poems and songs by primitive people from
all over the world. Represented are the Sioux, Zulu, Iroquois, Winnebago, Inca,
Aztec, Maori, Apache, Bantu, Chippewa, Bushmen, Eskimo, Borneo, Aborig-
inies, Pygmy, Pawnee, Papago, Navaho, Dakota, and Hawaiians. Common
themes are morning, children, hunting, prayer, animals, and love.

Grade Level/Content Area: Students in grades 3-6 studying communities
and cultures of the world in social studies enjoy these poems that enrich their
understanding of primitive people the world over.

 Oliver, Robert. *Cornucopia.* New York: Atheneum, 1978.

Summary: These poems use the alphabet as a foundation for describing animals and insects in amusing and informative ways.

Grade Level/Content Area: In science units on living things, these poems provide information on many familiar and not so familiar animals and insects for grades 1–3.

 Prelusky, Jack. *The New Kid on the Block.* (Illus., James Stevenson). New York: Greenwillow, 1984.

Summary: These poems are written about an assortment of odd characters, creatures, animals with human likenesses, and *whatevers* invented by the author, from Stringbean Small to the Gloppy Gloopers.

Grade Level/Content Area: In grades 2–6, these poems are enjoyed for their humor and craziness. They support a unit on poetry appreciation and writing and stimulate vocabulary growth and use of the imagination.

 Prelutsky, Jack. *Read-Aloud Rhymes for the Very Young.* (Illus., Marc Brown). New York: Knopf, 1986.

Summary: This is a collection of over 200 short poems, written by both traditional and contemporary poets, that appeal to young children with short attention spans. The poems deal with children's concerns such as waking, animals, bedtime, seasons, holidays, special events, and play and show children that life is happy and fun.

Grade Level/Content Area: Children in K–3 enjoy these poems as part of a language arts unit on poetry or a social studies unit on the community.

 Seuss, Dr. (T. Geisel) *I Am Not Going to Get Up Today.* (Illus., James Stevenson). New York: Random House, 1987.

Summary: In this example of rhyming narrative poetry, a young boy decides he is going to sleep in and convinces others to leave him alone. The story describes numerous ways to wake the boy up.

Grade Level/Content Area: Children in grades PreK–2 enjoy this poem that stimulates creative thinking and discussion of the effects of doing something unusual.

 Viorst, Judith. *If I Were in Charge of the World and Other Worries.* New York: Macmillan, 1981.

Summary: This book of 41 poems, most of which rhyme and are humorous, reveals the worries, wishes, and secret thoughts that everyone may have.

Grade Level/Content Area: This book appeals to children in grades K–6 and promotes appreciative listening, a discussion of feelings, or the writing of personal essays or individual poems on the same topic, which can be collected in a class book.

*Wood, Nancy. ***Spirit Walker.*** (Illus., Frank Howell). New York:Bantam, 1993.

Summary: This collection of poetry by the author reveals the unique wisdom and vision of the Native Americans.

Grade Level/Content Area: Students in grades K–6 who are studying Native Americans or poetry will enjoy these poems and may be motivated to write their own as a result of listening to these being read aloud.

Information Books

*Ancona, George. ***The Piñata Maker/El Pinatero.*** New York: Harcourt Brace Jovanovich, 1994.

Summary: This is the story of how seventy-seven-year-old Tio Rico makes piñatas. It follows one of his creations to a party where it is broken in traditional play. Color photographs and text in both English and Spanish give this story added appeal.

Grade Level/Content Area: Students in grades 1–5 who are studying Mexico or holiday traditions from other cultures will enjoy this story. It is also of interest to teachers of Spanish-speaking or English-as-a-second-language (ESL) students because of the dual text.

Arnosky, Jim. ***I See Animals Hiding.*** New York: Scholastic, 1995.

Summary: In this strikingly illustrated book, the reader is given a glimpse of the natural world that reveals many of the clever ways animals hide. Examples such as a snake that looks like a stick, an owl that blends into a snowy landscape, and a moth that vanishes on a tree trunk demonstrate the ways animals adapt in order to avoid danger.

Grade Level/Content Area: This book is appropriate for students in K–3 who are studying living things, adaptability, or specific animals. Arnosky is an award-winning naturalist and author.

*Atkin, Beth. ***Voices from the Fields: Children of Migrant Farmworkers Tell Their Stories.*** Boston: Little Brown, 1993.

Summary: This is a look at the bleaker side of immigrant and migrant farming life in California. It presents portraits of children, as young as six or seven, who are exhausted by their work and who must struggle to get an education. It is interspersed with their poetry translated from Spanish and individual interviews with them. Atkin is a photojournalist whose portraits of these children enrich the text.

Grade Level/Content Area: Students in grades 5–8 studying the life of migrant workers, California's economy, or Spanish immigrants will learn much about the personal side of migrant workers' lives through these children's personal stories. The book contains optimism, heartbreak, and the message that education and communication can improve the lives of these children and young people.

Brown, Laurene Drasny, & Brown, Marc. *Dinosaurs Divorce: A Guide for Changing Families.* New York: Atlantic, 1986.

Summary: After a table of contents and glossary of terms come sections on reasons why parents divorce, possible repercussions and reactions, dealing with visitations, living in two homes, celebrating holidays, and adjusting to parent dating, remarriage, and step-siblings. Humor and sensitivity distinguish this book and the dinosaur characters allow children to distance themselves emotionally from the characters yet identify with the issues.

Grade Level/Content Area: This book fits nicely into the family life segment of a social studies curriculum in grades K–4.

Brown, Mary Barrett. *Wings Along the Waterway.* New York: Orchard Books, 1992.

Summary: This book examines the lives of waterbirds such as coots, limpkins, and snowballs and the technological threats to their fragile environments. A bibliography of other books on the topic is provided.

Grade Level/Content Area: This book supports study of birds, water life, ecology, or the balance of nature for students in grades 4–8.

Clark, Margaret Goff. *The Endangered Florida Panther.* New York: Cobblehill, 1993.

Summary: Through text and color photographs this book looks at the plight of the panther and what is being done to save it from extinction. It offers suggestions for the reader who chooses to become involved.

Grade level/Content Area: Students in grades 3–8 who are studying endangered species, extinction, Florida wildlife, or panthers will enjoy this book which includes a time line of Florida panther milestones and an index.

*Cohn, Amy. *From Sea to Shining Sea.* New York: Scholastic, 1993.

Summary: This is a collection of multicultural stories and songs from all periods of U.S. history. It is illustrated by various Caldecott winners and contains background information, notes about the artists, and a glossary.

Grade Level/Content Area: This edited collection will support studies of diversity, art, or U.S. history by students in grades K–9.

— Cone, Molly. ***Come Back Salmon: How a Group of Dedicated Kids Adopted Pigeon Creek and Brought It Back to Life.*** (Illus., Sidnee Wheelwright). San Francisco: Sierra Club, 1992.

Summary: This is the story of a group of elementary students who save a creek and prepare it for the salmon that were being grown at their school. Color photographs are interspersed with actual dialogues among teachers, students, and other adults.

Grade Level/Content Area: This book supports study of the environment, ecology of a stream, fish, conservation, or the empowerment of children.

— Cottonwood, Joe. ***Quake! A Novel.*** New York: Scholastic, 1995.

Summary: This is the story of the recent Loma Prieta/San Francisco earthquake from the perspective of three children who were home alone during the quake. The author relives his first-hand experiences of the quake and writes of the bravery, compassion, and generosity of people in the midst of a natural disaster.

Grade Level/Content Area: This book supports theme instruction on topics such as earthquakes, disasters, or recent California history and is appropriate for students in grades 3–6.

— Cowcher, Helen. ***Rainforest.*** New York: Farrar, Straus & Giroux, 1988.

Summary: A brief cautionary tale about the destruction of the South American rainforests accompanied by vivid full-color paintings. The fragile balance of nature is explored in this story about the exotic animals and lush vegetation that are found in the usually peaceful rainforest.

Grade Level/Content Area: This story can be used in grades K–6 to support study of man's impact on ecology and the environment, the destruction of the rainforest, or animals and plants of the rainforest.

— Crisman, Ruth. ***Racing the Iditarod Trail.*** New York: Dillon (Macmillan), 1993.

Summary: This book, illustrated with photographs, takes the reader on Alaska's exciting International Iditarod Sled Dog Race. It contains a bibliography of other sources of information about the Iditarod, a list of Iditarod winners, and official checkpoints and distances.

Grade Level/Content Area: Students in grades 3–6 studying Alaska or international sports will learn much from this factual story about the Iditarod with its accompanying informative references and lists.

— Gibbons, Gail. ***Recycle! A Handbook for Kids.*** Boston: Little Brown, 1992.

Summary: Paper, glass, aluminum cans, plastic, and polystyrene are followed through colorful drawings and clear text as they are recycled from trash into useful products.

Grade Level/Content Area: This book supports study of environmental conservation or recycling for students in grades K–6.

— Godkin, Sheila. ***Wolf Island.*** New York: W.H. Freeman, 1993.

Summary: This story is about the balance of nature on one island and just how easily it can be disturbed and restored. Beautiful language and illustrations convey the message.

Grade Level/Content Area: This book is appropriate for students in grades K–6 who are studying ecology, the balance of nature, environmental conservation, or food chains.

— *Graff, Nancy Price. ***Where the River Runs: A Portrait of a Refugee Family.*** (Illus., Richard Howard). Boston: Little Brown, 1993.

Summary: This is the remarkable story of one refugee family that came from Cambodia to the United States. It includes striking photographs.

Grade Level/Content Area: Students in grades 3–8 who are studying immigration, refugees, or Asian or Cambodian life will enjoy this sensitive story that concludes with questions and answers.

— Guthrie, Donna. ***The Young Author's Do-it-Yourself Book.*** (Illus., Katy Keck Arnsteen). Fresno, CA: Millbrook Press, 1994.

Summary: An introduction to writing, assembling, and producing a book, this story discusses the writing of fiction and nonfiction, story structure, and different kinds of informational texts such as interview, how-to, and factual reports. Explanations of illustrations, page layouts, and binding are excellent.

Grade Level/Content Area: This book will help students in grades 2–4 who are studying writing or publishing, or who want to make their own books to showcase their own written work.

Harrison, Ted. *O Canada.* New York: Ticknor & Fields, 1993.

Summary: Through vibrant paintings and narrative descriptions, the reader is taken on a wonderful journey across Canada's provinces and territories.

Grade Level/Content Area: This book is a good introduction or resource for students in grades 4–8 who are beginning a study of Canada.

Hisock, Bruce. *The Big Storm.* New York: Atheneum, 1993.

Summary: This story presents information on basic weather phenomena as it describes a devastating storm that moved across the United States for six days in March and April of 1992. With accurate watercolor paintings, it follows the storm in all its beauty and strength as it caused avalanches in the Sierra Nevadas, blizzards in the Rocky Mountains, tornadoes in Texas and the Midwest, snow in Michigan, rain and hail in the South, and snow in New York City.

Grade Level/Content Area: In grades 2–4, this contemporary look at the many faces of a storm and the geography of the United States is perfect for a unit on the weather, storms, or geography of the United States.

*Intrater, Roberta. *Two Eyes, a Nose and a Mouth.* New York: Scholastic, 1995.

Summary: More than 100 full-color photographs show the eyes, noses, and mouths of people of all shapes, sizes, ages, and races in this book with rhyming text by a photojournalist.

Grade Level/Content Area: This book can introduce or be used in a unit on multicultural studies with students in grades PreK–3.

Isaacson, Philip M. *A Short Walk Around the Pyramids and Through the World of Art.* New York: Knopf, 1993.

Summary: This book teaches the reader to examine color, images, sculpture, photographs, and daily objects from a global perspective. It is illustrated with photos.

Grade Level/Content Area: This volume supports a study of art, diversity, or the global world for students in grades 4–12.

Iverson, Diane. *I Celebrate Nature.* Nevada City, CA: Dawn, 1993.

Summary: This story teaches a conservation ethic to young children as it elicits curiosity, joy, and wonder. A simple rhyming storyline and lovely illustrations portray a group of children in a variety of settings and seasons as they discover the wonders of the natural world.

Grade Level/Content Area: Students in grades K–3 studying conservation, ecology, or the seasons will find much to enjoy and learn in this story.

— Jasperspon, William. *How the Forest Grew.* (Illus., Chuck Eckart). New York: Mulberry Books, 1992.

Summary: This book is a description of different stages in the growth of a forest over a period of 200 years.

Grade Level/Content Area: This book is appropriate for students in grades 3–6 studying the environment, forests, or trees.

— Johnson, Rebecca L. *Investigating the Ozone Hole.* Minneapolis, MN: Lerner, 1993.

Summary: This book describes ozone research in Antarctica including destructive chlorofluorocarbon (CFC) use and the long-range ultraviolet problems that will result. It contains profiles of scientists at work along with photos, maps, and charts.

Grade Level/Content Area: Students in grades 3–8 who are studying Antartica, environmental pollution, scientists, or the atmosphere will enjoy this comprehensive work.

— Lasky, Kathryn. *Surtsey: The Newest Place on Earth.* (Illus., Christopher G. Knight). New York: Hyperion, 1992.

Summary: With exquisite color photographs, this book documents the birth of an island as a result of a volcanic eruption off the coast of Iceland and the emergence of life there.

Grade Level/Content Area: Students in grades 5–8 will enjoy this photo essay that supports study of the evolution of life or the life cycle on an island.

— Lauber, Patricia. *Volcano: The Eruption and Healing of Mount St. Helens.* New York: Bradbury, 1987.

Summary: In this Newbery Honor book, which is a full-color photographic essay, Lauber explains the most destructive volcanic eruption in the history of the United States. With the help of scientists and naturalists and the careful eye of her camera, she describes and shows the return of life to the mountain's barren landscape.

Grade Level/Content Area: This book fits science units in grades 2–9 on the earth's changing surface, animals, and plants.

Lavies, Bianca. ***Monarch Butterflies: Mysterious Travelers.*** New York: Dutton, 1992.

Summary: Brilliant photographs accompany the text of this story about the remarkable life cycle and migratory patterns of the Monarch butterfly.

Grade Level/Content Area: Students in grades 2–6 who are studying migration or insects will gain an enlightened picture of this insect after reading this book.

Le Tord, Bijou. ***Elephant Moon.*** New York: Bantam, 1993.

Summary: This book follows the world's largest living animal, the African elephant, through woodlands and hills and helps the reader see these majestic creatures with a renewed sense of respect and connection.

Grade Level/Content Area: Students studying Africa, grasslands, or elephants will enjoy this text with its watercolor illustrations that evoke a poetic style and message.

*Lindblad, Linda. ***The Serengeti Migration: Africa's Animals on the Move.*** (Illus., Sven-Olaf Lindblad). New York: Hyperion, 1994.

Summary: This story follows two herds of zebras and wildebeests as they migrate through the Serengeti National Park, a conservation area in Tanzania and Kenya, in a struggle for survival. Color photographs of many animals and their natural surroundings bring the reader immediately to the wilds of Africa.

Grade Level/Content Area: This book develops the concept of the interconnectedness of life and migration as a struggle for survival. It is appropriate for students in grades 3–6 who are studying grasslands, Africa, or animals.

London, Jonathan. ***Gray Fox.*** (Illus., Robert Sauber). New York: Viking, 1994.

Summary: A young boy finds a gray fox that has just been hit by a car and carries it through fields and woods to a stream bank where it dies. But Gray Fox's mate continues to raise their family and the young foxes grow up, disperse,and have young foxes of their own, and "the spirit of Gray Fox runs with them like the wind."

Grade Level/Content Area: Children in grades K–3 will enjoy this sad but realistic tale that fits well in a study of foxes, animals, man's impact on the environment, or the web of life. Sauber's rich and wonderful illustrations help communicate the subtle message that life goes on even when one light is extinguished.

\=\= *Lyons, Mary E. **Stitching Stars: The Story Quilts of Harriet Powers.** New York: Scribner's, 1993.

Summary: This is the story of how Harriet Powers preserved, piece by piece, a part of African-American history in the nineteenth-century United States with her quilts. Photographs and text show how she was inspired by the Bible, African tradition, and the world around her.

Grade Level/Content Area: Students in grades 6–12 who are studying discrimination, African-American history, notable women, or the art of quilting will enjoy this story that includes sources for further reading.

\=\= Macy, Sue. ***A Whole New Ball Game: The Story of the All-American Girls Professional Baseball League.*** New York: Holt, 1993.

Summary: This story, illustrated with prints and photographs, tells of the U.S. professional women's baseball league. From Ruth Richard, who caught back-to-back no-hit, no-run playoff games, to Betty Weaver Foss, who had a lifetime batting average of .340, the All-American Girls Professional Baseball League (AAGPBL) fostered some of the best female athletes in the United States.

Grade Level/Content Area: Students in grades 4–9 who are studying women, athletes, or baseball will learn much from this history that also provides notes on sources and suggestions for further reading.

\=\= *Margolies, Jacob. **The Negro Leagues: The Story of Black Baseball.** Chicago: Watts, 1993.

Summary: This book documents the history of African-American league baseball teams that flourished in the early twentieth century in spite of discrimination. It includes prints and photographs and profiles of some of the leading figures, outstanding players, and their achievements.

Grade Level/Content Area: Students in grades 5–9 who are involved in a study of discrimination, African American history, or organized sports will learn much from this book, which also provides a bibliography of further readings.

\=\= Morris, Campbell. **The Best Paper Aircraft: New and Expanded.** New York: Perigee, 1986.

Summary: This book includes easy-to-follow instructions and drawings of 28 flyable paper airplane models, including super loopers, a kamikaze water bomber, the space shuttle, jump jets, and more.

Grade Level/Content Area Use: Students in grades 3–6 enjoy this how-to book that enriches a science unit on rocketry or space exploration and helps teach the principles of lift and aerodynamics.

Morris, Desmond. *The World of Animals.* (Peter Barrett, Illus.). New York: Viking, 1993.

Summary: This book is filled with carefully researched information, anecdotal stories, and color illustrations that make it a good resource. It includes how animals such as the panda, armadillo, sea lion, and whale sleep, mate, rear their young, and survive.

Grade Level/Content Area: Students in grades 3–6 who are studying animal life, life cycles of animals, or reproduction will find many interesting facts in this resource.

Murphy, Jim. *The Great Fire.* New York: Scholastic, 1995.

Summary: A you-are-there account of the Great Chicago Fire of 1871 that began when a fire broke out in O'Leary's barn and ended the next day with the city almost totally devastated. Personal accounts from survivors make this a riveting book.

Grade Level/Content Area: Students in grades 3–6 who are studying U.S. or Illinois history or disasters will enjoy this story that also includes archival photographs and illustrations.

Presnall, Judith Janda. *Animals That Glow.* Chicago: Watts, 1992.

Summary: This is a study of bioluminescent insects and other animals with full-color photographs accompanying. Included are anglerfish, firefleas, fireflies, glowworms, millipeds, and squid among others.

Grade Level/Content Area: Students in grades 3–6 who are studying oceanography, insects, or living things will enjoy this high-interest book.

Pringle, Lawrence. *Antarctica: The Last Unspoiled Continent.* New York: Simon & Schuster, 1992.

Summary: Through color photographs and descriptive text, the reader learns about Antarctica, a land of extraordinary contrasts that has become a natural laboratory for the study of the earth and its environmental future.

Grade Level/Content Area: This book is suitable for students in grades 3–8 who are studying Antarctica, world ecology, or the role of environmental scientists.

Rand, Gloria. ***Prince William.*** (Illus., Ted Rand). New York: Holt, 1992.

Summary: This story, with accompanying watercolor illustrations, is about one of the seals rescued from the 1989 oil spill off Prince William Sound and the work of the volunteers who helped with the clean up.

Grade Level/Content Area: This book supports study of ocean life, the balance of nature, or environmental disasters and conservation for students in grades K–6.

Ride, Sally, & O'Shaughnessy, Tam. ***Voyager: An Adventure to the Edge Of the Solar System.*** New York: Crown, 1992.

Summary: With color photographs and illustrative diagrams, this book tells the story of two space probes, Voyager I and Voyager II, and the scientists who accompanied these probes.

Grade Level/Content Area: This book is appropriate for students in grades 5–8 who are studying space exploration, the solar system, or space scientists.

Ryder, Joanne. ***Dancers in the Garden.*** (Illus., Judith Lopez). San Francisco: Sierra Club, 1992.

Summary: Pertinent facts and close-up drawings reveal the life and habits of hummingbirds, which are found all across the United States. Background information and suggestions about how to attract hummingbirds are found in an author's note.

Grade Level/Content Area: K–3 students who are studying birds or animals will enjoy this book about the tiny, rapidly moving hummingbird.

Simon, Seymour. ***Snakes.*** New York: Harper Collins, 1992.

Summary: Color photographs accompany this informative text, which presents the colors, movements, strengths, eating patterns, and other behaviors of a variety of snakes.

Grade Level/Content Area: This book supports studies of the balance of nature, reptiles, or food chains for students in grades 3–6.

Simon, Seymour. ***Storms.*** New York: Mulberry Books, 1992.

Summary: The atmospheric conditions that lead to the creation of thunderstorms, tornadoes, and hurricanes are explained with concise text accompanied by full-color photographs.

Grade Level/Content Area: Students in grades 3–6 studying weather or the atmosphere will appreciate this straightforward explanation of various weather phenomena.

Skurzynski, Gloria. *Get the Message: Telecommunications in Your High-Tech World.* New York: Bradbury, 1993.

Summary: This book describes the technology behind a telephone call, cellular telephones, fax machines, interactive telephones, video systems, and much more. Colorful illustrations and pictures accompany textual explanations.

Grade Level/Content Area: Students in grades 3–8 who are studying telecommunications or technology will find this book full of easy-to-understand explanations.

Sobol, Richard, & Sobol, Jonah. *Seal Journey* (Illus., Richard Sobol). New York: Cobblehill, 1993.

Summary: Photographs show a father and son team as they have an exciting adventure that reveals the life cycle of the harp seal and emphasizes the need for wildlife conservation.

Grade Level/Content Area: This story supports a study of ocean life, the life cycle, or wildlife conservation. Author endnotes provide extended information for the reader.

*Turner, Dee. *1000 Facts About People.* New York: Kingfisher Books, 1992.

Summary: Little-known and amazing facts about the world's people are found in this colorful, picture-packed book. It is full of facts about how people live together and talk to each other, what they wear and eat, government, the arts, famous people, and inventions, as well as facts on the body and the first people.

Grade Level/Content Area: Students in grades 3–6 who are studying man, diversity, and multicultural awareness will enjoy learning about the world's people. An index and inviting visual graphics help make the knowledge contained in this book easy to grasp

Teacher Resources

Professional Books

Beach, R. (1993). *A Teacher's Introduction to Reader-Response Theories.* Urbana, IL: National Council of Teachers of English.
This third volume in the Teacher's Introduction series provides a comprehensive overview of the wide range of reader-response theories that have revolutionized the fields of literary theory, criticism, and pedagogy. Beach discusses the relationships between reader and text from five theoretical perspectives: social, cultural, psychological, experimental, and textual. Also included is an extensive bibliography with additional readings on reader-response.

Benedict, S. & Carlisle, L. (Eds.). (1992). *Beyond Words: Picture Books for Older Readers and Writers.* Portsmouth, NH: Heinemann.
This text contains anecdotes from teachers in grades one through twelve focusing on the uses of picture books in reading and writing classrooms. Professional writers and illustrators discuss their creative insights. Included are explorations of books by Chris Van Allsburg, David Macaulay, Maurice Sendak, and Dr. Seuss.

Bishop, R. S. (Ed.). (1994). *Kaleidoscope: A Multicultural Booklist for Grades K–8.* Urbana, IL: National Council of Teachers of English.
A detailed booklist that focuses on people of color, especially African Americans, Asian Americans, Hispanic Americans/Latinos, and Native Americans. Highlighting both commonalities and differences among cultures, the books are grouped by genre or theme rather than by cultural considerations. Including both fiction and nonfiction annotations, a list of resources, and a directory of publishers, authors, illustrators, and titles are included.

Bromley, K. (1994). *Journaling: Engagements in Reading, Writing, and Thinking.* New York: Scholastic.
This is an in-depth discussion of how teachers use many different types of journals in K–8 classrooms. The literature response journal is described, and examples are included of its use with specific literature and in several classrooms.

Burke, E. M., & Glazer, S. M. (1994). *Using Nonfiction in the Classroom.* New York: Scholastic.
This handbook presents the why and how of using quality nonfiction to promote an integrated approach to inquiry-oriented instruction. Classroom vignettes illustrate activities and environments that use specific nonfiction titles to promote learning across the curriculum.

Ernst, K. (1994). *Picturing Learning: Artists and Writers in the Classroom.* Portsmouth, NH: Heinemann.
This book connects literacy and art development through an exploration of the relationships among seeing and telling, drawing, and writing. The author, a former middle school English teacher, includes descriptions of students who use picturing and writing to express imagination and expand writers workshop.

Favorite Paperbacks for 1994. (1994). Newark, DE: International Reading Association.
An annotated listing of more than 100 popular paperbacks recommended by elementary school teachers, university students, and children. This informational booklist includes such categories as *Fiction for young readers, Poetry and verse, Easy to read, Folklore, Fiction for older readers,* and *Nonfiction.*

Hart-Hewins, L. & Wells, J. (1990). *Real Books for Reading: Learning to Read with Children's Literature*. Portsmouth, NH: Heinemann.
This informative guide to selecting and using real books for three- to eight-year-olds includes chapters on realistic, practical criteria for choosing books for use in the classroom, library, or home.

Harwayne, S. (1992). *Lasting Impressions: Weaving Literature into the Writing Workshop*. Portsmouth, NH: Heinemann.
A valuable resource that explores the diverse roles of literature in the writing workshop. Written for elementary and middle school teachers, this text also reexamines the familiar workshop structure and adds new ideas for building classroom community while improving student writing skills.

Heimlich, J. E., & Pittelman, S. D. (1986). *Semantic Mapping: Classroom Applications*. Newark, DE: International Reading Association.
This 48-page paperback contains several practical classroom suggestions about the use of semantic mapping. Five applications and numerous examples make it immediately useful to classroom teachers.

Jensen, J. M. & Roser, N. L. (Eds.). (1993). *Adventuring with Books: A Booklist for Pre-K through Grade 6* (10th ed.). Urbana, IL: National Council of Teachers of English.
This enlarged tenth edition, illustrated with photographs featuring the covers of many of the books included, contains summaries and brief synopses of nearly 1800 children's books published between 1988 and 1992. Indexes of authors, illustrators, subjects, and titles are included as well as a directory of publishers, lists of award-winning books, and possible applications in the classroom.

Kiefer, B. (Ed.). (1991). *Getting to Know You: Profiles of Children's Authors Featured in Language Arts, 1985–1990*. Urbana, IL: National Council of Teachers of English.
Selected from *Profile* features in *Language Arts* between 1985 and 1990, these articles provide an excellent starting point for students and teachers who would like to know more about the presented novelists, editors, translators, poets, folklorists, and illustrators. Included are profiles of Lilian Moore, Arnold Lobel, Alvin Schwartz, Cynthia Voigt, and many others.

Lukens, R. J. (1995). *A Critical Handbook of Children's Literature* (5th ed.). Glenview, IL: Scott Foresman.
This well-written and thoughtful book examines character, plot, setting, theme, point of view, style, tone, and the genres of children's literature using examples of children's books. Reading it gives one a better vantage point from which to make judgments about quality in literature.

McBride, W. G. (Ed.). (1990). *High Interest–Easy Reading: A Booklist for Junior and Senior High School Students* (6th ed.). Urbana, IL: National Council of Teachers of English.
Containing nearly 400 annotations, this booklist is targeted at and written for reluctant adolescent readers. Titles are organized into twenty-three categories. Also included are author, title, and subject indexes as well as a directory of publishers.

Norton, D. E. (1995). *Through the Eyes of a Child: An Introduction to Children's Literature* (4th ed.). Columbus, OH: Merrill.
In this comprehensive text on children's literature, webs and the webbing process using children's literature are explained.

Pearson, P. D., & Johnson, D. J. (1978). *Teaching Reading Comprehension*. New York: Holt Rinehart & Winston.
Chapter 3 contains a long section on the use of semantic maps as a way of organizing concepts. It includes several examples that illustrate how maps improve comprehension.

Pehrsson, R. S., & Denner, P. R. (1989). *Semantic Organizers: A Study Strategy for Special Needs Learners*. Rockville, MD: Aspen.
This book is about teaching students to organize their ideas and improve memory and learning through semantic webbing. It is divided into two parts: (1) theory and practice and (2) practical

applications to school subjects. Readers will find the examples of many different types of webs used to represent specific content and concepts extremely helpful since they can be easily adapted to the elements of story.

Rudman, M. (1995). *Children's Literature: An Issues Approach* (3rd ed.). New York: Longman.
This book contains annotations of quality literature for children and youth both fiction and nonfiction arranged by topic, such as divorce and death. It includes multicultural literature and provides a guide in the selection process.

Short, K. G. & Pierce, K. M. (Eds.). (1990). *Talking About Books: Creating Literate Communities.* Portsmouth, NH: Heinemann.
Featuring the beliefs of fourteen authors, this text focuses on the creation of classrooms in which students, using reading as a way to learn, become members of a literate community. Classroom experiences involving whole-class reading aloud and small-group discussions of literature are also included.

Stweig, J. W. & Sebesta, S. L. (Eds.). (1989). *Using Literature in the Elementary Classroom: Revised and Enlarged Edition* (2nd ed.). Urbana, IL: National Council of Teachers of English.
This text addresses the challenge of putting the several hundred fragmented skills of reading together again. Presented in the framework of the whole-language approach, the essays contained in this book provide rationales, explanations, applications, and examples of using children's literature in the classroom.

Teachers' Favorite Books for Kids: Teachers' Choices 1989-1993. (1994). Newark, DE: International Reading Association.
A compilation of five years of Teachers' Choices Lists, these exceptional trade books have been selected for use across the curriculum. Grouped by suggested reading levels, bibliographic information and annotations are provided for each title.

Trelease, J. (Ed.). (1992). *Hey! Listen to This: Stories to Read Aloud.* New York: Penguin.
This anthology of outstanding read-aloud tales contains 48 stories to share with children ages 5-9. Trelease provides a special introduction to each story, ranging from folktales to excerpts from classics, and suggestions for further reading.

Computer Software

Inspiration 4.0: The Easiest Way to Brainstorm and Write. Portland, OR: Inspiration Software, Inc. (2920 S.W. Dolph Court, Suite 3, 97219, 800-877-4292).
This tool models the thinking process by allowing the user to brainstorm ideas, create a web or diagram, and then write an outline. It permits quick movement between the web and outline, and changes made in one appear automatically in the other. Probably for computer whizzes and adults. IBM and MAC versions.

Kid Pix. San Rafael, CA: Borderbund Software, Inc. (17 Paul Drive, 94903-2101).
This program provides an elementary way for younger students to visualize concepts and then label them. The software allows for the creation of semantic maps as well as for outlining and diagramming at the same time. It is the easiest to use of the software programs that produce maps. IBM- and MAC-compatible.

The Literary Mapper. Gainesville, FL: Teacher Support Software. (1035 NW 57th St., 32605-4486, 800-228-2871).
This program contains predeveloped maps for *Character, Setting,* and *Action* so that students of any age can fill them in at the keyboard as they read a story. Brainstorming, listing, mapping, and editing for expanding and changing maps are also possible with this software. MAC-compatible.

The Semantic Mapper. Gainesville, FL: Teacher Support Software. (1035 NW 57th St., 32605-4486, 800-228-2871).
This program allows students of any age to create their own webs or maps and add labels. It allows for brainstorming, listing, mapping, and editing for expanding and changing maps. This software allows students who are doing research to see visual representations of their research as it progresses. MAC-compatible.

Visuals

CP Graphic Organizers (1994). Elizabethtown, NJ: Continental Press. (520 East Bainbridge St., 17022-2299.)
This set of laminated posters (24" x 37") includes 12 of the most common graphic organizer formats, for example, Venn diagram, story grammar map, time line/continuum scale, Know-Want to Know-Learned (KWL), and concept/attribute web. These formats are also available in 60-sheet student tablets for individual use. Helpful for teachers, students, and/or presenters to display information to be communicated visually.